Contesting Malaysia's Integration into the World Economy

"Through celebrating the work of Shahril Talib Robert, the authors in this volume remind us of a deeper economic and political heritage that is often lost in the rubble of confusing national politics. All who care for Malaysia will find the studies here an uplifting affirmation of the value of open-minded and dedicated scholarship. I congratulate the editors and their colleagues for bringing so much more of the country's varied foundations to our attention."

—Prof. Wang Gungwu, *National University of Singapore, Singapore*

Rajah Rasiah · Azirah Hashim ·
Jatswan S. Sidhu
Editors

Contesting Malaysia's Integration into the World Economy

palgrave
macmillan

Editors
Rajah Rasiah
Asia-Europe Institute
University of Malaya
Kuala Lumpur, Malaysia

Azirah Hashim
Faculty of Languages and Linguistics
University of Malaya
Kuala Lumpur, Malaysia

Jatswan S. Sidhu
Asia-Europe Institute
University of Malaya
Kuala Lumpur, Malaysia

ISBN 978-981-16-0649-6   ISBN 978-981-16-0650-2 (eBook)
https://doi.org/10.1007/978-981-16-0650-2

Cover credit: MAEKFOTO/Alamy Stock Photo

This Palgrave Macmillan imprint is published by the registered company Springer Nature Singapore Pte Ltd.
The registered company address is: 152 Beach Road, #21-01/04 Gateway East, Singapore 189721, Singapore

Foreword

ISTANA ISKANDARIAH

KUALA KANGSAR

This publication provides a most fitting tribute to the life and work of the late Professor Shaharil Talib Robert, in the depth and richness of the scholarship that it brings together, as well as in its range and scope. It embodies Shaharil's concept of history as being something that is actively constructed, through the critical interrogation of existing perspectives, and robust use of evidence. This approach is what we see on display here in all the individual contributions, while the broader question the book addresses—of the intersection of the national, regional, and global scales—also, of course, lay right at the heart of his work.

Among Shaharil's fundamental concerns was the way in which narratives are shaped, and how the presentation and interpretation of the facts determine what becomes the accepted version of historical or current events. As he saw it, the role of historians is to ensure that a 'better' truth can be told, or a more accurate and comprehensive version of events. To achieve this, historians must critically engage with the manipulation of information by those who seek to gain from so doing. They must employ rigorous scientific methods. And they must bring to the foreground the view from below, by highlighting the stories and actors more often excluded from the dominant narrative.

These concerns appear ever more pertinent today, in our post-truth world of social media, conspiracy theories, and the systematic distortion of facts to serve the interests of particular groups. Shaharil's approach of meeting this challenge through well-crafted historiography, focused on previously marginalized perspectives, was inspired in part by the work of historian and French resistance hero, Marc Bloch. Bloch's pioneering insights evolved during a period when fascism was in the ascendent. The total control and manipulation of the public discourse is an essential element of fascism, and in such conditions, the need to question constructed discourses, and to work tirelessly against the distortion of the facts by special interests, becomes even more urgent.

Shaharil was committed to this search for historical accuracy and truth, to trying to make sense of the 'bewildering' and 'tangled' relationships and dynamics of the complex world we are navigating through. I am often reminded of his metaphor of history as being like a ship charting a course through the dangerous waters of ideology and interests, 'in order to arrive at some unified and holistic understanding of our past and present,' as he put it. He thus conceptualized history as something we must actively engage with and shape ourselves, as historians and actors, in order to challenge and correct its biases and omissions.

Shaharil's intellectual legacy, with all its various facets, is honored in this volume most ably by his former colleagues, peers, and students. All of the chapters question accepted truths, and apply carefully considered new evidence to existing orthodoxies, or unexplored aspects of our past and present. In this vein, there is even a questioning and extension of his own work on the Malay aristocracy, which I'm sure he would have welcomed and enjoyed. The depth and breadth of the contributions, all under the rubric of Malaysia's integration with the world economy, and the multi-scalar ramifications of this process, attest to the deep impact Shaharil's work has had. The book underscores its immense influence on the practice and study of history in this country and beyond.

Shaharil and his work have had a profound influence on my own academic research, particularly in relation to my choice of methodology and use of archival source material. The pursuit of this research has proved both fulfilling and, I hope, useful, and I thus owe him an immense debt for his guidance and inspiration. I know there are many others who feel similarly, including many of those who have contributed chapters to this volume.

I want to congratulate the editors for this most fitting celebration of the life and work of Shaharil Talib. As a whole, the book fulfills admirably the historian's ultimate goal of helping us to better understand from where we have come, so that we can navigate more effectively the choppy waters of our current times, in keeping with the late professor's vision. And it serves to reassure us that his intellectual legacy will continue to resonate strongly, despite his passing. This legacy will help to ensure that our historical narrative will continue to be informed from below, and that those who seek a more accurate and holistic version of events will prevail over those who deliberately seek to manipulate and distort the facts.

Kuala Kangsar, Malaysia
November 2020

HRH Sultan Nazrin Shah

Preface

This book seeks to celebrate the contribution of the late Professor Dato' Shaharil Talib Robert to scholarship in general, and history and foreign policy in particular. He was a rare academic who was a bundle of intellectual energy that synergized others in his company. Always bubbling with his charming smile, Shaharil Talib never stopped motivating the young on the responsibility of a scholar to seek truth and novelty in furthering their fields. He wasted little time with academics with closed minds, even shying away from shallow critics to spend his precious time on worthy discourse. Groomed in the spirit of Marc Bloch and Fernand Braudel, Shaharil Talib sought to and encouraged others to recraft history by using cutting-edge methodologies and innovative analytical techniques to generate new insights for establishing greater rigor. In doing so, he called for scholarship to be sterilized from ideology and self-interest. Shaharil Talib campaigned for historical interrogation to be sensitive to the multi-scalar nature and plurality of social relations. While he was damning in his condemnation of the repression the masses faced under colonialism, he also pressed for such accounts to be told truthfully with concrete evidence. Shaharil encouraged research on undocumented developments unrelated to colonial intervention that were important to understanding Malaysian history. While Shaharil's historical research stretched beyond Malaysia to include Southeast Asia, he took great pride in serving his nation, Malaysia. Among contributions he made to the country include his key advisory role on tracing the historical maps of the Islands of Pedra Branca, Middle

Rocks, and South Ledge to assist the Malaysian team contesting their national location in a dispute between Malaysia and Singapore that was heard at the International Court of Judgement, The Hague.

In the scholarly spirit of Shaharil Talib, this book brings together a collection of chapters that either document developments that are new to the universe, or contest existing documentations in a wide range of topics that constitute pre-colonial, colonial and post-colonial relations in Malaya. Indeed, I would argue that each of the chapters provides a refreshingly new perspective to Malaysian history.

Shaharil was born in 1946 and passed away in 2018 leaving behind his dancer wife, Datuk Azanin Ahmad and daughter Shein Shanin Shaharil. He was a family man who was fond of them both. Shaharil was educated at the Victoria Institution before undertaking his degree at Universiti Malaya and his doctorate at Monash University. He was made Professor and Head of the Southeast Asian Studies Department at University of Malaya before being appointed as the founding Executive Director of the Asia-Europe Institute at University of Malaya. He shared the same doctoral supervisor at Monash University, Michael Swift, with Shamsul Amri Baharuddin and Zawawi Ibrahim. Shaharil showed utmost respect for the monarchy, and even used to wear black clothes to work all the time. He would proudly tell me that we Malaysians are the subjects of our monarchy, and black attire simply denotes our acceptance of the royal norm. He was particularly close to His Royal Highness Sultan Nazrin Shah of Perak. Nevertheless, Shaharil criticized the elitist nature of typical historical accounts, and so encouraged others to document the histories of the poor, including the working class. He often told me of how happy he was in having supervised Maznah Mohamad to produce a seminal piece of scholarship documenting the disappearance of Malay handloom weavers in Malaysia. Unlike those with old ways of doing things, Shaharil was open to new ideas so long as it opened novel pathways to pursuing scholarship. In my mind, Shaharil Talib was a wonderful example of a scholar who carried enormous experience and tacitness with him, yet always kept his humility. Although he is no longer with us, his legacy, which includes the several graduate students he supervised, and the many friends he connected with, will carry the torch he lit. I for one have missed hearing his soft voice, engaging smile, and the many intellectual discussions. He was like an elder brother who cared not just for the research I did, but also for me personally.

I wish to take this opportunity to acknowledge the contributions of several individuals who were either directly or indirectly involved in the development of the Asia-Europe Institute when I served as Shaharil's Deputy Director between 2004 and 2005: His Royal Highness Sultan Nazrin Shah, Datuk Prof. Dr. Hashim Yaacob, Prof. Dr. Roziah Omar, Dr. Shamsulbahriah Ku Ahmad, Dr. Giovanni Capanelli, Omar Farouk, Professor Dato'D. Hassan Said, Tan Sri Ghani Patail, Tan Sri Visu Sinnadurai, Datuk Sothi Rachagan, Tan Sri Ajit Singh, Dr. Mokhtar Thamin, Gareth Api Richards, Prof. Amitav Acharya, Rajarethnam M., Dr. Azmi Sharom, Professor Ajit Singh, Professor Sanjaya Lall, Dr. Gabriel Palma, Prof. Carlo Pietrobelli, Prof. Tan Eu Chye, HE Thierry Rommel, Prof. Antony Bryant, Prof Fernando Rodrigo, Syed Farid Alatas, Dato Dr. Thillainathan Ramasamy, Gnasegarah Kandaiya, Harbans Singh Sohan Singh, Dr. Ichiro Sugimoto, Patricia Martinez, Tin Htoo Naing, Dang Minh Quang and Amer Hamzah Jantan. Finally, I would like to thank the three anonymous referees for their constructive comments on the chapters. The usual disclaimer applies.

Kuala Lumpur, Malaysia — Rajah Rasiah

Contents

Notes on Contributors

Shamsul Amri Baharuddin is a social anthropologist and the Founding Director, Institute of Ethnic Studies (KITA), The National University of Malaysia (UKM) since 2007. To date, he is one of the only five Distinguished Professors appointed by the Ministry of Education, Malaysia; recipient of the Academic Prize, Fukuoka Award, Japan in 2008; inducted as a Fellow, Academy of Science Malaysia in 2018; in January 2019 appointed as Chair, National Council of Professors (MPN), Malaysia and in September 2019 was awarded the UNESCO CHAIR (Communications and Social Cohesion) at UKM. He is known as the architect of Malaysia's *Blueprint for National Unity 2015* and its first-ever *National Unity Index 2018* (IPNas 2018) and *The National Unity Action Plan* (2021–2025). In July 2020 he was appointed as the Advisor on Unity, Ministry of National Unity, Malaysia.

Azirah Hashim is a Senior Professor in the English Language Department, Faculty of Languages and Linguistics. Her previous positions include Executive Director of the Asia-Europe Institute, Director of the Centre for ASEAN Regionalism, Dean of the Humanities Research Cluster and Dean of the Faculty of Languages and Linguistics. She is also a Fellow of the Alexander von Humboldt Foundation, Germany.

Zawawi Ibrahim retired as a Professor of Anthropology at University of Brunei Darussalam and is currently a visiting Professor at Taylor's University. He was previously a Professor of Anthropology at University Malaysia

Sarawak and University of Malaya. He is also an acclaimed song composer, musician and singer.

Anthony Milner is an Emeritus Professor, Australian National University; Professorial Fellow, University of Melbourne and Visiting Professor, University of Malaya. He has published widely on Malay history and political culture—and on Southeast Asian regional relations.

Rahul Mishra is a Senior Lecturer at the Asia-Europe Institute. Before this, he was a Consultant at the Foreign Service Institute of India's Ministry of External Affairs. He has also worked with the Indian Council of World Affairs and Institute for Defence Studies and Analyses for four years each. Recipient of the Asia Fellowship of the East-West Center in Washington, DC, Korean and the Australian Government Fellowships, he was also previously affiliated with Nanyang Technical University and the National University of Singapore.

Maznah Mohamad is an Associate Professor and Head of the Department of Malay Studies at the National University of Singapore. Her areas of research and publications are Gender and Islam, Bureaucratic Islam, Malaysian Politics and the Historical Deconstruction of the Malay World.

Sivachandralingam Sundara Raja is an Associate Professor at the Faculty of Arts and Social Sciences, University of Malaya. He formerly headed the Department of History, Faculty of Arts and Social Sciences, University of Malaya. His main area of specialization is in the field of Malaysian economic history and also works on British imperial history of the late nineteenth and early twentieth century and contemporary Indians in Malaysia.

Rajah Rasiah is a Distinguished National Professor of Economics at the Asia Europe Institute, University of Malaya. He is also holds visiting positions at Sunway University, Institute of Energy Policy and Research, UNITEN, Institute of Capital markets Research, Cambridge University, Oxford University and UNU-MERIT. He is the 2015 recipient of the Celso Furtado prize from the World Academy of Sciences for advancing the frontiers of social science (Economics) thought. He was made Distinguished Professor of Economics in 2017 by Malaysia's Ministry of Higher Education, and awarded the Merdeka Prize for scholastic excellence in 2018.

Johan Saravanamuttu is a Professor Emeritus at Universiti Sains Malaysia and Adjunct Senior Fellow at the S. Rajaratnam School of International Studies, Nanyang Technological University. He also held positions previously as Professor of Political Science at Universiti Sains Malaysia and Senior Visiting Fellow at the Institute for Southeast Asian Studies, Singapore.

Viswanathan Selvaratnam is a third-generation Malaysian and a World Bank retiree. He had previously taught at the University of Malaya and at the National University of Singapore.

Jatswan S. Sidhu is an Associate Professor in the Department of International and Strategic Studies, Faculty of Arts and Social Sciences, University of Malaya in Kuala Lumpur. He is also Executive Director of the Asia-Europe Institute (AEI), University of Malaya and Director, Centre for ASEAN Regionalism, University of Malaya (CARUM).

Peter Brian M. Wang has served in the Malaysian Government for more than 17 years holding various portfolios, the majority of which was spent at the Ministry of International Trade and Industry (MITI) of Malaysia. He is currently attached with the National Institute of Public Administration (INTAN) where he lectures and undertakes research on economic- and international relations-related policy. He is currently working on his Ph.D. on the architecture of regional orders at the Asia-Europe Institute.

Danny Tze Ken Wong is a Professor of History and Dean of the Faculty of Arts and Social Sciences, University of Malaya. He is a former Director of the Institute of China Studies at University of Malaya. His research focuses on the Chinese in Malaysia, Sino-Malaysia relations and history of Sabah.

List of Figures

CHAPTER 1

Introduction: Problematizing Historicization

Rajah Rasiah, Azirah Hashim, and Jatswan S. Sidhu

History has remained a fascinating field for scholars and followers seeking to know how the world's civilizations have evolved, as well as the complex social relations that have advanced. However, the dominant account of colonialism has been one of the colonizers seeking to help uncivilized kingdoms to free the masses from cannibalism that characterized them, and hence, the establishment of the doctrine of the 'White man's burden'. For example, writing on colonial India, Marx (1853) drew on colonial reports to argue that colonialism was good for material accumulation as he equated Kingdoms that existed before to European antiquity, and that colonialism will create the conditions to bypass feudalism to open

R. Rasiah (✉) · A. Hashim · J. S. Sidhu
Asia-Europe Institute, University of Malaya,
Kuala Lumpur, Malaysia
e-mail: rajah@um.edu.my

A. Hashim
e-mail: azirahh@um.edu.my

J. S. Sidhu
e-mail: jatswanh@um.edu.my

R. Rasiah et al. (eds.), *Contesting Malaysia's Integration into the World Economy*, https://doi.org/10.1007/978-981-16-0650-2_1

the path for capitalist accumulation. Such depictions also did not recognize the scientific progress achieved by the Kingdoms of especially the Incas, Mayas, Indians, Chinese, Egyptians, and Arabs. These accounts, shaped by the conquerors, (which have often been colored by powerful interest groups) (Polanyi, 1944), buried out of sight contributions of the conquered. In addition, the limited attention given to precolonial histories has often prevented a material comparison of it with colonial and post-colonial histories, thereby denying readers an equal footing for a symmetric understanding of the social relations and material conditions between the two phases.[1] Indeed, Reid (2011) had lamented over the marginalization of African precolonial history as historians began to focus on colonial history.

In line with the spirit of the late Shaharil Talib's works, this book seeks to interrogate Malaysia's integration into the capitalist world economy with a special focus on the colonial period. However, given the entrenched nature of social relations it is inevitable that the span of inquiry should be lengthened to cover pre-colonial and post-colonial social relations. In this introductory chapter, we discuss the critical issues and introduce the book's chapters.

Critical Issues

While several Western historicizations of pre-colonial, colonial, and post-colonial economies have been bereft of scientific logic, there has also been an obsession among local scholars to equate colonial actions to simplistic claims of being triggers of underdevelopment. Influenced heavily by Bloch (1954) and Braudel (1969), Shaharil (2005: 4) argued that attempts to recraft history should not only use essential methodologies and existing techniques, but also utilize innovative techniques to generate new insights for greater rigor, and there should be efforts to stay clear of ideological predilections and vested interests. Shaharil (2005: 7) also argued that efforts to interrogate history must be sensitive to the multi-scalar nature and plurality of social relations, and that attempts to articulate them would require the acceptance of organized randomness that provide semblance of causality, contingency, contradictions,

[1] As Shaharil Talib had often noted, it is also the case that much of documented history is elitist in nature. Exceptions in the case of Malaysia include the work of Abraham (1970) and Fauconnier (1990).

and connections.[2] For example, it is certainly important to record the devastation that Britain wreaked on India during colonial rule, including robbing the country of USD44.6 trillion over the period 1765–1938 (Patnaik, 2018). However, it is also necessary to examine the changes that took place under colonialism as India succumbed to capitalist integration. Indeed, a dynamic Marxist analysis of capitalist integration, and how it affected the productive forces in India is no less important (Marx, 1853; Luxembourg, 1951). However tumultuous the destructive experience India went through, as Carr (1961) argued, it is pertinent for historians to also document these changes without being emotionally drowned into romantic moralism. Indeed, one can argue that the fragile social fabric of the ruling class in India, (which had become extremely repressive towards the end) had already left India vulnerable to external control. The Moghul Empire for one had become decadent and highly parasitic, thereby causing mass sufferings. Also, India was technologically stagnating at the time India's conquest began with the Battle of Arcot in 1751 (Henty, 1999) and the battle of Plassey in 1757 (Harrington, 1994). Kumar and Desai (1983) provide evidence to show that the Indian textile industry had for hundreds of years been characterized by handloom weaving, which made clothing a luxury that only a few could afford. Imports of waterjet looms from Britain provided the initial technological leap to support mass production.

Fitting Shaharil's (2005) call for innovative interrogation, Syed Muhd Khairudin (2015) provided a nuanced elucidation of the radical experience of Malays fighting to end colonialism in Malaya. This fascinating account is a classic example of historical interrogation that not only added to rich historicization that unfolded opposition against colonialism but also how such resistance groups were organized against the colonial power. Lees (2017) work qualifies in that spirit as she demonstrated that the relationships between rulers and the ruled were both complex and conflicting with, in the way they dealt with their subjects, as well as the colonial officials. The scope and methodological approach used enabled a fresh revisit that produced new findings on imperialism, urbanization, immigration, labour, and commodity production, including social mobility, and cross-cultural learning in British Malaya.

[2] Unfortunately, mainstream economics has gone in the opposite direction, which is driven by mechanistic and deterministic postulations.

The historical interrogation called for by Shaharil (2005) also opens the debate on macro-developments shaped by past governance structures and how such structures are sometimes reconfigured by changing social relations. In this regard, using a broad-brush macro approach with micro-evidence, Azlan (2012) discusses whether democratization is necessary and if it was whether it was sufficiently achieved during Malaysia's efforts to industrialize covering a period from 1824 till 2011. The novelty in the book generally relates to how colonial rule shaped the nature of social relations in the country following independence. British colonial efforts to shape Malaysia's external relations, he argues led to the support of Western-educated elites to govern the country. Nevertheless, he provides evidence to show that the post-colonial state has lost some of its political legitimacy owing to widening social disparities, increased ethnic polarization, and prevalent corruption. The new media is seen to have driven informational globalization that has empowered Malaysians in a new struggle for political reform, thereby reconfiguring the balance of power between the state and civil society.

While general accounts of history, especially those documented from oral histories, continue to flag the accounts of the dominant powers, drawing on archival research several historians have increasingly questioned such accounts. Among the famous contrapositions of such accounts include Alatas' (1977) famous work debunking colonial reference to the natives as being lazy. Others include Swift's (1965) dismissal of Western notions that the Malays preferred large numbers of children to work in their farms. Indeed, unlike the reductionist Western accounts which were conjectured without careful evidence, and which produced an economistic assessment of the conduct of Malays, Swift (1965) provided evidence to lucidly argue that the Malays enjoyed having children who gave them entertainment and fulfilment. In establishing the local account of the actors involved in the Terengganu rebellion, Shaharil (1984) offered evidence on the local actors who were involved.

The contestation of history is also laced with analyses suggesting the existence of socially cohesive societies that were not dominated by classes prior to colonization. It is in this context that historical accounts of capitalist integration often portray the governance of precolonial kingdoms as more caring to the masses than colonial regimes (see, for example, Lim (1977)). In fact, the Malay provinces were considered to have been ruled by Sultans through a tribute-paying mode of production (Jomo, 1986). Such accounts suggest that the Sultans took a nominal payment through farm surpluses in return for protection from the royalty. The tribute-paying mode of production can be viewed as an extension of the Asiatic production that was examined by Alavi (1975) and Currie (1984). Such romantic accounts may well be true when benevolent kings ruled these kingdoms. However, the social relations then lacked the organization essential to engender the conditions for rapid growth and technical change (Luxembourg, 1951). Albeit it remains controversial among historians and scholars from the South, it is for these reasons Luxembourg (1951) had argued that the destructive penetration of colonization should be taken as an opportunity to galvanize post-colonial national accumulation.

Shaharil Talib emerged from a celebrated Department of History in the University of Malaya that produced internationally recognized historians. Led by world-renowned historians, such as Wang Gungwu, Anthony Reid and William Roff among others, the department produced outstanding historians, including Sharil Talib, Khoo Kay Kim, Amarjit Kaur, Chandran Jeshrun, Jeyamalar Kathirithamby-Wells, Omar Farouk, Ranjit Singh, Lee Poh Ping, Lee Kam Hing, and M. Santhanaban. In addition to the works reviewed in this chapter, several other incisive works on Malaysian history exists (e.g. Arasaratnam, 1970; Sandu, 1969; Khoo, 1972, Sharom, 1984; Ariffin, 1993; Kaur & Meltcalfe, 1999; Ranjit Singh, 2003).

Shaharil carried two traits that defined Carr's (1961) expectation of a historian. First, Shaharil's (1977) works show detailed assessments of power structures between the royalty and other elites and the commoners, for example, in Terengganu. He mapped the lineage of the royal class in Terengganu in the late nineteenth century. Second, Shaharil (1984) narrated the developments that filled up the gaps left behind by Western scholars in capturing the relations between them.

Western accounts of colonial integration tend to show a deterministic bias towards colonial strategies with little account of local settings that together shaped the processes. However powerful Roff's (1967) arguments on how the British colonial policy shielded the Malay peasantry from secularization, it still lacked a profound account from the Malay elites and peasantry on how they responded to these developments. In doing so, Shaharil (1984) showed tremendous courage and conviction to compliment Western accounts of colonial integration in Malaysia and the struggle put up by the royalties to resist European encroachment into their domain. Shaharil (1984) evidently captured the spontaneous nature by which local resistance began as social friction grew from disagreements between the local rulers and British appointees, which included the British resident. Using his extensive evidence accumulated from both local and foreign sources, Shaharil (1984) was able to trace in a nuanced way the survival strategies of the Terengganu royalty.

Like Carr (1961), the political history lenses that Shaharil had honed allowed him a sound footing in international relations, as he made his mark on how Southeast Asian foreign policy should be shaped. He extended his logic of the Malay states to the Southeast Asian states. His notion of the *tanah air* (water land) referred to Malaysia as characterized by the water-faring Malays of different ethnicities, including the Bugis, Minangkabaus, Javanese, Achinese, Bataks, and Mandalings, freely sailing from one land to another. Hence, Shaharil took a leaf out of history to promote Southeast Asia as a place bound by waters, free of boundaries, where different ethnic groups with commonalities interacted over the centuries to produce their cultures.[3] Although economic interests have eventually taken control over the development of the Asian Economic Community (AEC), Shaharil's (2005) call to draw strength from the historical shaping of the *tanah air* cultures, stills resonate in some as an important channel that should be harnessed to build social bonds between the Southeast Asian states. The late Surin Pitsuwan once narrated to the first author of this chapter at the Institute of Economic Research in ASEAN and East Asia (ERIA) that such cultural bonds should be considered when negotiating problems of the global common, such as the haze, (which continues to affect Indonesia, Malaysia, and Singapore).[4]

History is also about events and what had happened. While the causes of the events can be deduced through logical argumentation, because of information imperfections logic can be blurred. Hence, while the predictive powers using historical evidence can always be questioned (Popper, 1944), making sense of particular conjunctures can also have limits. As Popper (1945a, b) had famously argued, predictions of the future on the basis of just the past alone can be futile. Just because we have seen the sun every day in the past, it does not mean that we will see it forever. In

[3] In his inaugural lecture, Shaharil (2005: 32) argued that the pre-colonial world was 'witnessed by a liquid world—literally encompassed by the sea-borne ties of commerce and kinship, and metaphorically represented by the *tanah air*... In the colonial world by contrast, we see the making of the region as a fixed bounded, annexed, and territorialized and then connected to the centres of empire through a series of hubs-and-spokes'.

[4] Interview with Surin Pitsuwan on 22 April 2011 in Jakarta.

other words, there are limits to attempt ex-post rationalization of events purely based on past events. Even more so, humans with their subjective minds, often act irrationally to conjure events that could be mindboggling for researchers. In this context, one can also question some of the sociological explications used to construct capitalist history. However, any attempt to refute past historical accounts must be backed by scientific evidence (Popper, 1959). An incisive attempt to reconstruct Malaysia's history using scientific evidence can be seen from the works of Sultan Nazrin Shah (2017, 2019). These works for the first time constructed a historical GDP series that, among others, allowed for a consistent assessment of growth and structural change in Malaysia over the period 1900 till 1939 and subsequently, the years after 1945. Scholars in the past were often restricted by scant data, which was not only discontinuous but also presented at different prices.[5]

While the book seeks to offer a reinterpretation and undocumented elements of developments, events, and issues, it does not attempt to provide an exhaustive account of these elements, which is neither possible nor necessary. Attempts to historicize will continue as researchers discover undocumented and inadequately treated issues that are critical to history. In other words, historical interrogation shall remain a continuous exercise.

Outline of Book

This book focusses on issues that are largely confined to colonial history, issues that connect pre-colonial developments with colonial rule, and post-colonial developments that have their origins in colonial rule in Malaya. In doing so, the prime thread that ties each of the chapters is the use of novel interpretations to rethink these issues. Given the enormous contribution Shaharil Talib made to our understanding of Malaysian history, it is only right that scholars of high standing are allowed the space to problematize issues for which reinterrogation offers new light, as well as extending novelty by those who have carried his torch into other fields.

After the introductory first chapter, in Chapter 2, Rajah Rasiah revisits colonial industrialization in Malaya with a focus on the key drivers. While

[5] (1995a, b), for example, used factor prices and only selected sectors over particular periods, and market prices and other sectors over other periods to examine how economic *laissez fairism* within the British empire impacted on colonial Malaya.

official trade regulations in colonial Malaya did not impose tariffs on several imports from within the British Empire, he argues that significant departures from the doctrine of free markets did take place as Malaya's location, specificity of production, and nature of the embedding environment were critical in shaping the nature of manufacturing that evolved in colonial Malaya. Although markets were important, given the inherently uneven and segmented nature of labour markets in emerging economies, he provides evidence to show that firms gradually adopted capital-intensive technology in a number of operations to improve coordination between supply and demand. As local manufacturing was exposed to international competition in which large-scale demand was met from imports, local manufacturing firms remained small despite absorbing capital-intensive power-driven technology. Rajah argues that colonial industrialization in Malaya was shaped by a myriad of institutions. While markets were important, so were other institutions that promoted the development of productive capacity at proximate locations, which gave rise to the manufacture of heavy machinery and equipment, and ships, and foundries, especially trust, which was instrumental in overcoming uncertainties and risks to ensure smooth coordination in tin mining and smelting, and rubber cultivation and processing.

Zawawi Ibrahim discusses in Chapter 3 how a continuous anthropological interest in the Malay peasantry from the 1930s has created a rich theoretical and empirical literature, which offers a critical genealogical account of knowledge production spanning four generations of anthropologists. He notes that the first two generations were dominated by Western anthropologists, (especially Raymond Firth and Michael Swift), who focussed on late colonialism. The latter two generations were led by indigenous scholars who consciously grappled with the intellectual legacies of the past while, at the same time, opening up new research vistas. Using a close reading of some of the key anthropological texts produced on the Malay peasantry, as well as an analysis of the institutionalization of professional anthropology in Malaysia, this chapter discusses the tensions of intergenerational continuities and ruptures. While acknowledging the enormous debt that many indigenous scholars owed to their Western mentors, the chapter argues that there emerged a qualitative break with the past during the late 1970s and 1980s. This saw indigenous anthropologists grappling with post-peasantry studies and opening up new fields of inquiry on the larger issues of agrarian change, capitalist modernity, ideational formation, and contemporary politics.

In Chapter 4, Shamsul Amri Baharuddin argues that colonial knowledge has been the most powerful form of knowledge in decolonized societies but is increasingly less recognized because it has become naturalized and embedded within those societies. Indeed, he asserts that it remains the single most dominating source of power and legitimacy for the post-colonial state, particularly those surviving on ethnic nationalism. In doing so, the chapter explores the role of the literary component, as part of colonial knowledge, in the construction of 'Malay ethnicity'. In the process, it demonstrates that the literary component is an integral and indispensable part of the colonial investigative modality. In fact, Shamsul demonstrates that the literary component of 'Malay' is an integral and indispensable part of the colonial investigative modality, and hence, the construction of classifications and categories that elaborate, refine, and even embellish the invented ethnic category of 'Malay'.

In Chapter 5, Anthony Milner seeks to define the contribution of Shaharil Talib to the study pre-modern Malaya political systems. His essay outlines the extraordinary range of analytical approaches employed over the years up to Shaharil's time. Beginning with the work of Thomas Stamford Raffes and John Crawfurd two centuries ago, then considering such later scholar-officials as Hugh Clifford and Rochard Winstedt, and finally noting the influence of different anthropological and Marxist-influenced perspectives developed in the post-colonial period, the chapter then examines the major study on Terengganu, which Shaharil published. Milner's main focus is on the significant shifts and contests in the historiography of pre-colonial Malay societies, seeking to show in particular where Shaharil's endeavours can be appropriately positioned. In Milner's view, Shaharil innovatory in adopting a diachronic approach—portraying the Malay states as societies in motion. Milner notes that Shaharil's conclusions, and interpretive framework, which he employed, have provoked scholarly debate—and this, Milner says, underlines the fact that Shaharil produced a classic work in the field of Malay history.

Maznah Mohamad uses Shaharil's innovative scholarly lenses to revisit her work on handloom weavers in Malaysia in Chapter 6. In doing so, Maznah attempts to enliven Shaharil's legacy in sharpening our understanding of the concept of social class, its condition, and the colonial state within a historical trajectory in an attempt to deconstruct critical elements of the past. Going beyond the typical paternalistic colonial narratives, Maznah discusses passionately the handloom weaving industry of Terengganu, Kelantan and Pahang. Although the handloom weavers engaged in textile weaving were wiped out during colonial integration, she documents the form of industrialization that took place, which was the lifeblood of the urban-based 'middle-class' of the old Malay world then.

Chapter 7 by Sivachandralingam Sundara Raja analyses case studies in the late nineteenth and early twentieth centuries to argue that Malay aristocrats were not just interested but were also directly involved in business activities before British intervention, and became more active during British rule in the Federated and Unfederated Malay States. The expansion in their business activities arose from both a drastic reduction in their allowances during the British administration, as well as the growing capitalist opportunities during colonialism. In doing so, he argues that the colonial government actively approved applications by the aristocrats to do business in mining and agriculture. The British also supported the Chettiar to help the aristocrats to retain their lavish lifestyle.

In Chapter 8, Viswanathan Selvaratnam argues that the British Empire's political intervention, territorial expansion, administrative dominance, land grabbing, and importation of indentured 'coolie' labour was to exploit the natural resources of Peninsular Malaya for the accumulation of capital at the metropolitan Britain, which evolved as an asymmetric race-class power structure between the imperial power and its colonies targeted at institutionalizing an empire-wide cheap, exploitative, and repressive coolie trade. The chapter outlines the impact of the constellation of exploitative and repressive policies of British imperialism, the colonial state, and colonial capitalism on South Indian coolies. The continuation of the changing capitalist structure combined with the perpetuation of the pro-capitalist and class-cum-race policy strategies has infantilized the subjugated South Indian 'coolies' to be relegated to the status of an oppressed, marginalized, dispossessed and precarious underclass to be 'mercilessly left to their fate'.

Using a longitudinal historical approach, Danny Wong Tze Ken documents, in Chapter 9, the development of the Hakka identity in Sabah since 1882, including its ties to the Basel Church, as well as the way the church provided impetus to reinforce the Hakka identity. In doing so, he argues that the Basel Church's institutionalization of Hakka-ness, both through language and activities (e.g. churches and schools), have been instrumental in enhancing the Hakka identity among the Chinese in Sabah, though the admission of other members and influences have begun to pose new challenges.

Johan Saranamuttu discusses, in Chapter 10, the steady decline in Western dominance in post-colonial Southeast Asian geopolitics since the Vietnam War. He argues that the post-Cold War period has witnessed a continuance of a system of watered-down American-led arrangements aimed at maintaining regional stability among Southeast Asian states, which was tempered by the emergence of the Association of Southeast Asia (ASEAN) regionalism in the late 1960s and the progressive fashioning of ASEAN constructs for regional stability. ASEAN over time evinced its own agency in crafting regional institutions and norms to leverage on the notion of 'ASEAN centrality' in stabilizing regional politics into the twenty-first Century. Hitherto, the notion of hegemonic stability in the international relations literature implied that a major hegemon, such as European power like Britain or the United States, would undergird regional stability. With the apparent decline of American hegemony, the changing character of global politics has allowed for a large measure of agency and flexibility in the foreign policy of small and medium states in ASEAN, which include Malaysia.

The final chapter by Rahul Misra and Peter Brian M. Wang presents arguments to show that instead of merely being one of many, Malaysia's colonial past has had a deep and meaningful effect on not only the shaping of Malaysia's foreign policies per se but also on the men responsible in its shaping. The chapter focusses on Malaysia's foreign policy during the administration of Tunku Abdul Rahman, the first Prime Minister of Malaysia. In the process, the chapter looks into the role of colonialism, particularly the relations with Britain, in influencing Malaysia's politico-security and military outlook and its approach towards international multilateral forums such as ASEAN and the Non-Aligned Movement. Rahul Misra and Peter Brian argue that Malaysia's pursuit of a pro-western and anti-communist foreign policy in the early post-independence years, instead of being a paradox, was a direct by-product of Malaysia's experience with colonialization.

Overall, the chapters in the book meet the *raison d'être* for reinterrogating Malaysia's integration into the world economy. Chapters 2 and 6 by Rajah Rasiah and Maznah Mohamad reinterpret and introduce the emergence of modern industrialization and the disappearance of cottage industrialization respectively during colonial rule. Zawawi Ibrahim and Shamsul Amri Baharuddin discuss using anthropological lenses, the indigenous perspective of understanding the Malays and their social relations to debunk colonial constructs about them in Chapters 3 and 4. Anthony Milner reminds us that Shaharil's major study on Terengganu is a case study of early Malay elite endeavours to engage in the growing international economy (though Milner also argues that such a materialist approach is only one way to interpret socio-economic and cultural activities in Malay states on the eve of colonial rule).

Sivachandralingam Sundara Raja provides fresh evidence in Chapter 7 to argue that the Malay royalty was involved in business prior to colonialism, an activity that expanded strongly during colonial rule owing to reduced revenue brought about by colonial rule. Viswanathan Selvaratnam offers in Chapter 8 a rigorous assessment of Indian coolie history during colonial rule, which adds further to existing accounts of the repressive nature of their relocation from India and subsequent exploitation in Malaya. Danny Wong Tze Ken documents the role of the Basel Church in shaping the Hakka identity in Sabah in Chapter 9. Finally, Chapters 10 and 11 by Johan Saravanamuttu and Rahul Misra link the foreign policy of independent Malaysia, and ASEAN to their colonial past.

References

Abraham, C. E. R. (1970). *The political economy of race relations in Malaya: A historical perspective*. Madison, WI: University of Wisconsin.

Alatas, S. H. (1977). *The myth of the lazy native: A study of the image of the Malays, Filipinos and Javanese from the 16th to the 20th century and its function in the ideology of colonial capitalism*. London: Frank Cass.

Alavi, H. (1975). India and colonial mode of production. *Economic & Political Weekly, 11*(33), 1235–1262.

Arasaratnam, S. (1970). *Indians in Malaysia and Singapore*. Kuala Lumpur: Oxford University Press.

Ariffin, O. (1993). *Bangsa Melayu: Malay concepts of democracy and community, 1945–1950*. Singapore: Oxford University Press.

Azlan, T. (2012). *Malaysia in the world economy (1824–2011)*. Lanham, MD: Lexington Books.

Bloch, M. (1954). *The historian's craft*. New York, NY: Vintage Books.

Braudel, F. (1969). *On history*, Translated in 1982 (Chicago, IL: Chicago University Press). Paris: Flammarion.

Carr, E. H. (1961). *What is history?* New York, NY: Random House.

Currie, K. (1984). The Asiatic mode of production: Problems of conceptualizing state and economy. *Dialectical Anthropology, 8*(4), 251–268.

Fauconnier, H. (1990). *The soul of Malaya*. Singapore: Oxford University Press.

Harrington, P. (1994). *Plassey 1757, Clive of India's finest hour; osprey campaign series no. 36*. London: Osprey Publishing.

Henty, G. A. (1999). *With Clive in India, or, the beginnings of an empire*. London: Adegi Graphics LLC.

Jomo, K. S. (1986). A question of class: Capital, the state, and uneven development in Malaya. Singapore: Oxford University Press.

Kaur, A., & Meltcalfe, I. (1999). *The shaping of Malaysia*. Basingstoke: Palgrave Macmillan.

Khoo, K. K. (1972). *The western Malay states 1850–1873: The effects of commercial development on Malay politics*. Kuala Lumpur: Oxford University Press.

Kumar, D., & Desai, M. (1983). *The Cambridge history of India*. New York: Cambridge University Press.

Lees, L. H. (2017). *Planting empire, cultivating subjects: British Malaya, 1786–1941*. Cambridge: Cambridge University Press.

Lim, T. G. (1977). *Peasants and their agricultural economy in colonial Malaya 1974–1941*. Singapore: Oxford University Press.

Luxembourg, R. (1951). *The accumulation of capital*. Abingdon: Routledge & Kegan Paul.

Marx, K. (1853, June 25). The British Rule in India. *New-York Daily Tribune*. https://www.marxists.org/archive/marx/works/1853/06/25.htm. Accessed on 12 Mar 2021.

Patnaik, U. (2018, November 20). How much money did Britain take away from India? About $45 trillion in 173 years, says top economist. *MSN News*.

Polanyi, K. (1944). *The great transformation: The political and economic origins of our time*. New York: Farrar & Rinehart.

Popper, K. R. (1944). *The poverty of historicism. Economica, 11*(42), 86–103.

Popper, K. R. (1945a). *The open society and its enemies: The spell of Plato*. London: George Routledge & Sons.

Popper, K. R. (1945b). *The open society and its enemies: The high tide of prophecy—Hegel and Marx*. London: George Routledge & Sons.

Popper, K. R. (1959). *The logic of scientific discovery*. London: Hutchinson Education.

Ranjit Singh, D. S. (2003). *The making of Sabah 11865–1941: The dynamics of indigenous society*. Kuala Lumpur: University of Malaya Press.

Rasiah, R. (1995a). Laissez Fairism and industrial development in colonial Malaya. *Journal of Contemporary Asia, 25*(4), 524–538.

Rasiah, R. (1995b). *Foreign capital and industrialization in Malaysia*. Basingstoke: Macmillan.

Reid, R. (2011). Past and presentism: The 'precolonial' and the foreshortening of African history. *Journal of African History, 50*(2), 135–155.

Roff, W. (1967). *The origins of Malay nationalism*. New haven, CT: Yale University Press.

Sandu, K. S. (1969). *Indians in Malaya: Some aspects of their immigration and settlement 1786–1957*. Cambridge: Cambridge University Press.

Shaharil, T. (1977). The Terengganu ruling class in the late nineteteeth century. *Journal of the Malaysian Branch of the Royal Asiatic Society, 50*(2), 25–47.

Shaharil, T. (1984). *After its own image: The Trengganu experience, 1881–1941*. Singapore: Oxford University Press.

Shaharil, T. (2005). *Interrogating the state and craft of history: The Malaysian historiographical journey*. Inaugural Lecture, Kuala Lumpur: University Malaya Press.

Sharom, A. (1984). *Tradition and change in a Malay State: A study of the economic and political development of Kedah 1878–1923*. Kuala Lumpur: The Malaysian Branch Of The Royal Asiatic Society.

Syed Muhd Khairudin, A. (2015). *Radicals: Resistance and protest in Colonial Malaya*. Ithaca, NY: Cornell University Press.

Swift, M. G. (1965). *Malay peasant society in Jelebu*. London: Athlone Press.

Sultan Nazrin Shah. (2017). *Charting the economy: Early 20th century Malaya and contemporary Malaysian contrasts*. Shah Alam: Oxford University Press.

Sultan Nazrin Shah. (2019). *Striving for inclusive development: From Pangkor to a modern Malaysian state*. Shah Alam: Oxford University Press.

CHAPTER 2

Revisiting Colonial Industrialization in Malaya

Rajah Rasiah

Introduction

Historical narratives on colonial industrialization have tended to vacillate between one of largely free trade within the domain of particular sphere of colonial empires (e.g., Bauer, 1948; Benham, 1949; Corden & Richter, 1963; Little, 1982) and hostile interventionist efforts by colonial grandmasters to protect colonial interests (e.g. Puthucheary, 1960; Lim, 1977; Jomo, 1986). As colonies acted as labour-surplus economies dominated by disguised unemployment, the neoclassical dictum should have seen a specialization in agriculture and labour-intensive industrialization. Using the experience of colonial Malaya, we show in this article that colonial rule in Malaya saw the aggressive opening of tin mines and rubber plantations to serve the interests of the British empire rather than capitalist accumulation in Malaya. However, in its quest to extract surplus from tin mines and rubber plantations, the colonial government did effect institutional change that left the country with fairly good basic infrastructure, security and political stability for the post-colonial government

R. Rasiah (✉)
Asia-Europe Institute, University of Malaya,
Kuala Lumpur, Malaysia
e-mail: rajah@um.edu.my

R. Rasiah et al. (eds.), *Contesting Malaysia's Integration into the World Economy*, https://doi.org/10.1007/978-981-16-0650-2_2

to pursue, inter alia, industrial development. While the brutal methods through which surplus extraction evolved raised serious questions about British rule (Fauconnier, 2003; Cheah, 2012), colonial rule did quicken capitalist integration and sowed the seeds for industrial transformation in the country.[1]

Both plantation agriculture and physical infrastructure benefitted from technology transfer as the deployment of farming instruments, such as rubber processing and coagulation, hybrid seeds in agriculture, hydraulic sluicing, gravel pumping and dredging in tin mining, and the construction and maintenance of infrastructure relied on foreign technology (Allen & Donnithorne, 1957; Thoburn, 1977). However, colonial rule also limited industrialization to servicing agriculture and services, as well as into petty commodity manufacturing. While British rule under an imperial power focussed on protecting British capitalist interests restricted the potential for local industrial accumulation, it also exposed Colonial Malaya to modern manufacturing targeted at servicing the agricultural and infrastructure sectors.

I begin my analysis by arguing that the colonial government generally limited its role to supporting capitalist interests by assuming market-enhancing policies but on a number of times departed from deterministic relative price arguments owing to asset specificity and production control requirements affected by distance and war-time disruptions. Subsequently, I examine the extent and shortcomings of industrialization achieved under colonial policies. In doing so, we seek to use evidence to present the history of colonial industrialization in Malaysia in the tradition of Carr (1961) rather than rationalizing it *ex post* in the, which is consistent with the historical accounts undertaken by Shaharil (1995, 2005).

Theoretical Considerations

While colonial trade was largely laissez faire in nature within colonial spheres of influence, governments did intervene to protect the colonial

[1] While Chinese labour recruitment and control were handled by Chinese headman without direct management by Western owners (Cheah, 2012), the colonial government was more directly involved in Indian labour recruitment and management. The oppressive labour conditions in estates were pursued through repressive labour control methods, which included supervisors from different ethnicities and castes, and aggressive treatment meted out to those attempting to organize labour (Jomo, 1986; Jain, 1988, 1993).

interests. Three significant institutions were critical in shaping colonial economic governance.[2] Relative prices (markets) had a critical role in that the mining and smelting of tin and cultivation, tapping and processing of rubber were driven strongly by relative resource endowments. This line of economic argument was advanced by Ricardo (1817), Heckscher (1935) and Ohlin (1933),[3] which was later modelled mathematically by Samuelson (1948) to form the neoclassical model of specialization on the basis of relative factor endowments. Although subsequent refinements have taken place, the free trade arguments of Bhagwati (1988) and Krueger (1997) essentially emphasize the dominant role of markets.

The new institutionalists of Coase (1937), North (1990) and Williamson (1985) made the case for circumstances when market failures occur and how institutions, such as trust help correct market failures.[4] Scale effects and frequency of transactions, and asset specificities are examples of when markets are adapted to correct market failures. However, Veblen (1915), Nelson and Winter (1982) and Rasiah (2011) argue that markets often do not dictate circumstances when economic agents seek to pursue trust and other non-formal institutions to determine their choices.[5] It is in this way that economic agents often capture opportunities to introduce technologies that deviate from relative factor prices. For example, the economics of distance and war-time disruptions, as well as the need to coordinate adaptations to capital goods (e.g. heavy) machinery by locating their manufacture close to mining, cultivation and processing operations offer the opportunity for economic agents to enter in the manufacture of complementary goods that defy relative factor endowments. Albeit specific examples are scant, Hirschman (1958, 1970) made the case that the expansion in exports offers host-governments the opportunity to stimulate institutional change to promote backward linkages that often enter into the production of intermediate and capital

[2] Institutions are defined as influences that shape the conduct of economic agents (individuals, firms and organizations) (Veblen, 1915).

[3] In the two factor model of free trade, Heckscher (1935) and Ohlin (1933) used assumptions of perfect mobility of capital and labour within country borders and their perfect immobility across country borders.

[4] Such views are often referred to the new institutionalist account of institutions (Rasiah, 2011).

[5] These views are popularly known as the evolutionary view of institutions (Rasiah, 1995a, b; 2011).

goods. Businesses and governments closely working with them often appropriate these pecuniary and technical external economies to stimulate structural transformation.

Given the risks and uncertainties involved in entering the production of scale- and capital-intensive goods, the extent of entry of economic agents into such economic activities often require support from host-governments and business associations to check cut-throat competition and that the right incentives are in place to underwrite risks and uncertainties (Rasiah, 2019).

However much the colonial state avoided and in some cases discouraged the growth of manufacturing in Malaya, one can expect that the smooth functioning of the export-oriented colonial mining and agriculture would have required some departures from the role of markets as an institution of governance. Hence, in this chapter, we explore the interactions of a myriad of institutional influences in the emergence of manufacturing under colonial rule.

Precolonial Production

Although there are considerable accounts of precolonial Malaya that include other states, such as Kedah, Kelantan, Perak and Johore (Wong, 1965), Malacca is the most decorated precolonial kingdom that was involved in trading of Indian piecemeal goods for spices, aromatics and dyewoods, what Reid (1993) classified as early mercantilism in Malaya. Trade was mainly confined to few ports (especially Malacca), though Indian traders visited other parts of Malaya, such as Kedah. The Malays were largely involved in subsistence farming and fishing, locating their settlements close to the rivers (Ooi, 1961: 350). Only small-scale off-season mining was carried out with the Mandailings from Sumatra, important participants who used *Dulang* (bucket) to hand mine tin ore from the rivers (Burns, 1982). Petty commodity production characterized manufacturing, which was limited to craft-work and cottage industries. Handicrafts (e.g., floor mats, blinds and rattan baskets) and simple food processing (e.g. keropok [fish crackers]) were among the main manufactures. Traditional human skills characterized the technology deployed in such manufacturing activities. Traditional wood- and rattan-based home and boat making were the most sophisticated manufacturing operation then.

Production organization in precolonial Malaya was based on a tribute-paying mode of production in which the debt bondsman and the commoner tilled the land, which was in the control of the rulers and chieftains (Jomo, 1986). The social relations that existed then were organized around the palace with a strong emphasis on culture, religion, ceremonies and security. Except for the emerging tin and cash crop trade involving foreign labour along the West coast, free wage labour was largely non-existent. There were often plots and counter plots involving the rulers and chieftains, which continued after British colonialism emerged (Shaharil, 1977, 1995).

Colonial Production

Western influence, especially since the advent of British colonialism in 1874, turned Malaya into a major raw material exporter, starting with tin and later rubber to feed the industries of the West, including the United States, which became a major importer of natural rubber. Tin and later rubber became the two most important revenue earners. Other primary commodities of significance included oil palm, pineapple and coconuts. Malaya was endowed with rich deposits of tin ore. However, commercially produced rubber and oil palm owed much to seeds brought originally from Brazil and Nigeria, respectively. While immigrants were brought by the British from India to farm, weed and tap natural rubber, Chinese settlers were brought by Chinese headmen to mine tin initially using chain pumps, and later through acquisition from the British, hydraulic sluicing and gravel pumps (Thoburn, 1977).

Furthermore, there is also considerable debate on the preferential treatment provided by the colonial government to foreign estate owners and dredging companies (see Yip, 1964; Bauer, 1948; Silcock, 1948; Knorr, 1945).[6] The bulk of colonial Malayan revenue came from import tariffs and excise duties on opium, tobacco and liquor.[7] Income taxes were only introduced in Malaya and Singapore in 1948 (Loo & McKerchar, 2014: 245). Tariffs on goods imported from non-British empire were

[6] British ownership in tin mining began to rise following the introduction of dredging through the Malayan Tin Dredging Company, which was opened in 1912 (Fermor, 1939: 74; Allen & Donnithorne, 1957: 152).

[7] For instance, In Kedah revenue from opium accounted for 40% of total revenue in 1919 (Sultan Nazrin Shah, 2019: 41).

important, but also important were tariffs on exports of tin and rubber, which together accounted for a peak of 36.8% in 1906 and a trough of 5.2% in 1947 (see Fig. 2.1). The contribution of tin revenue was strong in the early years owing to massive output, which fell in trend terms owing to exhaustion in tin deposits despite the introduction of dredging from 1912. While claims that the colonial government selectively imposed tariffs to favour British owners are misplaced as tariffs were a function of prices (cf. Lim, 1967; see Rasiah, 1995a, 1995b), the colonial government did allocate favourable lands to foreign companies (see Drabble, 1973: 72–74, 249; Lim, 1977; Yip, 1964: 151–152), and excluded taxation from merchants and professionals (Sultan Nazrin Shah, 2019: 41). Research was largely concentrated among large foreign companies with

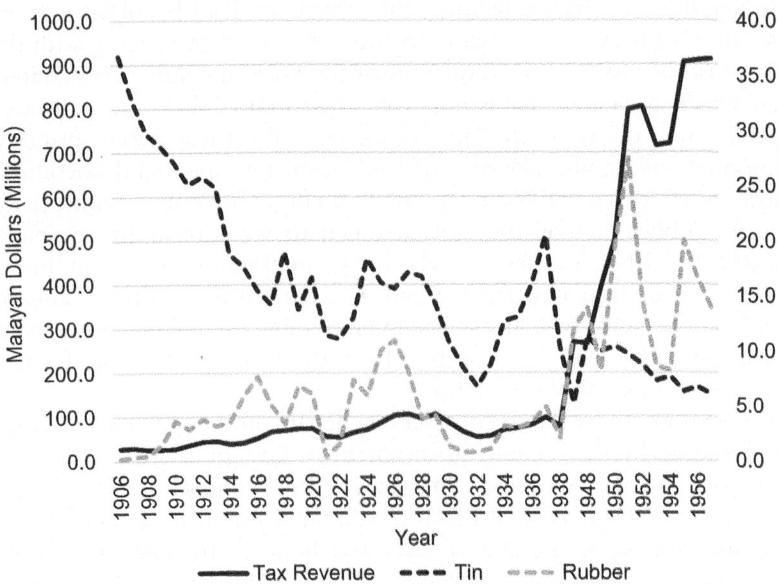

Fig. 2.1 Contribution of export taxes from tin and rubber in colonial revenue, Malaya, 1906–1957 (*Source* Plotted from Federation of Malaya [1957])

local interests confined mainly to small firms that lacked the capital to engage in such activities.[8]

The colonial government's four most important developmental functions helped modernize Malaya, namely, establish and maintain order and security, infrastructure and labour supply (Sultan Nazrin Shah, 2017, 2019). The most obvious interventions were tariffs and quotas imposed on manufactured imports from non-British spheres of control (especially Japan and the United States) (see Jomo, 1986: 145–147), and the Stevenson Restriction Scheme introduced in 1935 to regulate rubber supply following the depression of the 1930s (see Bauer, 1948). The colonial government also generated revenue from export taxes, which were determined based on prices.

The first task the colonial government assumed after the Pangkor treaty in 1874 was to establish law and order. Anarchy in the states had reached such proportions that tin mining output had begun to fall (Turnbull, 1964: 135–136); from 6 thousand tons annually in 1871–1872, output fell to 5 thousand tons and 4 thousand tons, respectively, in the years 1873 and 1874 (Lim, 1967: Appendix 2.1). The feuding Malay chiefs and sultans showed little signs of establishing a peaceful platform for the extraction and transfer of tin ore, which was escalated by gang fights among the Chinese miners. British efforts to intervene directly were economic in nature, which was dominated by efforts to protect and strengthen tin trade. Although colonialism was repressive and the Malay chiefs were increasingly frustrated with foreign governance,[9] the British helped reduce chaos and establish law and order. In addition, British rule also reduced the threat of other Western powers (especially the Netherlands, Germany and Japan) intervening in the Malay states. It was only after security was established did Western capital invest extensively in the extraction and export of raw materials from Malaya.

Secondly, the colonial government embarked on a massive development of infrastructure. Transport networks, health service, education and public utilities were developed and maintained. The colonial government's policy promoted capitalist production and distribution, which was driven by demand from the West. Railways and roads were constructed

[8] Schumpeter (1934) had argued that entrepreneurs are too small to have the financial capacity to invest in research and development activities.

[9] Among the resistance from local forces that emerged include that by Maharaja Lela in Perak and Tok Janggut in Kelantan (Cheah, 1995, 2006; Shaharil, 1995).

to connect administrative centres and ports with mining and plantation centres. Over the period 1884–1937, the colonial government spent MS228 million on building railways. By 1931, it had laid 1028 miles of railway lines (Lim, 1967: 272). From the short stretches of cart tracks in 1874, the colonial government had also built 6060 miles of roads by 1948. The port facilities at Georgetown, Port Swettenham, Dungun, Malacca, Port Dickson and Telok Anson were also expanded. Health facilities were built at the towns (especially at administrative centres) and the estates. There were 70 hospitals and 72 mobile dispensaries in 1947 (Lim, 1967: 310), and 80 rural health centres in 1949. The Federated Malay States' (FMS) expenditure on health rose from MS3.4mn in 1924 to M$15.8mn in 1957 (Lim, 1967: 304). While the hospitals and schools were built at towns, dispensaries were established at estates. The FMS expenditure on education rose from M$1.8mn in 1927 to M$l7.9mn in 1957. By 1957, there were 1.l (1.1?)mn school students and 35.7 thousand teachers in Malaya. Technical training institutes were located close to the major public utilities and railway maintenance departments. Albeit demand for skilled labour in the erection and maintenance of mining operations (e.g. pumps, sluices and dredges) and agricultural milling (e.g. latex sheeting machines) machinery rose strongly (Thoburn, 1977), the government did little on its own initiative to raise skilled labour supply for manufacturing.

Nevertheless, in its efforts to boost tin mining and rubber cultivation, the government had to violate a number of free market tenets because of the specific technologies essential to mine tin and cultivate rubber effectively. This is the third contribution the colonial government made to modernize the extraction of surplus from the primary sector. For example, Perak's British Resident, Hugh Low introduced the first steam engine and centrifugal pump to overcome flooding in tin mining. Its technology, as with dredging, was capital-intensive. Indeed, the Railway and Public Works departments had to pay for British instructors to train local employees to maintain their huge structure. That largely explains why the government placed priority on establishing technical schools in the twentieth century. Third, the British introduced the Torrens system (which with the mukim register started off free ownership of land), resulted in the transfer of significant patches of lands to the foreigners. The prime objectives of this policy were to alienate land for commercial use smallholdings under government control (Kratoska, 1975: 135). However, the reluctance of the British colonialists to engage the peasants meant that the peasants did not experience large-scale emancipation from pre-capitalist relations. Nevertheless, free ownership of land attracted foreign investors. Immigrant labour formed the main mass of free wage labour in colonial Malaya.

Fourth, the colonial state encouraged and administered the import of immigrants from India and China as the main source of labour supply (Amarjit, 2014). Although Malay-centric politicians in independent Malaysia have often contended that imports of foreign labour undermined national unity and disfigured Malaya's cultural identity, one can also argue that imports of foreign labour laid the foundations for capitalist development through the participation of free wage labour.[10] Although wage labour (especially Chinese) was already emerging prior to direct intervention, colonialism accelerated the deployment of free wage labour in production relations. Officials from Ceylon were also engaged to manage and administrate port facilities, postal service and estates (see Drabble & Drake, 1981: 309). Free wage labour was initially dominated by Chinese and Indian labour in tin mining and rubber production, respectively. The British were cautious in utilizing the indigenous Malay labour who derived their livelihood from sedentary farming and shifting cultivation. The large reserves of impoverished masses from India and China offered a better source of cheap labour. By excluding the Malays from the main mining and plantation agriculture, the government also ensured that the food supply (especially rice) to mining and plantation workers was not disrupted.[11] Obviously, the government stimulated the movement of a generally immobile factor to harness the growing potential offered by Malaya. By 1938, 80.4% of the estate labour force constituted Indians (Jomo, 1986: Table 7J). By 1946–1950, the Chinese contributed 60.9% of the tin mining labour force in Malaya (Yip, 1964: Table V-19). Although the government subsidized imports of foreign

[10] See Sultan Nazrin Shah (2019) for a lucid account of the emergence of foreign labour, and the political arrangements agreed upon by the ethnic representatives at the time of independence, which included, inter alia, the provision of citizenship to foreign labour in return for recognition of the special position of the Malay royalty, and the Bumiputras.

[11] The Japanese colonial government strengthened paddy cultivation in Malaysia over the period 1941–1945 through heavy promotion of paddy cultivation, though a significant share of the surplus was exported through highly regulated procedures (Yoji & Mako, 2008).

labour (Thoburn, 1977; Jomo, 1986), they were more than compensated by tariffs levied on commodity exports (Rasiah, 1995a, 1995b).

Industrial Development

The only area where the British colonial government was involved directly in manufacturing is in the promotion of rural industry. However, as the government's main intention here appears to have been in offering off-season employment for the rural population, especially to the paddy cultivators whose produce was crucial in supporting the mining and plantation labour force, and to arrest support for the growing communist insurgency, it hardly took-off (see Rasiah, 1995a, 1995b). Thus, despite the promotion of rural industry such as handicraft (e.g. rattan and attap basketware), employment in related industries, which was started by the Japanese over the period 1941–1945 fell sharply between 1947 and 1957 (see Fig. 2.2).[12] Although the government also offered loans to smallholder associations to erect latex processing plants (e.g. Johore Smallholders Association), albeit in small scale, they were market related.

The British colonial government's fiscal revenue (which was accumulated largely from export taxes on primary commodities with tin and rubber) amounting to over 90% of it in the period 1947–1957 (Lim, 1967: 267–269), was also used to provide indirect subsidy to manufacturing firms from the utilization of infrastructural support services. Meanwhile geographical distance that separated Malaya from the industrial West offered the best natural protection for several industries, especially during the war and between colonial spheres. Especially tin smelting and rubber processing grew strongly in Malaya. Other agricultural processing activities also grew substantially. For example, by 1906, 16 factories with strong associations with the local Chinese produced over 29,000 cases of canned pineapples a year (Kennedy, 1962: 218; Rasiah, 1995b: 538). Output rose to 2.7 million cases in 1939 before falling sharply as a consequence of destruction during the Second World War. Following rehabilitation efforts after the war, output reached 102,000 cases in 1947 with 86,600 cases exported to Britain and the Middle East (Benham, 1951: 33). Meanwhile, in 1947 the 24 palm oil factories in

[12] Japanese economic interests in Malaya started well before the Second World War, including in plantations, iron mines, and commercial fishing (Kratoska, 1988).

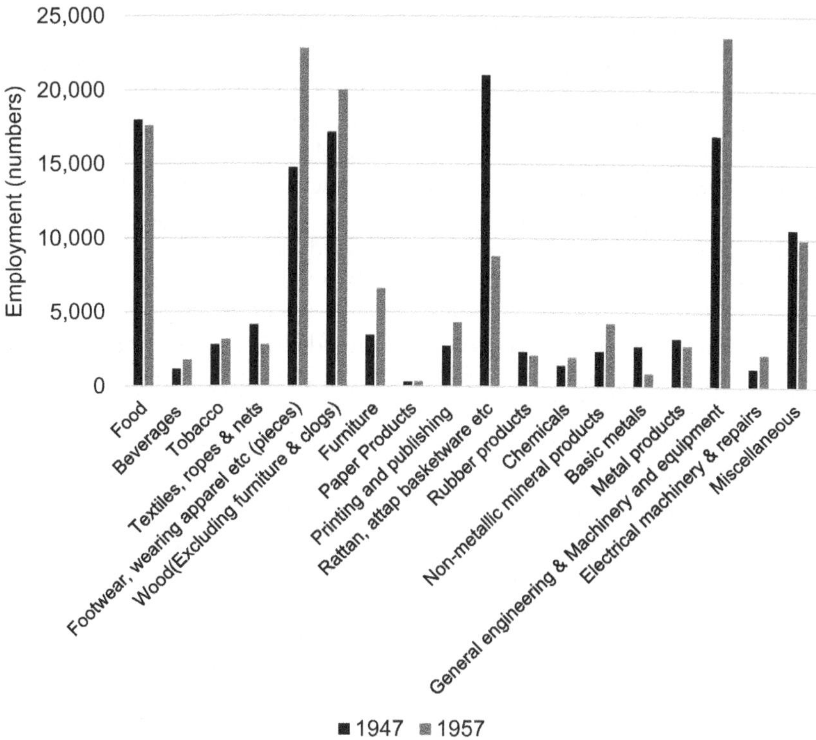

Fig. 2.2 Manufacturing employment, Malaya, 1947 and 1957 (*Source* Federation of Malaya [1957])

Malaya generated 5700 tons of palm kennels (Benham, 1951: 24), while coconut oil and copra-cake production totalled 138,000 tons.

The Japanese colonial government introduced more comprehensive central control than the British, whereby the sale of essential goods was regulated and a Five-Year Production Plan was introduced in 1943 (Kratoska, 1988). Also introduced was a Five-Year Industrial Plan with the goal of transforming Malaya from a liberal to a planned economy largely because of war-time restrictions on imported manufactured goods from Japan while supplies from Europe and the United States were cut. Consequently, the Japanese colonial government promoted the smelting of iron, and chemical industries (Kratoska, 1998: 174–175), and essential light consumption goods, such as soaps and toothpaste (Kratoska, 1998: 178–179; Rasiah, 1995b: 528). Although some of these industries re-emerged following the introduction of import-substitution following the enactment of the Pioneer Industry ordinance by the post-colonial state in 1958 (Rasiah, 1995a), Japanese participation in modern manufacturing ended upon the return of the British. Japanese involvement in the processing of agricultural food crops to food items, such as biscuits and beverages, also complimented such activities by local Chinese (Kratoska, 1998: 178).

Efficiency improvements from the introduction of technically superior smelting methods soon attracted the attention of other Southeast Asian miners. Until 1933, about 30% of all tin smelted in Malaya came from Indonesia and Siam (Fermor, 1939: 79–80; Allen & Donnithorne, 1957: 160–161). Both the large-scale nature of Western smelting and transport facilities, which the colonial state built using mainly revenue collected from tax on tin exports, supported vibrant smelting operations at major ports, such as Georgetown and Port Swettenham. Although the smelting of tin imports fell after 1933 (following Indonesia's introduction of its own smelter in Arnhem), it was still around 25% in 1937 with new supplies coming from Burma, French Indo-China and China.

In rubber milling, the replacement of paired rollers with continuous sheeters enabled continuous processing, which helped reduce rubber processing costs from 5 cents per pound in the early 1920s to 0.5 cents per lb in 1932–1933 (Bauer, 1948: 265). It was during colonial rule that the first massive rubber research ground was founded in Malaya. From its conception in 1925, the research land was started at Sungai Buloh in 1927 with 2000 acres. The research institute itself was started initially at Bungsar Estate in 1926 before it was moved to Ampang in Kuala Lumpur in 1937.

The specificity of machinery and equipment required in both tin mining and smelting, and rubber cultivation and processing increasingly made them capital-intensive. Thus, although primary production in Malaya emerged as largely labour intensive ventures (e.g. dulang washing by the Malays and chain pumping by the Chinese in tin mining and charcoal furnaces in smelting, and simple planting and tapping methods in plantation agriculture), competition and the quest of raising productivity necessitated a shift towards capital-intensive technology. The problems of organizing and controlling labour, and inefficient smelting and processing methods were the prime forces that forced the introduction of capital-intensive methods in tin production. For example, the dredge, first introduced by Malayan Tin Dredging Company in 1912, reduced sharply the utilization of labour and therefore problems of control. Meanwhile, the regenerative gas-fired reverberator furnaces, first introduced in 1902, improved tin smelting efficiency considerably (see Fermor, 1939: 74; Allen & Donnithorne, 1957). In addition, dredging enabled mining in deep and swampy grounds. The exhaustion of surface ores and the efficiency of capital-intensive methods led to the Chinese displacing their traditional chain pumps with gravel pumps and hydraulic sluices. As dredges required lump sum investment, local firms generally could only afford them after independence in 1957. Rubber and oil palm milling machines were located in estates.[13] Even smallholders usually sent their produce to the estates for milling. Thus, although market forces were important, the drive to sustain competitiveness and efficiency meant that planters and miners in Malaya were increasingly resorting to power-driven machinery. This is endemic to capitalist production.

The specificity of particular technologies and restrictions imposed on foreign trade through colonial spheres of influence and hostile war zones were instrumental in the emergence of heavy consumer, intermediate and capital goods industries in colonial Malaya. The utilization of power-driven technology offered immense potential for diffusion in colonial Malaya. A subsidiary of United Engineers started building small crafts and repairing ships in Singapore in 1881 (Allen & Donnithorne, 1957: 261), which gradually spread its activities to the construction of dredges and rubber machinery. These industries were supported by its iron and steel plants, and machine and boiler shops especially in Ipoh (Perak), where it fabricated the machines and parts. This firm formed the training ground for local Chinese workers who carried the skills to the local firms, including foundries that they foundered subsequently (Thoburn, 1977: 201). From simple foundry work, power-driven machinery gradually diffused into several other industries (see Fig. 2.3). By 1955, even the once traditionally human-skills dominated pottery making industry had become mechanized. Strong cooperation among the Chinese ensured that cut-throat competition was avoided. This development led to foreign mining companies increasingly subcontracting servicing and later dredge

[13] British miners also had difficulty controlling Chinese labour (Rasiah, 1995b).

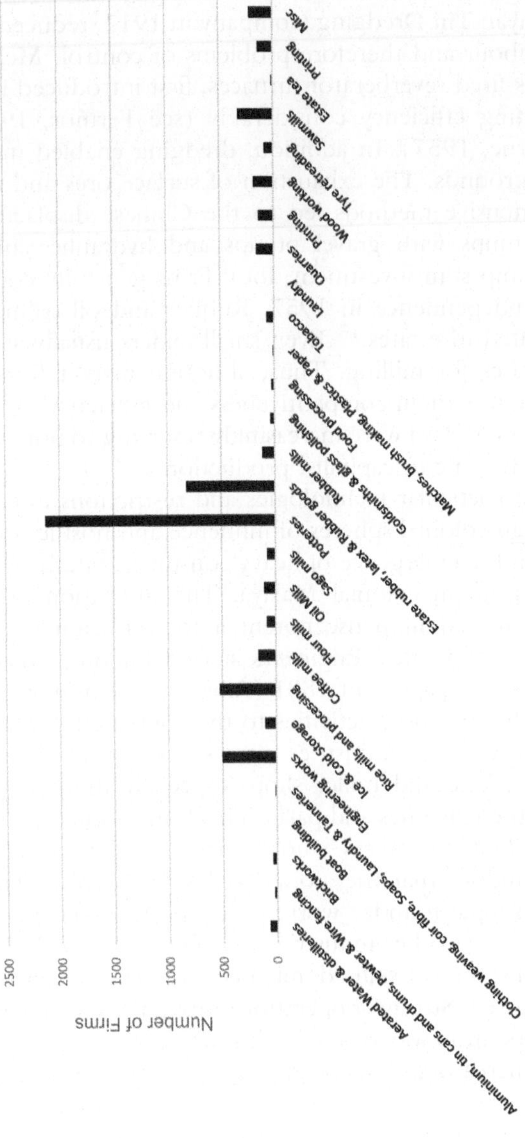

Fig. 2.3 Manufacturing firms using power machinery, Malaya, 1955 (*Source* Adapted from Federation of Malaya [1957])

construction work to local firms, followed by a complementary two-tier system in which United Engineers did the designing while the local firms did the fabrication and assembly (Thoburn, 1977: 201). From foundry, machining, fabrication and other engineering works, foreign firms acted as training grounds for consumer industries. Singapore Rubber Works, which was founded in 1889 to extract gutta-percha, branched into the manufacture of rubber-based products. Bata started its shoe factory in Singapore in 1937 and Port Swettenham in 1939 (Allen & Donnithorne, 1957: 261).

In addition, local firms (e.g. Ho Hong and Tan Kah Kee) opened operations to manufacture steam ships, cement, milled oil, sheet rubber, sweets, boots, shoes, bicycle tyres, hoses, biscuits, bricks and soaps. Indeed the production of these items grew strongly as local demand increased with the development of the cash-based primary commodity economy (Rasiah, 1995a, 1995b), which enjoyed considerable impetus from war-time disruptions of 1914–1918 and 1939–1945, the communist insurgency in the late 1940s and 1950s and the Korean war boom in the 1950s. Production of plywood and cement met around three-quarters and half, respectively, of domestic demand (Federation of Malaya, 1957: para 78). Exports of rubber footwear, and bicycle tyres and tubes accounted for 5.3 million and 0.4 million pieces, respectively, in 1955 (Federation of Malaya, 1957: Appendix V, Table A). Manufacturing, albeit on a small scale, was indirectly subsidized by the mining and agricultural sectors during colonial rule through the infrastructure developed and maintained by the colonial government using taxes collected from primary exports.

Other than the skilled staff and technology offered by the foreign companies operating in Malaya, local companies also gained from the government's technical training programmes developed largely to support the railway, port and public works departments. Several skilled personnel from these departments eventually left to work in the more lucrative private sector. Compared to the M$5 bonus offered by the state departments, private firms were offering M$20–25 monthly wages in the early 1900s (Chai, 1967: 260–262). Indeed the acute shortage of skilled labour in state departments led to the government introducing various incentives and training schemes. Perak and Selangor offered scholarships of M$3000 and M$2000, respectively, in 1899 to enable boys from English schools to undergo training in the workshops of the public works and railway departments. This was boosted by an engineering instructor hired from England in 1906. They were augmented by technical schools. The four junior technical schools in Penang, Ipoh, Kuala Lumpur and Johore Bharu trained a total of 784 residential and 235 non-residential students in 1955 (Federation of Malaya, 1957: Appendix VI). The government also set up a techno-factory in Kuala Lumpur and nationally coordinated training schemes by 1957. Learning by doing, adaptive engineering and in-house apprenticeship training schemes were also important in enhancing technology of the local Chinese firms (Song, 1923). Unlike Western firms, which had difficulty controlling local Chinese labour, Chinese firms, housed in backyard workshops enjoyed closer cooperation, which often ran along family and clannish lines.

The planning framework that the Japanese colonial government introduced in 1941–1945 resembled strong pro-active industrial policy elements but was quickly ended by the returning British colonial government. Thus, although Malaya was largely labour- and natural resource-rich, the nature of production and institutional framework that emerged encouraged the utilization of capital-intensive power-driven technology. Nonetheless, the natural protection offered by distance, and the war-time trade disruptions enhanced production for domestic use. However, as the demand for engineering support services were generally infrequent and fluctuated considerably, the engineering firms remained relatively small despite using power-driven machinery. Consequently, these small firms did not enjoy the scale to grow into large machine tool manufacturers. Besides, large orders were met from imports from Britain. Thus, the World Bank (1955: 422) noted that the average manufacturing firms in Malaya were small, employing on average of 20 employees but mostly less than 10 employees. Nevertheless, the economics of flexibility, where small firms specialized horizontally in similar technologies, switching quickly production to adjust with demand, ensured that these firms continued to utilize power-driven machinery.

Nevertheless, the impetus offered by war-time disruptions in trade, growing local demand as the cash-based raw material economy flourished, and massive government efforts to build new villages to quell the communist threat, and the Korean war boom generated sufficient demand to draw a handful of Western consumer and intermediate firms. Bata, Ford Motors, Unilever Brothers, Imperial Chemical Industries (ICI), Metal Box, OU Associated Portland Cement Manufacturers and Malayan Collieries were some of the big firms that opened production in consumer and intermediate goods' manufacturing. Unilever Brothers opened in 1952 equipped with the latest machinery to manufacture soaps and cooking fats from local oil palm costing M$10 million with an employment size of 700 workers (Allen & Donnithorne, 1957: 262).

Between 1947 and 1957, employment in the beverages, tobacco, wearing apparel, furniture, printing and publishing, non-metallic mineral products, general engineering machinery and equipment, electrical machinery and equipment rose (Fig. 2.2).

Unilever began operations with a planned capacity of 10 million tons of oil per year (Nanjundan, 1953: 162). Domestic production of light consumption goods, such as soaps, tobacco and biscuits grew strongly in the period 1953–1955 (Rasiah, 1995a, 1995b). Domestic cement and plywood production met nearly half and three-quarters of domestic requirements, respectively, in 1955 (Federation of Malaya, 1957: para 78). Within simple modern manufacturings, the economy had become quite diversified. Food products, general engineering, machinery and equipment and wood products contributed 9.1, 18.9 and 14.1% of total manufacturing value added in 1947 (Benham, 1951: Table 3). Indeed, employment in the intermediate and capital goods' industries grew strongly in the period 1947–1957 (see Fig. 2.2), which happened alongside a sharp decline in the labor-intensive handicrafts industry (e.g. textiles, ropes, nets, rattan, and attap basketware). Employment in the basic metals' (mainly tin smelting) fell in the same period owing to a rise in capital-intensity as tin smelting value added did not decline in the period 1947–1957 (Rasiah, 1995a). The extent of structural change is reflected in a rise in the composition of imports of intermediate and capital goods as the share of import as of machinery and equipment, and transport vehicles and equipment increased, while the share of food, beverages and tobacco decline in the period 1953–1957 (Corden & Richter, 1963).

While expansion in the primary sectors and infrastructure powered the emergence of modem manufacturing, the lack of a profound industrial policy restricted large-scale manufacturing growth. Nevertheless, the expansion in local owned firms (especially Chinese firms) owed much to linkages that emerged in the engineering industries. In addition, as the mining and milling machines needed heavy engineering support, local firms gradually acquired power-driven technology, which was influenced by a blend of institutions, including markets and cooperation. Also, colonial policy encouraged the utilization and diffusion of heavy engineering technology to expand output to meet increasing demand in the West.

While markets were important, various extra-market institutions, such as transport costs, processing costs of plantation output, war-time blockages and asset specificities acted as critical propellants of early modern manufacturing. A combination of learning by doing, adaptive engineering and employee transfers stimulated the diffusion of power-driven technologies across industries such that even traditional pottery malting firms had begun to mechanize production; pottery making contributed more than a third of factories using power-driven machinery in Malaya in 1955 (see Fig. 2.3).[14] That significant amounts of technology that was transferred into colonial Malaya was capital-intensive shows that production is a dynamic process in which relative prices reflecting factor endowments were only one influence. However, in the absence of strong subsidies (e.g. in research and development [R&D], and exports) and elaborate industrial policies, the local firms remained small. Where large-scale manufacturing appeared profitable, foreign firms (which enjoyed strong R&D support and high technology from their parent plants) set up operations.

A network of institutions linking the primary sectors, infrastructure, engineering and technical support (both machinery and personnel) and training institutions evolved to support the extraction of surplus from mining and agriculture in colonial Malaya. While markets were important, capitalist interests resorted to the most effective technologies at their disposal to generate surplus.

Despite the opportunities that emerged, it appears that its potential for promoting large-scale industrialization was lost during colonial rule. As Hirschman (1958, 1970) and Warren (1980) had argued in the case of the developing economies, the massive exports generated from Malaya offered considerable room for promoting backward linkages. However, the colonial state was not focussed on national interests to pursue a policy of large-scale industrial promotion.[15] The colonial government's preoccupation with promoting British interests meant that even Malaya's precolonial socio-cultural social formation was not

[14] See Schumpeter (1934) for a lucid account of incremental innovations that entrepreneurs typically generate.

[15] As Bagchi (1982) argued on India, Rodney argued on Africa, Kay (1989) argued on Latin America, and Jomo (1986) and Shaharil (2005) had argued on Malaya, colonialism was not aimed at accumulation at host-sites. Instead, colonial plans were targeted at enriching the colonial grandmasters.

entirely broken down. Imperialism under the rule of a foreign power, as Charlesworth (1982: 70–71) had noted in the case of India, denied the local state an independent nationalist political drive necessary to promote local industrialization. However, it will be simplistic to argue that the colonial state denied colonial Malaya rapid industrialization as the counterfactual of an extension of the tribute-paying mode of production offers no evidence of any elements of modern manufacturing. Malaya did not possess the institutional framework for modem manufacturing to take-off prior to the establishment of colonial rule (see also Rasiah, 1995a, 1995b). Indeed, despite the repression and destruction brought about by colonialism, it did provide the early shake-up essential to initiate modern industrialization (Marx, 1976; Luxemburg, 1951).

Conclusions

With the exception of export taxes, it is clear that liberal trade policy instruments were used by the government in colonial Malaya within the British empire to extract surplus for accumulation in Britain. Official trade regulations in colonial Malaya did not impose tariffs on imports from within the British Empire but restricted them from other spheres of influence. However, significant departures from the doctrine of free markets did take place as Malaya's location, specificity of production, and nature of the embedding environment necessitated greater role for non-market institutions. Apart from intermittent restrictions on imports from non-British spheres of control, the colonial government hardly intervened in manufacturing. Its only direct promotional role within manufacturing was limited to rural industry, especially the traditional handicrafts sector. Although the government did offer loans to local petty producers, the extent was very small.

The economics of distance encouraged the emergence of modern manufacturing in colonial Malaya to support tin mining, smelting and processing, and rubber cultivation and processing. Given asset specificities, power-driven technology became an essential driver of these activities, which diffused to local firms (especially Chinese owned). The transfer of skilled staff from the government's railway and public works departments, and the technical schools started by the government provided sufficient supplies of technical labour to support such activities. Although markets were important, given the inherently uneven and segmented nature of labour markets in emerging economies, firms gradually adopted capital-intensive technology in a number of operations to improve coordination between supply and demand. As the Chinese firms enjoyed a significant advantage in organizing local Chinese labour, foreign firms resorted to subcontracting various aspects of manufacturing to them. Consequently, collaboration became an important institution that blended with markets to shape production organization.

Although the British were more involved in the recruitment of Indian labour for rubber cultivation and processing, similar structures of control were established using Indian and Ceylonese supervisors. Since the early management among the big plantations were from the West, an ethnic division of labour differentiated by caste was used to control labour. Trade unionism was suppressed, while Indian supervisors were left with the task of managing the oppressive working conditions (Fauconnier, 2003). Since off-estate processing of latex into sheet rubber was undertaken in estates, similar labour controls were used in rubber processing.

As local manufacturing was exposed to international competition in which large-scale demand was met from imports, local manufacturing firms remained small despite absorbing capital-intensive power-driven technology. The two war-time disruptions and growth in effective demand locally and regionally stimulated the opening of large foreign firms. However, as the market economy was still in its early stages of development, even foreign firms operating in Malaya hardly competed against one another in the domestic product market. Therefore, the lack of a dynamic industrial policy restricted spill-over effects of technology diffusion from generating large-scale manufacturing expansion in Malaya.

Resources and later end-product markets were decisive in attracting capitalists to Malaya whose ventures to extract surplus led to the development of infrastructure and the other institutions to maintain them. This emerging institutional framework offered the potential for modern manufacturing to evolve. Despite its repressive imposition and administration, which are characteristics of capitalist integration (see Luxemburg, 1951), colonial rule created the conditions for the transformation of Malaya from one of traditional and stagnant economies to a market economy. The rich resources enabled the colonial state to support its fiscal, security and administrative role. The development and maintenance of infrastructure (especially railways, ports and public works) and the primary sectors offered considerable spin-off potential. However, governed by a foreign power to support British imperial interests, the Malayan state lacked a nationalist focus, and with that, the nationalist drive to pursue pro-active industrial policies to stimulate rapid industrialization (e.g. targeting, prioritization and subsidies and tariffs to shelter local firms). However, although it is impossible to imagine the counterfactual accurately without colonial rule, given the sluggish social formation that existed prior to British intervention and the lack of dynamic industrial policies after independence (see Rasiah, 1995a), there is little evidence to suggest that industrial transformation would have rooted more deeply if Malaya had not been colonialized.

Returning to the theoretical argument on what shaped colonial industrialization in Malaya, it is obvious that a myriad of institutions were critical. Markets were important and so were the different initiatives that defined *laisse fairism* within the colonial sphere of influence, though even here distance and the need to situate productive capacity at proximate locations gave rise to the manufacture of heavy machinery and equipment, and ships and foundries. Uncertainties and risks also drove the emergence of manufacturing to ensure smooth coordination of tin mining and smelting, and rubber cultivation and processing. Trust and collaboration between shipping companies, miners and smelters, cultivators and processors and infrastructure providers were also important to effectively manage risks and uncertainties for the transfer of tin and rubber to final markets, which helped make Malaya the prime earner of US dollars in the Sterling area (Sutton, 2016). Expanding trade offered considerable opportunities for widening industrialization,[16] but the colonial government was engrossed mainly on accumulation in Britain, which denied the requisite interventions essential to support full-scale industrialization in Malaya. Consequently, the task of industrializing Malaya was left to the post-colonial state, which became independent in 1957.

References

Allen, G. C., & Donnithorne, A. G. (1957). *Western enterprise in Indonesia and Malaya: A Study in Economic Development*. London: Routledge.

Amarjit, K. (2014). Plantation systems, labour regimes and the state in Malaysia, 1900–2012. *Journal of Agrarian Change, 14*(2), 190–213.

[16] *A la* Hirschman's (1958, 1970) argument on the role of expanding export markets on the potential for developing backward linkages at host-sites.

Bagchi, A. K. (1982). *The political economy of underdevelopment*. Cambridge: Cambridge University Press.
Bauer, P. T. (1948). *The rubber industry: A study in competition and monopoly*. London: Longmans.
Benham, F. C. (1949). The rubber policies. *Economica, XIV*(64): 355–368.
Benham, F. (1951). *The National Income of Malaya, 1947–49: With a Note on 1950*. Washington, DC: U.S. Government Printing Office.
Bhagwati, J. (1988). *Protectionism*. Cambridge: MIT Press.
Burns, P. L. (1982). Capitalism and the Malay states. In H. Alavi, P. L. Burns, G. R. Knight, P. Meyer, & D. McEachern (Eds.), *Capitalism and colonial production*. London: Croom Helm.
Carr, E. H. (1961). *What is history?* New York: Random House.
Chai, H. C. (1967). *The development of British Malaya 1896–1906*. Kuala Lumpur: Oxford University Press.
Charlesworth, N. (1982). *British rule and the Indian Economy 1800–1914*. London: Macmillan.
Cheah, B. K. (1995). Hunting down the rebels in Kelantan, 1915: The Sultan's 'double game'. *Journal of the Malaysian Branch of the Royal Asiatic Society, 68*(2), 9–32.
Cheah, B. K. (2006). *To' Janggut: Legions, histories and perceptions of the 1915 rebellion in Kelantan*. Singapore: Singapore University Press.
Cheah, B. K. (2012). *Red star over Malaya—Resistance and social conflict during and after the Japanese Occupation of Malaya, 1941-46* (4th ed.). Singapore: NUS Press.
Coase, R. H. (1937). The nature of the firm. *Economica, 4*(16), 386–405.
Corden, W. M., & Richter, H. V. (1963). Appendix B: Malayan Trade statistics and the entrepot trade. In T. H. Silcock & E. K. Fisk (Eds.), *The political economy of independent Malaya: A case study in development* (pp. 282–298). London: Angus and Robertson.
Drabble, J. H. (1973). *Rubber in Malaya: The genesis of the industry*. Kuala Lumpur: Oxford University Press.
Drabble, J. T., & Drake, P. J. (1981). The British agency houses in Malaysia: Survival in a changing world. *Journal of Southeast Asian Studies, 12*(2), 297–328.
Fauconnier, H. (2003). *Soul of Malaya*. Singapore: Archipelago Press.
Federation of Malaya. (1955). *Report of the Industrial Development Working Party, Kuala Lumpur.*
Federation of Malaya. (1957). *Report of the Industrial Development Working Party*. Kuala Lumpur: Government Printers.
Fermor, L. L. (1939). *Report upon the mining industry in Malaya*. Kuala Lumpur: British Malaya.

Heckscher, E. F. (1935). *Mercantilism* (M. Shapiro, Trans.). London: Allen & Unwin.

Hirschman, A. O. (1958). *Strategy of economic development*. New Haven: Yale University Press.

Hirschman, A. O. (1970). *Exit, voice, and loyalty: Responses to decline in firms, organizations, and states*. Cambridge: Harvard University Press.

Jain, P. C. (1988). Exploitation and reproduction of migrant Indian labour in colonial Guyana and Malaysia. *Journal of Contemporary Asia, 18*(2), 189–206.

Jain, R. K. (1993). Tamilian labour and Malayan plantations. *Economic and Political Weekly, 28*(43), 2363–2370.

Jomo, K. S. (1986). *A question of class: Capital, the state and uneven development in Malaya*. Singapore: Oxford University Press.

Kay, C. (1989). *Latin American theories of development and underdevelopment*. Abingdon: Routledge.

Kennedy, J. (1962). *A history of Malaya AD1400-1959*. London: Macmillan.

Knorr, K. (1945). *World rubber and its regulation*. Palo Alto: Stanford University Press.

Kratoska, P. (1975). *Peasants, yeomen and rice farmers: Cultural categories in British Malaya*. Doctoral dissertation, University of Chicago, Chicago.

Kratoska, P. H. (1988). The post-1945 food shortage in British Malaya. *Journal of Southeast Asian Studies, 19*(1), 27–47.

Kratoska, P. H. (1998). *The Japanese occupation of Malaya 1941-1945: A social and economic history*. Sydney: Allen and Unwin.

Krueger, A. O. (1997). Free trade agreements versus customs unions. *Journal of Development Economics, 54*(1), 169–187.

Lim, C. Y. (1967). *Economic development of modern Malaya*. Kuala Lumpur: Oxford University Press.

Lim, T. G. (1977). *Peasants and their agricultural economy in colonial Malaya*. Kuala Lumpur: Oxford University Press.

Little, I. M. D. (1982). *Economic development: Theory, policy and international relations*. New York: Basic Books.

Loo, E. C., & McKerchar, M. (2014). The impact of British colonial rule on the Malaysian income tax system. *eJournal of Tax Research, 12*(1), 238–252.

Luxemburg, R. (1951). *The accumulation of capital*. London: Routledge and Kegan Paul.

Marx, K. (1976). *Pre-capitalist economic formations*. London: Lawrence and Wishart.

Nanjundan, S. (1953). Economic development of Malaya. In B. K. Madan (Ed.), *Economic problems of underdeveloped countries in Asia* (pp. 145–168). New Delhi: Oxford University Press.

Nelson, R. R., & Winter, S. (1982). *An evolutionary theory of economic change*. Cambridge: Belknap Press of Harvard University Press.
North, D. (1990). *Institutions, institutional change and economic performance*. Cambridge: Cambridge University Press.
Ohlin, B. (1933). *Interregional and international trade*. Cambridge: Harvard University Press.
Ooi, J. B. (1961). Mining landscapes of Kinta. In T. H. Silcock (Ed.), *Readings in Malayan economics* (pp. 345–403). Singapore: Eastern University Press.
Puthucheary, J. J. (1960). *Ownership and control in the Malayan economy*. Singapore: Eastern University Press.
Rasiah, R. (1995a). *Foreign capital and industrialization in Malaysia*. Basingstoke: Macmillan.
Rasiah, R. (1995b). Laissez fairism and industrial development in colonial Malaya. *Journal of Contemporary Asia, 25*(4), 524–538.
Rasiah, R. (2011). The role of institutions and linkages in learning and innovation. *International Journal of Institutions and Economies, 3*(2), 165–172.
Reid, A. (1993). *Southeast Asia in the age of commerce, 1450-1680: Expansion and crisis* (Vol. 2). New Haven: Yale University Press.
Ricardo, D. (1817). *On the principles of political economy and taxation, collated text of all three editions*, published in 2004. Indianapolis: Liberty Fund Press.
Rasiah, R. (2019). Building Networks to Harness Innovation Synergies: Towards an Open Systems Approach to Sustainable Development. *Journal of Open Innovation: Market, Technology, and Complexity, 5*(3), 70.
Samuelson, P. (1948). International trade and the equalisation of factor prices. *Economic Journal, 58*(230), 163–184.
Schumpeter, J. A. (1934). *Theory of economic development*. Cambridge: Harvard University Press.
Shaharil, T. (1977). The Terengganu ruling class in the late nineteeth century. *Journal of the Malaysian Branch of the Royal Asiatic Society, 50*(2), 25–47.
Shaharil, T. (1995). *A history of Kelantan, 1890-1940*. Singapore: Malaysian Branch of the Royal Asiatic Society.
Shaharil, T. (2005). *Interrogating the state and craft of history: The Malaysian historiographical journey*. Inaugural Lecture. Kuala Lumpur: University Malaya Press.
Silcock, T. H. (1948). A note on the working of Rubber Regulation. *Economic Journal, 58*(230), 228–235.
Song, O. S. (1923). *One hundred years' of history of the Chinese in Singapore*. London: J. Murray.
Sultan Nazrin Shah. (2017). *Charting the economy: Early 20th century Malaya and contemporary Malaysian contrasts*. Shah Alam: Oxford University Press.
Sultan Nazrin Shah. (2019). *Striving for inclusive development: From Pangkor to a modern Malaysian state*. Shah Alam: Oxford University Press.

Sutton, A. (2016). British imperialism and the political economy of Malayan independence. *Journal of Imperial and Commonwealth History, 44*(3), 470–491.

Thoburn, J. T. (1977). *Primary commodity exports and economic development: Theory, evidence and a study of Malaysia*. London: Wiley.

Turnbull, M. (1964). The nineteenth century. In G. Wang (Ed.), *Malaysia: A survey* (pp. 128–137). London: Pall Mall Press.

Veblen, T. (1915). *Imperial Germany and the Industrial Revolution*. Kitchener: Batoche Books.

Warren, B. (1980). *Imperialism: Pioneer of capitalism*. London: NLB and Verso.

Williamson, O. (1985). *The economic institutions of capitalism: Firms, markets, relational contracting*. New York: Free Press.

Wong, L. K. (1965). *The Malayan tin industry to 1914*. Tucson: Arizona University Press.

World Bank. (1955). *The economic development of Malaya*. Baltimore: John Hopkins Press.

Yip, Y. H. (1964). The Mining Industry. In G. Wang (Ed.), *Malaysia: A survey* (pp. 293–306). London: Pall Mall Press.

Yoji, A., & Mako, Y. (2008). *New perspectives on the Japanese occupation in Malaya and Singapore, 1941–1945*. Singapore: National University of Singapore Press.

CHAPTER 3

The Anthropology of the Malay Peasantry: Reflecting on Colonial and Indigenous Scholarship

Zawawi Ibrahim

Introduction

There has been a continuous anthropological interest in the Malay peasantry for the past 70 years. This has resulted in a rich theoretical and empirical literature. We can identify at least four distinctive generations

The author wishes to thank University of Malaya as this chapter is based on his Inaugural professorial address: 'The Malay *peasantry: Reflecting on Colonial Indigenous Scholarship*. presented to the University of Malaya Kuala Lumpur Dewan Kuliah A Faculty of Arts Social Sciences University of Malaya 6th October 2009. The author also wishes to acknowledge Professor Shaharil Talib as an integral part of the Malaysian Monash postgraduate circle of anthropologists who were supervised by Professor M.G Swift,constituting of H.M Dahlan Abdullah Taib Shamsul A.B (Wan) Zawawi Ibrahim Halim Salleh Wan Hashim Norazit Selat.

Z. Ibrahim (✉)
Taylors University, Kuala Lumpur, Malaysia

R. Rasiah et al. (eds.), *Contesting Malaysia's Integration into the World Economy*, https://doi.org/10.1007/978-981-16-0650-2_3

of anthropologists who have each left us with an interesting, sometimes controversial, legacy of knowledge. Their work is the inevitable starting-point for any young scholar embarking today on the journey to understand some of the major questions of social, political and cultural change in recent Malaysian history. This chapter identifies and maps out a critical genealogy of knowledge production on the Malay peasantry in the works of these four generations of social anthropologists. The first and second generations were the domain of two British anthropologists, Raymond Firth and his student Michael Swift. Both researched and published their respective ethnographies on Malay society, focusing on its peasantry. By contrast, the next two generations of anthropologists were constituted from within. The so-called third generation came to be referred to as the "local pioneers" in the "social anthropology of the Malays" (Shamsul, 2003b: 21). They were Abdul Kahar Bador, Syed Husin Ali and the late Mokhzani Abdul Rahim—all of whom ended up as professors and like Swift, who studied under Firth for his doctorate, "they [also] went to the LSE to do their postgraduate studies in Anthropology, obtained their Ph.Ds from the same institution and were supervised by the same *cikgu* (teacher), Sir Raymond Firth" (Ibid.). S. Husin Ali's early postgraduate work at the University of Malaya was also supervised by Swift (King, 2003: 64). Abdul Kahar Bador and S. Husin Ali, in particular, were responsible for establishing the first Department of Anthropology and Sociology in Malaysia, at the University of Malaya, while Mokhzani introduced anthropology into his rural development courses in the Faculty of Economics and Public Administration of the same university, where he finally ended up as its Dean and later Deputy Vice-Chancellor. Though S. Husin Ali was the most prominent and "political" academic, all three scholars contributed to the accumulation of "new knowledge" on the Malay peasantry (see Mokhzani, 1973; Abdul Kahar Bador, 1978; Husin Ali, 1964, 1972, 1975).

In a recent survey entitled *The Modern Anthropology of South-East Asia* (2003), Victor King and William Wilder highlight only S. Husin Ali's works to represent local/indigenous scholarship on the Malay peasantry (see King 2003: 159–170). What is most glaring in their account is an almost total omission of any discussion of the contribution to this field of study made by the "fourth generation", comprising local anthropologists. These were mainly younger Malay scholars who completed their postgraduate studies in the Department of Anthropology and Sociology at Monash University, Australia under the *guru*ship of Swift who remained the

Chairman of the Department until his death in 1985. Long before King and Wilder published their survey in 2003, the writings on the Malay peasantry generated by this fourth generation had already been widely published, reviewed and referred to by the scholarly community. Indeed, almost all of these indigenous anthropologists undertook their own "peasantry journey" and, as scholars, they too have made their respective mark in the field. In doing so, they have arguably gone beyond the theoretical lessons and empirical findings bequeathed by their colonial-era *gurus*.[1] Among those of this generation who still remain practising anthropologists, most have moved on to what we can describe as post-peasantry studies.

This chapter revisits the legacy of successive generations of anthropological writings and, in particular, it traces the constitution and reconstitution of knowledge production on the Malay peasantry. The purpose is to go beyond the rather truncated account offered by King and Wilder and make an assessment of the terrain beyond the original intellectual legacy left by the early generations. Understandably, then, the focus is rather more oriented towards the fourth-generation scholars and the content of their discourse in relation to that of their colonial-era mentors. While acknowledging the enormous debt that many indigenous scholars clearly owed to their Western mentors, it is suggested here that a qualitative break with the past occurred during the late 1970s and 1980s. This break saw indigenous anthropologists grappling with what we may call post-peasantry studies and opening up new fields of inquiry to do with larger issues of agrarian change, capitalist modernity, ideational formation and contemporary politics. This new terrain of inquiry has, in its turn, set the agenda for the most pressing questions that face anthropologists today—questions that grapple with issues of representation, ethnicity, identity and multiculturalism that lie at the very centre of social scientific inquiry.

[1] Two qualifiers are in order at this juncture of the chapter. In the first instance, the term 'indigenous' used in the text does not refer to a 'racial' or 'ethnic' identity as such; rather it is used as an ideological category, in contrast to that of 'colonial'. The fact that the 'indigenous' anthropologists referred to in the text happened to be Malay is purely a matter of historical coincidence, and should not be read as an attempt to 'ethnicise' social categories. Secondly, it is important to acknowledge that whilst historically, the author considers the 'Firth-Swift-indigenous anthropologists' axis as a dominant geneology in the knowledge production of the Malay peasantry, this by no means disqualifies the legitimacy of other 'geneologies' or modes of 'representation' of the same empirical subject, involving other western and/or 'indigenous' scholars.

The Anthropological Legacy of Firth and Swift

In the context of our present concern, the creation of an anthropological legacy by Firth and Swift points to the enduring ideational claims made in relation to both the theoretical and empirical knowledge of the Malay peasantry. Their ideas do not necessarily represent an integrated or fully developed body of knowledge. Certainly, some issues—such as economic structures and development—have been given more emphasis than others. While some of their anthropological commentaries on Malay peasant culture and its relationship to the economy are incomplete, with the benefit of hindsight they have proven to be relevant to the larger and contemporary issues of Malay modernisation. In acknowledging the specificities of the period in which they worked, it should be noted that both Firth and Swift were capturing the early phases of the reconstitution of the Malay peasantry by both the colonial and postcolonial states as well as capitalist penetration of the economy. And being anthropologists, their primary empirical emphases were the dynamics of the micro socio-economic and political processes occurring at the small-scale village level of Malay society. As we shall see, that does not always mean they neglected the linkages between the macro and micro levels of analysis in shaping "social change" in their fieldwork area. Nor did they ignore the wider implications emanating from what was happening in the localities they studied. As such, the first important element of their legacy is the body of empirical findings on the Malay peasantry (at both micro and macro levels) and the arguments they derived from these findings. This body of knowledge became the basis for later generations of anthropologists (in our case, the two waves of indigenous scholars) to follow through in their own journey.

In order to unpack the character of the initial legacy it is necessary to offer a brief review of Firth's and Swift's key writings on the Malay peasantry, which include not only the fieldwork-based ethnography but also other relevant publications. Of course, in the case of Firth, his major ethnography, *Malay Fishermen* (1968) constitutes only a small component of his overall anthropological research and contribution on peasant society and the field of economic anthropology more generally (see Firth, 1929, 1939, 1952, 1957, 1959, 1963, 1964, 1966b, 1968, 1970, 1975). Swift's contribution is more explicitly focused on the Malay peasantry both theoretically and empirically; apart from ***Malay Peasant Society in Jelebu*** (1965), his other writings on the Malay peasantry were recently made accessible in an edited volume of collected essays (Swift, 2003). In his introduction to this collection, Shamsul (2003b: 20) notes:

If measured against the present day "publish or perish" ethos of academia in the Anglo-American world, one would be amazed to realise that he achieved so wide a coverage in a collection of ten essays—a true measure of his intellectual ability. This was made possible by his extraordinary ability to present complicated arguments in a concise manner and in language that even a lay person understands.

In the foreword of the same volume, Firth (2003: 9) acknowledges Swift's contribution in the following terms: "In time, the pupil surpassed his teacher, not only in his profound knowledge on Malay society but also in command of his chosen field of economic anthropology". But he adds a caveat: "Because of Michael Swift's reticence in his public pronouncements, the keenness of his analytical mind tended to show more clearly in his talk and his correspondence than in his publications" (Ibid.). This creates an obvious difficulty when trying to assess the overall scope and influence of Swift to the initial legacy.

A sense of Firth's remark about Swift can be gleaned from some personal insights offered by his students and others. In a private communication, S. Husin Ali mentions that while he had a "love and hate" relationship and "quarrelled" a lot with Swift when the latter was initially supervising his Masters thesis at the University of Malaya, he readily admits that Swift's lectures on social stratification and capital formation in the Malay peasantry contributed to his early thinking on his research on social stratification in Kampong Bagan (Husin Ali, 1964). Similarly Swift's graduate students at Monash would remember his insightful commentaries and distinctive intellectual rebuttals in the regular staff seminar series held either in the Department of Anthropology or the Centre for Southeast Studies. When his students had to defend their presentations, Swift was reasonably "protective" but gave ample opportunity for them to fend for themselves against critical comments from other participants. In his own weekly modernisation seminar series with his senior graduate students in the late 1960s and early 1970s, he would constantly introduce the latest theoretical writings in the field ranging from Barrington Moore's work on comparative social history to Wallerstein's celebrated delineation of the "world system". Swift would constantly try to expose them to the latest critical knowledge in and beyond anthropology even if it meant inviting different intellectual experts for one-off sessions or longer-term interventions. In formulating research questions and related theoretical perspectives, or in the final writing of the thesis, he would give full freedom to his graduate students to explore their own independent thinking in relation to their respective intellectual prowess and creativity. Seldom would he come down in a heavy-handed way to push his own particular view onto students. While it is interesting to think of what constitutes a "legacy" in these terms, how to translate such a contribution into something more measurable can be both subjective and problematic and is beyond the immediate scope of this chapter.

Let us therefore return to the question of the concrete. Firth undertook two field trips to study Malay fishing communities in Kelantan and North Terengganu, with fieldwork predominantly focused on Perupok in Kelantan. The initial work was conducted during the period immediately prior to the Japanese Occupation (1939–1940) and followed up some 23 years later in the context of a recently independent Malaysia (Firth, 1966; Dahlan, 1976: 103–16; Wan Hashim, 1988: 132; Ishak Shari, 1990: 35–142; King, 2003: 159). The first fieldwork period was a period characterised by a fishing economy that was still Malay-based and essentially "non-capitalist", and shaped by rudimentary traditional technology. By the time of the second fieldwork period, Firth was able to observe the use of modern fishing technology, capitalisation, extensive market relations, the role of financial credit institutions and the greatly expanded presence of Chinese middlemen (Firth, 1966). All these factors had radically altered the nature of the traditional peasant fishing economy and its attendant class structure.

For his part, Swift's major fieldwork was conducted in the matrilineal community of Kampong Kemin, Jelebu, Negeri Sembilan (the only matrilineal state in peninsular Malaysia) between 1954–56, where he often faced serious difficulties due to the "Emergency" (Firth 2003: 8). The traditional, rice-based peasant economy was increasingly subjected to the imperatives of commercialisation through the cultivation of cash crops such as rubber. This had profound implications for the existing kinship system and peasant social differentiation. Swift also captured a period of transition in which the traditional kinship and authority system was increasingly overtaken by the modern state and administrative structure (Swift, 1965: 1–2, 173). He visited the area for frequent periods between 1957 and 1960, when he held a lectureship at the Department of Malay Studies in the University of Malaya in Singapore and later in Kuala Lumpur. The major results of his anthropological fieldwork, *Malay Peasant Society in Jelebu*, were published in 1965. He chose to further his career as an anthropologist in Australia, initially in Sydney and later in Melbourne, where he was able to make a substantial contribution to the development of Australian anthropology (and indirectly, to Malaysian anthropology) for twenty years until his untimely death in 1985. For some months in 1962–63, he was able to fulfil "a long-cherished ambition" to carry out research in Minangkabau. In 1971, he spent six months restudying Jelebu. In 1974–75 he was a visiting professor at Universiti Kebangsaan Malaysia, and in 1977 and 1979, he undertook a "dull" quantitative-based research project with a geographer from the University of Melbourne to study Malay urban settlements in Kuantan, Pahang. At the time of his death, he was apparently collaborating with S. Husin Ali on a research project at the University of Malaya, based at the newly established Institut Pengajian Tinggi (Institute of Higher Studies) (Firth, 2003: 13–14).

The empirically grounded ethnographies of both Firth and Swift are exemplars of the kind of fieldwork-driven research that dominated social anthropology in the middle decades of the twentieth century. In addition, both men had outstanding professional careers as teachers. The legacy is profound. It is on the theoretical front that there is greater controversy or at least contention as to the exact importance of their work. In their review of modern anthropology in the region, King and Wilder (2003: 173) note that peasant studies of the kind produced by Firth and Swift "certainly help draw our attention to the processes affecting village communities". But they go on to offer a more critical assessment of the worth of this legacy. They claim that it merely "confirmed" the fact that post-war anthropology in Malaysia and other parts of Southeast Asia "had to move away from its preoccupation with the defined, self-contained, autonomous social and cultural unit" in which "the horizons of these anthropologists, using mainly functionalist, structuralist and cultural analyses, usually only extended to the surrounding region or in rare cases to the nation-state… continued to concentrate primarily on the local situation".

This assessment cannot be allowed to pass without some major revision. It is simply inaccurate to label Firth and Swift as orthodox functionalists, at least in the mould of Radcliffe-Brown or Evans-Pritchard. For one thing, they were continuously involved in identifying and analysing the dynamics and processes of change in the communities that they studied, hardly the forte of classical functionalism. They strongly believed in the "rational conceptions" underlying choices but equally contended that the whole discourse of "rationality" must be mediated through the understanding of the relationship between the social and the economic system, and not simply understood to reside in the domain of the economy (see Firth, 1968, 1970). Even in his critical commentary on Marxist anthropology, Firth recognises "the analytical value of certain Marxist ideas… in non-capitalist or non-western societies" such as "the processes of radical social change… from the colonial period, the expansion of market relations, the development of wage labour and the emergence of new social classes and class conflict" (see King & Wilder, 2003: 179). In doing do, Firth (1975: 52–53) draws attention to "the basic significance of economic factors, especially production relations; the relations of structures of power; the formation of classes and the opposition of their interests; the socially relative character of ideology; the conditioning force of a system upon individual members of it". These views cannot be labelled functionalist in any meaningful sense.

In his re-study of *The Malay Fishermen*, Firth (1966: 344) was able to identify the emergence of a new *taukeh* class representing an "economic aristocrat of the fishing community". He notes different categories of burgeoning Malay capitalists—owners and entrepreneurs who had invested in the new technologies of fishing. Some of them had also combined forces with Chinese merchant capital, representing the "emergence of non-seagoing entrepreneurs who almost completely dominated the means of production and the marketing outlets" (Dahlan, 1976: 110). It was apparent that the fishing industry was then approximating a business enterprise of quite a new type rather than the former pattern of Malay peasant agriculture (Firth 1966: 7). In reviewing Firth's observation, Jomo (1986: 119) concludes:

> The trend towards concentration of land-ownership in peasant agriculture appears to be matched by a similar trend in peasant fishing, at least on the East Coast The transformation in the relations of production in fishing has also affected the relative income of the fishermen, as the rate of exploitation has risen in capital's favour.

As Firth (1966: 323) himself had noted some twenty years earlier: "Much greater returns to fishing in modern conditions, accompanied by or resulting from much greater capitalization, has resulted in a marked drop in the percentage of earnings going to labour". While he was an advocate of the "economic" being subordinated to "social ends" (Firth, 1968: 86), in the case of the emerging economic concentration and social differentiation observed in the "modern" Malay fishing industry, Firth (1966: 348) pinpoints the fact that the economic processes, which had widened the gap between capitalist entrepreneurs and propertyless fishermen, were not cushioned to any apparent degree by the elaborate network of kinship ties in the local social system... The kinship ties of these fishermen do not inhabit their economic calculation, though they may soften its intensity.

And he concludes:

> What seems to appear quite clearly from this analysis is the strength of economic forces in making a new kind of society. Initially at least these economic forces are not automatic; they operate through the choices of individuals. (Ibid.: 346)

In ways similar to Firth, Swift also focuses on the early processes of economic differentiation taking place in Jelebu. There was evidence of land concentration and the emergence of a group of wealthier landowning farmers, comprising the local political elite, in contrast to the presence of a class of tenants, labourers and sharecroppers. His explanation of the process anticipates some of the "new economic anthropology" arguments, specifically those of Henry Bernstein, couched in the notion of a "reproduction squeeze" as part of the conditions of the peasant household caught under the formal subsumption of capital (Bernstein, 1976, 1979). As Swift (1965: 169) astutely explains:

> A further necessary feature of this process is the commercialisation of the economy so that all needs and obligation tend to be mediated through money, which... becomes necessary for even simple day-to-day survival. In such circumstances the possession of a surplus income over ordinary consumption expenditure assumes enormous significance. The ordinary peasant who does not possess this surplus can only meet extra demands on his resources by selling land. The possessor of a surplus, on the other hand, can not only survive extraordinary expenditures without having to part with his main productive capital, but can also buy the property of others, often at very low prices, when the opportunity arises. As land is now a scarce resource, only to be acquired by purchase, and as he has now an even lower income than formerly, the peasant who is forced to sell his land has little hope of acquiring more, and is confronted with the alternatives of sharecropping or drifting to the town.

In framing his argument, Swift draws some hugely valuable lessons from the transformations affecting peasant societies.

> By studying the economy as an autonomous sector of the social structure we can show that there is an internal process making for the concentration of ownership in a few hands, with a corresponding increase in the economic differentiation of the society [T]here will be a move away from equalitarianism in the peasant society, and assuming this trend to continue unaffected by other forces, what will be seen is an increasingly large class of low status share-croppers, and a small group of wealthy men controlling an increasingly large share of the society's productive assets. (Ibid.: 168)

Swift is also unafraid to move his analysis of the micro-level processes to the macro situation. For example, he suggests that

> scattered evidence throughout Malaya indicates that this concentration of ownership is a general phenomenon Adopting a more general viewpoint I would stress the great and continuing increase in population which has caused a genuine land shortage for much of the country. The formerly low level of population and current population growth provide an explanation of why such a common feature of peasant economies as landlordism and impoverished tenantry are now beginning to appear in widespread form in Malaya. (Ibid.: 168–169)

In this regard, Swift also notes the transfer of peasant land to an upper class or an official class, an absentee landlord, who may not necessarily be an agriculturalist. He is, in short, an acute observer of the emergent class divisions in contemporary village life, right from the peasantry (*orang kampong*) to the many variants of the "upper class". He points out that while the class distinctions within the peasantry were almost entirely economic (rich, ordinary and poor), the distinctions with the "salariat" whose position was based on governmental position and education—were not purely economic despite the higher incomes of the Malay officials when compared with peasant incomes. Long before James Scott (1976, 1985) began to delve into the notion of the "everyday class struggle" of the peasantry, Swift (1965: 152) was already able to provide elements of these inter-class narratives ("class ideas") between the various peasant classes or in the official—peasant relationship, the latter being characterised by a combination of "hostility", "ambivalence", "subordination" and "respect" (Ibid.: 149–162). At the village level he notes how the economic-based stratification system in Malay society was being "tempered by the basically egalitarian kinship organisation" (Ibid.: 166). Moreover relations between social classes were handled through various non-economic or cultural terms emphasising a moral component based on generosity, mutual dependence, sharing and even a sense of egalitarianism. According to Swift, these values did not prevent class exploitation from taking place nor did they promote a radical consciousness or orientation among the peasantry: "such values are not demanding a change in the whole organisation of society" (Ibid.: 154). Indeed the "egalitarian values of the village are not radical in orientation towards the structure as a whole, but essentially conservative" although they did function, somewhat tenuously, as a social leveller of wealth between some of the social classes (Swift, 1967: 241). These initial ideas on class were later developed into a more complex discourse by Zawawi Ibrahim when elaborating the Malay proletarian content of "class consciousness" (Zawawi, 1998c). Swift's initial hypothesis is that the growth of a cash economy in Negeri Sembilan would prove a major factor for the decline of its matrilineal *adat perpatih*. However he later attributes the decline of the traditional adat system to the growth and development of a modern government administration, specifically the role of a centralised bureaucracy comprising educated and trained officials to administer justice and land matters, or to implement development policies and projects "made effective through a hierarchy of officials under the District Officer and the State Government" (Swift, 1965: 79, 172–173; see also King & Wilder, 2003: 164).

A final area of Swift's contribution is in the field of culture values and Malay modernisation. He remarks:

> A marked fatalism, presented in religious form, is also conspicuous among Malay economic attitudes. The Malay is very prone, after receiving a setback, to give up striving, and say that he has no luck, that it is the will of God. In economic affairs this is most clearly seen in the concept of *rezeki*, a person's divinely determined economic lot. (Swift, 1965: 91)

If the above sounds rather "orientalist", he makes certain qualifications in a later article, by emphasising that *rezeki*

> also has important overtones of luck in the economic sphere. The peasant who fails to prosper as much as his neighbours has no need to feel that he

is lacking in industry or ability, he does not have the *rezeki*. Or, if a man starts a small business, or experiments with a new crop or fails, "he hasn't the *rezeki*". The concept of *rezeki* is ultimately a religious one, but in every day life there is little specifically religious about it. It simply amounts to a predisposition to explain everything in terms of luck, and to neglect trying to improve one's position, for after all one has very little control over it. (Swift, 2003: 21).

In comparing the Malay with the Chinese economic orientation, Swift observes that the Chinese view "is essentially long term", in contrast to the Malay "who is interested in the short run". For the Chinese "[w]ealth is desired not only for consumption but for accumulation, to build up a fortune which can be handed on to future generations". In the case of the Malay, "[w]ealth is strongly desired but for consumption". However Swift was quick to qualify that: "Malay preference for the short run is not, in itself, uneconomic or irrational, but it does make for weakness in economic competition with groups or individual with a long run orientation" (1965: 29). The above arguments, it should be noted, bear much relevance to the unfinished discourse on Malay underdevelopment and development, and Swift's observations have also been taken up by some of the later indigenous anthropologists, as we shall see below.

In sum, both Firth and Swift provided certain "windows" to the understanding of the important socio-economic, political and cultural dynamics affecting the changes in the Malay peasantry of their time, from the late 1930s to the mid-1960s. In tracing their legacy, it is clear that their students began to open up these "windows" even further and, in doing so, formulated new questions and searched for new answers.

First Generation Indigenous Anthropologists

To a large extent, both S. Husin Ali and Mokhzani continued to focus on and provide the empirical elaboration of some of the important issues and processes in Malay peasant society observed by the British *gurus* in their own work. There is no evidence of any radical theoretical departure in the analyses of these first local anthropologists. While conflict theory was becoming increasingly in vogue in sociology, the translation of a Marxist or neo-Marxist perspective into the anthropology of the peasantry was as yet not forthcoming.

Of the two, S. Husin Ali became the better-known scholar compared to Mokhzani because of his publications. Both also made different choices in their final careers. Mokhzani, a close friend and an affine to Swift, decided to join the corporate world after retiring from academic life and, according to Shamsul (2003b: 21), "he is perhaps the first anthropology-trained millionaire in the world". Mokhzani's original Ph.D. thesis (1973) was only recently published (2006), and even then it was at a time when interest in peasant studies had already waned. But Mokhzani's work does provide the "missing link" in Malay peasantry studies, for his research presents a micro-level database to understand how different forms of usury practices led to indebtedness, hence facilitating the twin processes of land concentration and dispossession in village society (see Jomo, 1986: 49–54).

After initially working under Swift, S. Husin Ali (1964) focused on elaborating the issue of peasant social differentiation in his Masters thesis, during which time he undertook four months fieldwork in Kampong Bagan, Johor. Following Weber's qualifier of Marx on social stratification, he explores not only the class dimension of stratification but also the status structure of the Malay peasant community of Bagan. He locates Bagan both as part of the national administrative structure as well that of a wider market economy, i.e. characteristics of peasant incorporation which had already been recognised in both Firth's and Swift's works. However, there is no doubt that S. Husin Ali is more empirically substantive in elaborating his class delineations based on their "similar position in relation to the means of production' (Ibid.: 10). He takes great methodological care to categorise his 149 Malay household samples into the five class distinctions—landlords, landlord-cum-owner operators, owner-operators, owner operators-cum-tenants or farm labourers, and tenants or farm labourers. Like Swift, he also tries to identify those in the village who were not engaged in agriculture. In his later comparative research on peasant leadership, S. Husin Ali (1975: 84) notes a "more complicated" situation in which "[t]he concentration of ownership in the three areas has not led to a clear-cut two class system made up of landlords on the one hand and tenants on the other". He also undertook similar rigour in delineating four status groupings in Bagan—Muslim religious functionaries, village officials, government servants such as teachers, and those such as landlords who had good incomes (Ibid.: 69).

For his doctoral thesis at the London School of Economics, supervised by Firth, S. Husin Ali (1975) moved on to complement his earlier stratification research by focusing on Malay peasant leadership in three village communities: Kangkong (a rice and fishing community in Kedah), Kerdau (a rice and rubber community in Pahang) and again Bagan (a rubber and coconut growing community in Johor) based on fieldwork he had undertaken between 1964 and 1969. He points out the changing perceptions among young people towards some of the "traditional" leaders as a consequence of change, education and mobility. He also observes the strengthening of the "status" of some traditional leadership positions, such as the penghulus, by virtue of their being incorporated into the modern administrative bureaucracy. As both Firth and Swift had already highlighted, S. Husin Ali also notes that education and wealth were increasingly becoming dominant markers of "new" leadership composed of "a triad of landlord, party functionary and government official". This was especially true for political office in rural society which linked the Malay peasantry to national political parties (Ibid.: 162). These were the "new leaders" in the making.

There is little doubt that S. Husin Ali drew on the empirical and analytical insights that had been pioneered by Firth and Swift. Perhaps even more important, he anticipated crucial research questions that would be taken up by others. First, his work on changing patterns of leadership clearly identifies some early manifestations of "patronage politics" and its crucial role in underpinning local political leadership (Ibid.: 152). This insight would anticipate Shamsul's (1986) findings on the politics of the New Economic Policy (NEP) almost a decade later. As King and Wilder (2003: 170) succinctly summarise S. Husin Ali's observations:

> The provision of material assistance to rural Malays by the governing party UMNO in the form of rural development programmes became an important agency for retaining political support and for ensuring that local UMNO leaders associated with this largesse as 'brokers', performed as effective patrons.

Second, his research also anticipates James Scott's (1985) celebrated *Weapons of the Weak* published some ten years later. S. Husin Ali (1975: 97) is able to pinpoint to "the manifestations of class conflict confined… to the verbal level" and the presence of different forms of "foot dragging" undertaken by Malay peasants as part of their "everyday class struggle" against the rich.

> Some peasants express contempt of landlords who are mean and show their anger towards those who take advantage of them through debt-bondage. For instance, in these areas (i.e. Kangkong, Kerdau and Bagan) a number of peasants do not hide their feelings towards some landlords and shop-keepers who try to take advantage of them and they go a degree beyond verbal abuse by trying to inflict damage to property belonging to the latter. In Kerdau and Bagan, some poor peasants practise slaughter-tapping — careless stripping of the bark — so that the rubber trees belonging to some of the landlords are harmed. (Ibid.: 97–98)
>
> On the other hand, he also observes that up to a point, frustrated poorer peasants tended "to submerge their feelings towards the rich" owing to "kinship affinity and territorial proximity" and a desire not to "cause great disturbances to a harmonious way of living in society (*hidup bermasyarakat*)". (Ibid.: 99)

S. Husin Ali also provides a necessary "intervention" in the *rezeki* and fatalism discourse on the Malay peasantry. He argues that there has been too much emphasis on the dimension of *rezeki* in Islam in the above debate, revealing that "at the same time Islam also teaches its believers to use their faculty and effort in order to overcome difficulties and determine their own positions and future; and this is referred to as *ikhtiar*. To say that all Malays- or all Malay peasants — are fatalistic is mere indulgence in stereotypes...(T)he belief in 'fate' and 'divine lot'...cannot be elevated as being the cause of poverty or 'economic retardation'. The concepts of 'fate' and 'divine lot' need to be relegated to their proper places in trying to explain Malay economic behaviour" (1972: 111).

Revisiting the Paradigm Shift in Peasant Studies

As we follow the journey of what came to be called peasant studies it was increasingly obvious that the peasantry was no longer the exclusive theoretical subject matter of anthropologists (Redfield, 1960; Wolf, 1966; Shanin, 1971). By the early 1970s, it was also evident that the new problematique relating to the understanding of contemporary Third World peasants were now addressed not in the context of former theoretical frameworks but rather were being superseded by new perspectives. As opposed to the "descriptive" mode of analysis that had hitherto dominated peasant studies, the new perspectives took the view that the location of Third World peasants could only be adequately theorised in their historical relationship to capital. In other words, the fortunes of the peasantry should best be understood in relation to capitalism's world-historical expansion into pre-capitalist formations leading to the eventual destruction of the "natural economy" and their reconstitution as commodity producers in a social formation articulated with a dominant capitalist mode of production (see Ennew et al., 1977; Bradby, 1975; Bernstein, 1976, 1979; Kahn, 1978a; Boesen, 1979; Meillassoux, 1973; Deere & de Janvry, 1979).

This new theoretical reformulation was not initially generated by a concern for the "peasant question" per se. Rather it emerged mainly as an adjunct to a more general concern with the issues of development and underdevelopment in the Third World, associated mainly with theorists and scholars approaching them from a Marxist or neo-Marxist perspective. The works of a newer brand of anthropology, the so-called new economic anthropology (grounded in developing and elaborating Marxist ideas on pre-capitalist formations and drawing its initial inspiration from French Marxist anthropology), also found complementarities with those concerned to examine the changing character of the peasantry. The major focus was its concern with the nature of pre-capitalist relations and their articulation with capital during the different phases of imperialist contact (Frank, 1969; Laclau, 1971; Dupre & Rey, 1973; Amin, 1976; Bradby, 1975; Meillassoux, 1972, 1973, 1981; Godelier, 1977; Clammer 1975, 1978; Seddon, 1978; Foster-Carter, 1974, 1978a, 1978b; Taylor, 1979; Bloch, 1983). The theoretical "confrontation" between capital and peasants, as to be expected, was hardly simple and straightforward. Discussions and debates centred on various issues. They ranged from problems of conceptualising the different levels of capitalist penetration into rural society (Bernstein, 1976, 1979; also Kay, 1978), the issue of "articulation" (Dupre and Rey, 1973; Taylor, 1979; Foster-Carter, 1978a, 1978b), to the problem of defining what capitalism is in regard to agriculture (Alavi, 1975; Banaji, 1976a; Cleaver, 1976; McEachern, 1976, 1979; Patnaik, 1979). This storm of debate all took place in the longer-term framework of theories developed earlier by Lenin and Kautsky in the context of pre-revolutionary Russia (Lenin, 1974; Banaji, 1976b).

A dominant question in most of the new literature on the Third World peasantry was how peasants became structurally reconstituted by the process of capitalist penetration and the destruction of the natural economy. The answer was that their present location (in the 1970s) could not be understood outside their relationship with capital. From this perspective, the position of the peasantry is clear-cut at the level of their relations of exchange in the social formation. Through the circuit of merchant capital, peasants have been transformed into commodity producers, whose dominant orientation is towards the production of exchange rather than use-values. Through such commodity relations, capital indirectly determines the conditions of peasant household production and reproduction in which peasants are made "to work for capital" in various "exploitative" ways (Bernstein, 1976). But at the level of productive relations, the task of identifying the presence of capitalist relations of production in rural society is much more complicated. This is partially the product of merchant capital as the dominant form of capital dominating over rural society, as well as the reluctance of productive capital to bear the burden of organising peasant production (especially in the context of the colonial state, bearing in mind that it could still benefit from such "conservation"). Thus while the position of proletarianised peasants or capitalist farmers poses no theoretical problems in terms of the capitalist nature of their relations of production, complications arise when considering that many of the Third World peasants have not been reconstituted in this way (Zawawi, 1982). As a theoretical rule, however, it is quite acceptable to conclude that for these peasants, their position is one of non-capitalist producers formally subsumed under capitalism (Galeksi cited in Roseberry, 1976: 48–49; Clarke, 1977). However, insofar as colonialism had legally transformed land into a commodity which can be owned and transferred, it also meant that these peasants, though not actually expropriated by capital, were no longer located in pre-capitalist ("feudal") relations of production. Neither were these relations dissolved into a form which was classically capitalist (Alavi, 1975; McEachern, 1976; Zawawi, 1982).

The perspective of capital—peasantry relations does not stop here. It also intrudes into the relationship between the state and the peasantry in the peripheral social formation. Despite the "relative autonomy" of the postcolonial state (Alavi, 1972), it still mediates the penetration of capital albeit in new forms (such as through rural development programmes like the Green Revolution). Though the state is no longer the instrument of solely foreign capital, as in the colonial phase, capital is still capital whether it takes the form of "state capitalism", comprador or foreign capital (see Cleaver, 1972; Feder, 1979).

Despite the manifest sophistication of its analyses, the new theoretical perspectives that emerged in the 1970s left something rather incomplete in their emphasis. The concern with the analysis of peasants under capitalist domination tended to focus predominantly on the underlying structural changes and transformations. By contrast, there was very little consideration of how to explain changes at the level of consciousness or ideology, i.e. how peasant actors have become ideologically reconstituted as subjects by capital. This is not to deny the contribution on specific ideologies or "superstructures" in the work of some Marxist anthropologists with regard to concrete social formations (see Wolpe, 1972; Alavi, 1973; Terray, 1975; Feuchtwang, 1975; Godelier, 1977; Kahn, 1978b; Kahn and Llobera, 1981). On the question of peasant ideology and consciousness, Scott's seminal work in *The Moral Economy of the Peasant* (1976) and *Weapons of the Weak* (1985) did provide a useful framework, although the task of synthesising his mode of analysis with the new theoretical framework did not really materialise. In retrospect, it shows the limitations of neo-Marxism when dealing with "superstructures" and "ideologies". Slowly but surely it was the field of cultural studies that would address these shortcomings in any coherent manner.

New Generation Malay Anthropologists: Going Beyond the Legacy?

As we have seen, the research and writings on the Malay peasantry by a new generation of Malay anthropologists came at a time of paradigm transition. The longstanding descriptive and liberal economic anthropological framework which had dominated the study of the peasantry was evolving to incorporate ideas from various other macro-level and alternative theoretical sources. Yet the question remains: why did local scholars flock back to the Malay peasantry for their postgraduate fieldwork? It was clear from the start when the earlier generation of local anthropologists took to the field until the early 1980s that there was a kind of interactive synergy and convergence from the various disciplines on the Malay peasantry. From history, the pathbreaking and innovative analyses ushering in a new kind of economic historiography by Lim Teck Ghee (1976, 1977) and Shaharil Talib (1984) still occupy a prominent place in the evolution of local scholarship on the impact of colonial rule on the Malaysian peasantry. From economics, the preoccupation and arguments on the questions of Malay rural development and poverty by Ungku Aziz and others were already well known (see Abdul Aziz, 1957, 1964; Parkinson, 1967; for a summary some of the debates, see Snodgrass, 1980). Even from the Malay ruling class "intelligentsia", the discourse on Malay underdevelopment especially the relationship between economic development, achievement orientation and cultural values (the so-called "mental revolution") also became a major point of reference (see Mahathir, 1970; Senu Abdul Rahman, 1970). Indeed it was Mahathir's Malay Dilemma with its odd eclecticism of cultural, genetic and environmental determinism—that became one of the strongest ideological underpinnings of' the NEP. Of course, during the colonial period the orientalist writings of administrators such as Hugh Clifford (1903, 1927, 1926) and Frank Swettenham (1895, 1900) had already laid the basis for the ensuing debate and discourse on Malay values and development. From within the indigenous "intelligentsia", the writings of Munshi Abdullah and Zainal Abidin Ahmad (Za'ba) also provided some of the early rebuttals of culturalist explanations of Malay underdevelopment. It was only a matter of time before the deconstructionist and anti-orientalist writings of the late Syed Hussein Alatas (1972, 1977), criticising both the culturally based underpinnings of *Malay Dilemma* and *Revolusi Mental* (Senu Abdul Rahman, 1970) and the colonial construction and imagining of the "lazy native", took the debate to a new critical scholarship (see Zawawi, 2005).

Although Lim Teck Ghee (1984: 35) was soon announcing that "[t]he year 1980 appears to mark the beginning of an era of a majority worker class in Malaysia", there was I think "a sense of destiny" that inspired a new generation of young scholars to converge on the Malay peasantry as their research base. Also at the back of their minds was an opportunity to move beyond the arguments and analyses of their colonial *gurus*. After all, in the West, there was already an emerging discourse questioning the "colonial encounter" between anthropology (as "a child of western imperialism"), anthropologists (as "reluctant imperialists") and those of the colonised world (see Asad, 1973). As we have seen, this initial questioning later led to a postmodernist turn in anthropology which was critical of the authority and authorship of the colonial anthropologists and their fieldwork/ethnographic texts and methodology (see Marcus & Fischer, 1986; Clifford and Marcus, 1986; also Fontana, 1994; Smith, 1999; Yamashita et al., 2004). At another level, Edward Said's (1978) earlier deconstructionist Orientalism had already provided another landmark reference point to the whole knowledge encounter between the colonialism and "the Other" (see Gardner & Lewis, 1996: 22–25).

What is interesting in the work of many of this new generation of Malay anthropologists is the professional rigour by which they went about their work, both empirically and theoretically. Of course, at Monash, the postgraduate "apprenticeship" exposed the students to the discipline of independent scholarship; the first year was a reading preparation of all the relevant secondary theoretical and empirical literature; after this there was a compulsory presentation of the research proposal to both the staff departmental seminar and the postgraduate seminar series at the Centre of Southeast Asia Studies. The potential fieldwork candidates had to prepare for the critical commentaries coming from both peers and professors and had to be intellectually ready to fend for themselves. This tradition would be repeated after the respective candidate came back from the field.

Of the fourth generation of anthropologists, one of the earliest postgraduate Malay students to attend the department to work under Swift was the late H.M. Dahlan. After finishing his undergraduate studies in 1968 in the Malay Studies Department at University of Malaya based on research on *adat* and the land system in Naning, Malacca, he was drawn to the work of Andre Gunder Frank. His postgraduate project was a theoretically informed examination of the underdevelopment of the Malay peasantry via a detailed analysis of all the anthropological micro-based studies that had been undertaken on Malay village society (Dahlan, 1973). The result is a systematic historical reconstruction of the capitalist process of peasant encapsulation at the level of the concrete in the case of peninsular Malaysia (Dahlan, 1976). While in theoretical terms the thesis suffered from the usual Frankian limitations of the time, the initiative taken in applying the perspective to the Malaysian context was laudable. It was a first Malaysian scholarly attempt to locate micro-level anthropological writings in the context of a neo-Marxist political economy theoretical framework. In the Malaysian context, this wider economic analysis was dominated by conventional development economics or geography. On his return to Malaysia, Dahlan joined Universiti Kebangsaan Malaysia (UKM) and became involved in promoting what he considered a progressive Malaysian-based anthropology and social science. He later joined the expanding UKM university programme on Development Science in Sabah. He led new ethnographic research in Sabah and at the time of his death, he was theoretically moving to innovate in the field of social communication, specifically to explore what he calls the "formation of the urban social mind" (Dahlan, 1989, 1997).

A rising star under his tutelage at the time was Shamsul who was supervised in the final phase of his Masters course by S. Husin Ali while the latter was in detention under the Internal Security Act (ISA). Already enrolled as a Ph.D. student under Swift at Monash, Shamsul (1979) contributed an historical and macro-level overview of peasant underdevelopment in Malaysia to the *Journal of Contemporary Asia* that was inspired by the theoretical project of Dahlan. In fact, Zawawi Ibrahim was Swift's first Malay anthropology Ph.D. student and completed his thesis by 1978. In 1980, he returned to Malaysia to lead the Development Studies programme in the School of Social Science, Universiti Sains Malaysia (USM). There, he began to contribute theoretical overviews of the "peasant question" which were published in both local and international journals (Zawawi, 1982, 1983, 1984), complementing Shamsul's earlier contribution. Zawawi's theoretical forays were located very much within the new capital—peasantry paradigm shift with a stronger inclination towards the issue of ideology and class consciousness.

Shamsul's well-known ethnography on patronage politics in the context of the NEP in Kuala Selangor, *From British to Bumiputera Rule: Local Politics and Rural Development in Peninsular Malaysia* was published in 1986. His work is a rigorous study of the interconnections between state and the peasantry via the processes of bureaucracy and party politics. In some ways, he was filling in the missing "political gaps" in the study of the peasantry left by the two colonial *gurus*. At another level he was empirically following through, though at a different time frame, some of the initial leads given in S. Husin Ali's analysis on "patronage politics". In doing so Shamsul was able, through anthropological lenses, to unravel the political economy of rural development and the symbiotic relationship between the NEP and "money politics". In a telling passage he writes:

> From the beginning, UMNO was perceived as the political party which belonged to the official-entrepreneur class.... The biggest beneficiaries... have been the politicians, namely the "wakil rakyat", and their Malay and Chinese associates. They have managed to turn rural development projects, initially aimed at eradicating poverty, into rich financial resources for themselves, by establishing their own companies and the awarding them

> lucrative government contracts.... There exist numerous other development projects at the "mukim" and district levels The distribution of these projects is based on personal links of patronage within the political arena.... The beneficiaries have been small select group of peasants, not necessarily the poorest, although the projects are supposedly for them.... The situation is such that those closely-associated with the centre of power at the local level stand to benefit most from the implementation of the development programmes under the NEP....
>
> The NEP has transformed not only the image of the objective position of the "wakil rakyat" within the district... Their political power has been greatly increased by their control of the district development machinery which, in turn, places them in an unassailable position in distributing development benefits [and] the ability to buy continued political support with hard cash.... Thus the rise of "money politics", at all levels within UMNO is closely related, if not the direct result, of the NEP itself. (Shamsul, 1986: 237–244)

Thus Shamsul's work is a critical breakthrough in anthropological analysis of postcolonial politics delineating what really goes on at the local level behind the so-called "Malay modernisation project". His study captures empirically the beginning of "money politics" in Malay political culture. By the time of its publication, he was already back at UKM where he subsequently continued as a professor and became *guru* to many undergraduate and postgraduate students of anthropology. After being the Dean of the Faculty of the Social Sciences, he was made the Director of the Institute of the Malay World and Civilisation (ATMA) and co-founded the Institute of Occidental Studies (IKON) at UKM. He is now Director of the new Institute of Ethnic Studies (KITA) at the same university. He continues to be a prolific contributor to the discourses on ethnicity, identity and nation in postcolonial Malaysia (Shamsul, 1994, 1996a, b, 1998a, b, 2000a, b, c, d, 2002a, b, 2003a, b, 2004, 2005).

After USM, Zawawi decided to do a follow-up to his Ph.D. study in the oil palm plantations of Terengganu which had begun to be dominated by Indonesian migrant workers. In 1984, he moved as a rural sociologist to the Faculty of Economics and Public Administration, University of Malaya, a position which was once also occupied by Mokhzani. There he continued researching on the Malay peasantry working as settler tobacco farmers (Zawawi, 1990). Later he turned his attention to the Orang Asli under the impact of development (Zawawi, 1996, 1998a, b, 2000) and, most recently, to the field of popular culture and cultural studies (Zawawi, 2003a, b, 2004, 2007).

The echoes of the earlier anthropological concerns are evident in Zawawi's work. For example, in his study of tobacco farmers he expands on the Swift/S.Husin Ali's elaborations of *rezeki* in the following terms:

> An important ideological basis of their social existence is defined by a strong belief in *usaha* (literally "to make an effort" or "to strive"). It is through *usaha* that they can face the uncertainties of the new environment. It motivates them to learn the new ways, to innovate, to improve, or sometimes even to question and resist. But that is only half the story. There are things beyond their control, as when they are faced with the sudden "death" of their tobacco Such a misfortune does not mean that they have not made an effort in the past; it is still based on *usaha*, meaning that "even if there is disease (*penyakit*), we must *usaha*, then if they happen to die, its *nasib* (fate); if it's good, it's *nasib* " Their resort to *nasib* thus complements delicately with their belief in *timbang*. "*Usaha* first, if you can't overcome it, then surrender to *nasib*... *Rezeki* does not come by itself'. The resort to *nasib* is a crucial stabilising cultural [actor in the context of the Malay settlers' battle with the elements. At the subjective level of the individual such a balancing act is still necessary. It attenuates his disappointment and frustration. It calms him down and goads him to face the world of routine and work again after a setback. It absolves him of blame. It gives him a sense of reason rather than create a sense of anger or aggression against his neighbours who do not face the same misfortune; it serves to tone down the competition between them. In the end the whole notion of work, *usaha*, *nasib* and *rezeki* are all intertwined into a single religious cosmology. (Zawawi, 1990: 176–179)

By 1998, Zawawi's ethnographic work on the peasantry becoming proletarianised, *The Malay Labourer: By the Window of Capitalism*, was published with very major theoretical revisions and incorporating some of the new follow-up database (Zawawi, 1998c). His work again moved existing anthropological studies by following the peasantry beyond the village threshold to investigate the construction of "class" at the level of experience as capital confronted the emerging peasants becoming proletarians at the level of production relations. Inspired both by Swift's ideas on the moral component of class relations in the peasantry and the "moral economy" of Scott, he framed his own synthesis of the proletarian "moral economy". He drew on Gramscian ideas and neo-Marxist insights into the articulation of class and non-class contents (including humanness and ethnicity) in the make-up of what constituted "class consciousness" (see Laclau, 1971). In doing so, he was able to demonstrate how the encroachments of such a "moral economy" could lead to subalternism and protest. He was also able to identify the egalitarian cultural principle (*timbang rasa*) emerging from the proletarian experience which could be used to mediate class relations and exploitation. He also innovated on the idea of a new concept of exploitation, i.e. "status exploitation" (1998).

In a key article, Zawawi published a follow-up to his plantation study in which he attempts to develop an alternative mode of explanation for why immigrant labour had taken over the harvesting work previously done by Malays in the plantations (Zawawi, 2005). Inspired by the work of Syed Hussein Alatas, he concludes that the recent postcolonial discourse on "labour shortage" facing the Malaysian plantation industry—which saw the "return of the lazy native" concept—was essentially about capital deliberating on familiar ground, i.e. on the virtues of two different fragments of labour. One fragment was local and the other, the cheap and expendable immigrant labour coming in droves from across the Straits of Malacca and the surrounding low-wage sectors of Southeast Asia. Based on the Terengganu data and the multi-sited anthropological ethnographic data collected, he commented:

> I have tried to counter and subvert the return of the same orientalist thinking by demonstrating the "rational" strategies of local labour as they exercise their choices within and outside the changing landscape in the context of the Malaysian post developmentalist state.... The problem has to be analysed in terms of the logic of capitalist accumulation itself, which finds in immigrant labour the perfect 'model' for minimising costs and maximising productivity, and as a source of docile and cheap labour. (Ibid.: 66)

Halim Salleh was another Masters student of Swift who went on to research on the emergent ideology of urban Malays (including peasants) in Kota Bahru, Kelantan, employing a sophisticated articulation of modes of production analysis, again a first of its kind in Malaysian anthropology. Fully anchored in state-of-the-art neo-Marxism and the new economic anthropology he is also concerned to understand the role of non-material factors in attenuating the emergence of class consciousness. He argues that

> when capital preserves and defends the subservient indigenous mode of production in Kota Bharu, the classes and the class relations it generates become highly distorted; while the new productive system introduces the new classes, the non-economic instance (especially religiousness in the present case) of the indigenous mode of production negates the reality of such classes and its relations.... In short the consciousness of class and class relations in the town of Kota Bharu have been tranquillized, obviously for the benefit of the dominant capital to accumulate and expand. (Halim Salleh, 1981: xv)

For his Ph.D. Halim Salleh studied at the Institute of Development Studies, Sussex University, undertaking research on the relationship between Malay peasant settlers and capital–state relations in land settlement schemes (Halim, 1988, 1992). He moved his analysis into the infamous state-sponsored Federal Land Development Authority (FELDA) resettlement schemes which were part of the postcolonial development project's solution to the "peasant question". Landless families from the Malay peasantry were resettled in large-scale, managerially driven rubber or oil palm plantation schemes. According to the scheme's promise, after paying off their debts to the FELDA organisation, these "privileged" peasantries would eventually be fully fledged owners of their commercial lots. Halim (1992: 107) deconstructs the mythology of FELDA and argues that the state—through FELDA production—acts like capital in its "ability to control peasant labour force for large-scale production" which "is clearly shown in the fundamental FELDA—settler relationships relating to land ownership, finance and labour control which separate the settlers from the control over the means of production and the products". He goes on to conclude that:

> Essentially, this turns the settlers into proletarians but for obvious political and economic reasons, they are not transformed into pure wage workers. They are instead considered by the state as if they were independent if not privileged citizens who are enjoying the benefits of a major government sponsored rural (land) development project. Consequently, the protests and everyday forms of resistance that the settlers engage in are characterised by the desire to deproletarianise themselves and to assert their standing as individuals. (Ibid.)

Halim remained at Universiti Sains Malaysia as an Associate Professor in the Development Studies programme after which he moved to join the university's medical branch in Kubang Krian, Kelantan, where he now researches and teaches in anthropology and sociology of medicine.

Wan Hashim was another Masters student of Swift, who continued to study for his doctorate under Hamza Alavi at the University of Manchester. Like S. Husin Ali, Wan Hashim (1988) undertook comparative fieldwork of four different peasant communities in Perak, from padi growers, to rubber tappers, FELDA settlers and fisherfolk. Again, working from the neo-Marxist modes of production and capital–peasant perspective, he attempts to explain the different impacts on peasant relations of production and the attendant processes of differentiation arising from fishing as opposed to the land-based peasantry. He finds comparable processes occurring in his fishing village as Firth had, except that in the former the presence of Chinese capitalists rather than Malays was conspicuous. Wan Hashim concludes that in the light of the new technological and capital investment taking place in the modern fishing sector, the pace of the capitalist relations of production was faster when compared to the land-based peasant economy. He notes the emergence of a more rapid proletarianisation and marginalisation as the end product of capitalist development in the fishing sector and concludes that the dissolution of the peasantry may be delayed in the land-based sector since it is characterised by a preponderance of the middle peasantry. Wan Hashim was also a Professor at UKM and at one point of his career he was also appointed as the Deputy Vice-Chancellor at the university in charge of student affairs. He also held the position of Directorship at ATMA before Shamsul and was active in the Federation of Malaysia Writers' Associations (Gapena) focusing on the Malay diaspora. He finally left to join the government as a member of parliament but has now retired from active formal politics.

Another scholar of the fourth generation is Zahid Emby, currently an Associate Professor at Universiti Putra Malaysia (UPM). Zahid finished his Masters under Swift at Monash and continued to do his Ph.D. at Cornell University. His work also moved into the new post-peasantry phase in the study of Malay society by chronicling the last 140 years of the history of Kampong Alur Mas in Kedah (Zahid, 1992, 2003). This period saw a group of peasant rice cultivators switching from subsistence rice growing to rubber cultivation and then moving back to padi production again, but this time for the market. However, low yields forced them to turn to wage labour in order to secure a better income and livelihood in the towns and industrial areas where factories and construction companies were offering higher wages. By the end of the twentieth century the village which had been populated in the 1800s by subsistence rice farmers was transformed into a village of labourers.

The last scholar from the fourth generation is the late Norazit Selat, who died while serving as a Professor at the University of Malaya. He started his postgraduate studies at Monash under Swift but continued under Joel Kahn after Swift's death. Norazit's anthropological work, like that of Halim Salleh, took him to study another Malay urban population—the working class of Lorong Sembilang, Johor—where he examined Malay men and women involved in wage labour. He pinpoints to the totalising impact of capitalist social relations in these new conditions, which were "subjected to a capitalist economic rationality". He argues that in such a structural context, it is

> not only their work, but also their mode of expressing themselves, confirms and gives reality to this position. The people's relationships and mode of consciousness manifest in many ways the major governing institutions of the capitalist society: monetization and commoditization. (Norazit Selat, 1996: 180)

In an interesting twist on the discourse on *rezeki*, Norazit suggests that *rezeki*, *ikhtiar*, money and savings (including the beliefs in spirits *(hantu)* have been redefined as "working for capital", that is in "the quest for money, the commodity of all commodities" (Ibid.). This new logic is played out in the emerging consciousness of wage labourers as they justify new modes of behaviour:

> The concepts of *ikhtiar* and *rezeki* go hand in hand with the attempts of urban Malays to improve their lot. Gambling and the search for easy money are *ikhtiar* because one must go after them. Most of the men who engage in these acts agree that they are forbidden in Islam, but argue that they are not dosa besar (great sins) as are adultery, murder or calumny (*fitnah*). Yet through ideologically assimilating these morally questionable activities into an acceptable phenomenon, namely work, the people have taken the first step towards the acceptance of bourgeois values. (Ibid.: 179)

The fourth generation offers an instructive case study of important shifts in the production of knowledge in the field of anthropology. By any measure, they represent a relatively small group of scholars but one which has had a considerable impact on the theoretical and empirical issues that have shaped the research and teaching agendas in some of

Malaysia's leading public universities. In methodological terms, the fourth generation's approach to knowledge production has been both individual and collaborative, and they have been keen to bring together experts of interdisciplinary backgrounds to engage in specific projects. And given their seniority in leadership roles in the academic system, they have been able to influence new younger scholars and, to some extent, helped foster dialogue between anthropologists, policymakers and the wider public.

Conclusion

The genealogy of professional anthropology in Malaysia over a period of some 70 years offers a fascinating insight into both the continuities and the ruptures in knowledge production. Above all, it is the fourth generation of indigenous anthropologists who emerged to prominence in the late 1970s and 1980s that were able to demarcate an original niche in our understanding of the changing dynamics of Malay peasant society. This is not to deny the continuities with some of the initial ideas and windows opened up by the original masters, Raymond Firth and Michael Swift above all. These continuities are evident. But the Malay scholars were able to bring something fresh and invigorating to the table. Building on the outstanding work of their predecessors, scholars such as S. Husin Ali, Mokhzani Abdul Rahim and Syed Hussein Alatas also drew inspiration from the wider "radical turn" in the social sciences that marked the 1970s. The fourth generation was a product of a particular time when theoretical paradigms and research questions were evolving in interesting ways. The result was a shift from the classical concerns with the peasantry using data from micro-level fieldwork studies towards broader issues of agrarian change, capitalist modernity, ideational formation and contemporary politics. This research agenda has yet to run its course. But the signs are already there of a newer generation—exploring hugely important issues such as representations, ethnicity, identity and multiculturalism—who will once again reinvigorate anthropological debates in Malaysia for the foreseeable future (see Zawawi, 2008; Lim et al., 2009).

References

Abdul Kahar, B. (1978). Social rank, status honour and social class consciousness amongst the Malays. In H.-D. Evers (Ed.), *Modernisation in South-East Asia* (pp. 132–149). Kuala Lumpur: Oxford University Press.

Alatas, S. H. (1972). *Siapa Yang Salah: Sekitar Revolusi Mental dan Peribadi Melayu*. Singapore: Pustaka Nasional.

Alatas, S. H. (1977). *The myth of the lazy native: A study of the image of the Malays, Filipinos and Javanese from the 16th to the 20th century and its function in the ideology of colonial capitalism*. London: Frank Cass.

Alavi, H. (1972). The state in post-colonial societies. *New Left Review, 74*, 59–81.

Alavi, H. (1973). Peasant classes and primordial loyalties. *Journal of Peasant Studies, 1*(1), 23–62.

Alavi, H. (1975). India and the colonial mode of production. In Ralph Miliband & John Saville (Eds.), *The socialist register* (pp. 160–97). London: Merlin.

Amin, S. (1976). *Unequal development*. New York: Monthly Review Press.

Asad, T. (Ed.). (1973). *Anthropology and the colonial encounter*. Ithaca: Cornell University Press.

Banaji, J. (1976a). India and the colonial mode of production: A comment. *Economic and Political Weekly, 10*(49), 1887–1892.

Banaji, J. (1976b). Summary of selected parts of Kautsky's The Agrarian question. *Economy and Society, 5*(1), 1–49.

Bernstein, H. (1976). Notes on capital and peasantry. *Review of African Political Economy, 10*, 60–73.

Bernstein, H. (1979). Concepts for the analysis of contemporary peasantries. *Journal of Peasant Studies, 6*(4), 421–443.

Bloch, M. (1983). *Marxism and anthropology*. New York: Oxford University Press.

Boesen, J. (1979). On peasantry and the 'modes of production' debate. *Review of African Political Economy, 15*(16), 154–161.

Bradby, B. (1975). The destruction of natural economy. *Economy and Society, 4*(2), 127–161.

Clammer, J. (1975). Economic anthropology and the sociology of development. In I. Oxall, T. Barnett, & D. Booth (Eds.), *Beyond the sociology of development* (pp. 208–228). London: Routledge & Kegan Paul.

Clammer, J. (Ed.). (1978). *The new economic anthropology*. London: Macmillan.

Clarke, J. (1977). Some problems in the conceptualisation of non-capitalist relations of production. *Critique of Anthropology, 2*(8), 59–70.

Cleaver, H. (1972). The contradictions of the green revolution. *Monthly Review, 24*(2), 80–111.

Cleaver, H. (1976). Internationalisation of capital and mode of production in agriculture. *Economic and Political Weekly, 11*, 2–16.

Clifford, H. (1903). *In court and kampong: Being tales and sketches of native life in the Malay Peninsula*. London: Grant Richards.

Clifford, H. (1927). *Studies in Brown humanity: Being scrawls and smudges in sepia, white, and Yellow*. London: Richards Press.

Clifford, J., & Marcus, G. (Eds.). (1986). *Writing culture: The poetics and politics of ethnography*. Berkeley: University of California Press.
Dahlan, H. M. (1973). *Theories and policies of modernisation: An application of A.G. Frank's critique with reference to Malaysia (West Malaysia)*. M.A. thesis, Department of Anthropology and Sociology, Monash University.
Dahlan, H. M. (1976). Micro-analyses of village communities in Peninsular Malaysia: A study of underdevelopment. In H. M. Dahlan (Ed.), *The nascent Malaysian society* (pp. 99–132). Bangi: Universiti Kebangsaan Malaysia.
Dahlan, H. M. (1989). *Urbanisation in sabah: Probing into the Urban social mind*. Kota Kinabalu: Institute for Development Studies Sabah.
Dahlan, H. M. (1997). *Urbanisasi: Alam Kejiwaan Sosial dan Pembangunan*. Bangi: Penerbit Universiti Kebangsaan Malaysia.
Deere, C., & Janvry, A. D. (1979). A conceptual framework for the empirical analysis of peasants. *American Journal of Agricultural Economics, 61*(4), 601–611.
Dupre, G., & Rey, P.-P. (1973). Reflections on the pertinence of a theory of the history of exchange. *Economy and Society, 2*(2), 131–163.
Ennew, J., Hirst, P., & Tribe, K. (1977). Peasantry as an economic category. *Journal of Peasant Studies, 4*(4), 295–322.
Feder, E. (1979). The new World Bank programme for the Self-liquidation of the third world peasantry. *Journal of Peasant Studies, 3*(3): 343–354.
Feuchtwang, S. (1975). Investigating religion. In M. Bloch (Ed.), *Marxist analysis and social anthropology* (pp. 61–82). London: Malaby.
Firth, R. (1929). *Primitive economics of the New Zealand Maori*. New York: Duton.
Firth, R. (1939). *Primitive polynesian economy*. London: Routledge.
Firth, R. (1952). *The elements of social organisation* (2nd ed.). London: Watts.
Firth, R. (Ed.). (1957). *Man and culture: An evaluation of the work of Bronislaw Malinowski*. London: Routledge & Kegan Paul.
Firth, R. (1959). *Social change in Tikopia*. London: Allen & Unwin.
Firth, R. (1964). *Essays on social organisation and values*. London: Athlone Press.
Firth, R. (1966a [1943]). *Housekeeping among Malay peasants*. London: Athlone Press.
Firth, R. (1966b [1946]). *Malay fishermen: Their peasant economy*, revised and enlarged edition. London: Routledge & Kegan Paul.
Firth, R. (1968). The social framework of economic organisation. In E. E. LeClair & H. K. Schneider (Eds.), *Economic anthropology: Readings in theory and analysis* (pp. 65–87). New York: Holt, Rinehart and Winston.
Firth, R. (1970). Themes in economic anthropology: A general comment. In R. Firth (Ed.), *Themes in economic anthropology* (pp. 1–28). ASA Monographs 6. London: Tavistock.

Firth, R. (1975). The sceptical anthropologist? social anthropology and Marxist views on society. In M. Bloch (Ed.), *Marxist analyses and social anthropology* (pp. 29–60). London: Malaby.

Firth, R. (2003). Foreword. In A. B. Shamsul (Ed.), *Social anthropology of the Malays: Collected essays of Michael G. Swift*. M.G. Bangi: Penerbit Universiti Kebangsaan Malaysia.

Firth, R., & Yamey, B. S. (Eds.). (1963). *Capital, savings and credit in peasant societies: Studies from Asia, Oceania, The Caribbean and Middle America*. London: Allen and Unwin.

Fontana, A. (1994). Ethnographic trends in the postmodern era. In D. Dickens & A. Fontana (Eds.), *Postmodernism and social inquiry* (pp. 203–223). New York: Guilford Press.

Foster-Carter, Aidan. (1974). Neo-Marxist approaches to development and underdevelopment. In E. D. Kadt & G. Williams (Eds.), *Sociology of development* (pp. 67–105). London: Tavistock.

Foster-Carter, A. (1978a). Can we articulate 'articulation'. In J. Clammer (Ed.), *The new economic anthropology* (pp. 210–247). London: Macmillan.

Foster-Carter, A. (1978b). The mode of production controversy. *New Left Review, 107,* 47–78.

Frank, A. G. (1969). *Capitalism and underdevelopment in Latin America*. New York: Monthly Review Press.

Gardner, K., & Lewis, D. (1996). *Anthropology, development and the post-modern challenge*. London: Pluto Press.

Godelier, M. (1977). *Marxist perspectives in anthropology*. Cambridge: Cambridge University Press.

Halim, S. (1981). *Bureaucrats, Petty Bourgeois and Townsmen: An observation on status identification in Kota Bharu*. Monash Papers on Southeast Asia No. 8. Melbourne: Centre for Southeast Asian Studies, Monash University.

Halim, S. (1988). *Changing forms of labour mobilization in Malaysian agriculture*. Ph.D. thesis, University of Sussex.

Halim, S. (1992). Peasants, proletarianisation and the state: FELDA settlers in Pahang. In J. Kahn & FKW Loh (Eds.), *Fragmented vision: Culture and politics in contemporary Malaysia* (pp. 107–132). Sydney: Asian Studies Association of Australia in association with Allen & Unwin.

Husin Ali, S. (1964). *Social stratification in Kampong Bagan: A study of class, status, conflict and mobility in a rural Malay community*. Singapore: Malaysian Branch, Royal Asiatic Society.

Husin Ali, S. (1972). Land concentration and poverty among the rural Malays. *Nusantara 1*.

Husin Ali, S. (1975). *Malay peasant society and leadership*. Kuala Lumpur: Oxford University Press.

Ishak, S. (1990). *Ekonomi Nelayan: Pengumpulan Modal, Perubahan Teknologi dan Pembezaan Ekonomi*. Kuala Lumpur: Dewan Bahasa dan Pustaka.
Jomo, K. S. (1986). *A question of class: Capital, the state and uneven development in Malaysia*. Singapore: Oxford University Press.
Kahn, J. (1978a). Marxist anthropology and peasant economics: A study of the social structure of underdevelopment. In J. Clammer (Ed.), *The new economic anthropology* (pp. 110–137). London: Macmillan.
Kahn, J. (1978b). Ideology and social structure in Indonesia. *Comparative Studies in Society and History, 20*(1), 103–122.
Kahn, J., & Llobera, J. (Eds.). (1981). *The anthropology of pre-capitalist societies*. London: Macmillan.
Kay, G. (1978). *Development and underdevelopment: A Marxist analysis*. London: Macmillan.
King, V., & Wilder, W. (2003). *The modern anthropology of South-East Asia: An introduction*. London: RoutledgeCurzon.
Laclau, E. (1971). Feudalism and capitalism in Latin America. *New Left Review, 61*, 19–38.
Lenin, V. I. (1974 [1899]). *The development of capitalism in Russia*. Moscow: Progress Publishers.
Lim, T. G. (1976). *Origins of a colonial economy: Land and agriculture in Perak, 1874–1879*. Penang: Penerbit Universiti Sains Malaysia.
Lim, T. G. (1977). *Peasants and their agricultural economy in colonial Malaya 1874–1941*. Kuala Lumpur: Oxford University Press.
Lim, T. G. (1984). The growth of the worker class and its implications for social relations. In S. Husin Ali (Ed.), *Ethnicity, class and development*. Malaysia. Kuala Lumpur: Persatuan Sains Sosial.
Lim, T. G., Alberto, G., & Azly, R. (Eds.). (2009). *Multiethnic Malaysia: Past, present, future*. Petaling Jaya: SIRD.
Mahathir, M. (1970). *The Malay dilemma*. Singapore: Asia Pacific Press.
Marcus, G., & Fischer, M. (1986). *Anthropology as cultural critique: An experimental moment in the human sciences*. Chicago: University of Chicago Press.
McEachern, D. (1976). The mode of production in India. *Journal of Contemporary Asia, 6*(4), 444–457.
McEachern, D. (1979). *Colonialism and colonial modes of production*. Adelaide: University of Adelaide, Centre for Asian Studies.
Meillassoux, C. (1972). From Reproduction to Production. *Economy and Society, 1*(1), 93–105.
Meillassoux, C. (1973). The social organisation of the peasantry: The economic basis of kinship relations. *Journal of Peasant Studies, 1*(1), 81–90.
Meillassoux, C. (1981). *Maidens, meal and money*. Cambridge: Cambridge University Press.

Mokhzani, A. R. (1973). *Credit in the Malay peasant economy*. Ph.D. thesis, University of London.

Mokhzani, A. R. (2006). *Credit in a Malay peasant economy*. Kuala Lumpur: Faculty of Economics and Administration, University of Malaya.

Norazit, S. (1996). *Urban survival: The Malays of Muar*. Kuala Lumpur: Yayasan Penataran Ilmu.

Parkinson, B. K. (1967). Non-economic factors in the economic retardation of the rural Malays. *Modern Asian Studies, 1*(1), 31–46.

Patnaik, U. (1979). Neo-populism and Marxism: The Chayanovian view of the Agrarian question and its fundamental fallacy. *Journal of Peasant Studies, 6*(4): 375–420.

Redfield, R. (1960). *The little community and peasant society and culture*. Chicago: University of Chicago Press.

Roseberry, W. (1976). Rent, differentiation and the development of capitalism amongst peasants. *American Anthropologist, 78*(1), 45–58.

Said, E. (1978). *Orientalism*. London: Penguin.

Scott, J. (1976). *The moral economy of the peasant: Rebellion and subsistence in Southeast Asia*. New Haven: Yale University Press.

Scott, J. (1985). *Weapons of the weak: Everyday forms of peasant resistance*. New Haven: Yale University Press.

Seddon, D. (1978). *Relations of production: Marxist approaches to economic anthropology*. London: Cass.

Senu, A. R. (1970). *Revolusi mental*. Kuala Lumpur: Penerbitan Utusan Melayu.

Shaharil, T. (1984). *After its own image: The Trengganu experience, 1881–1941*. Singapore: Oxford University Press.

Shamsul, A. B. (1979). The development of the underdevelopment of the Malaysian peasantry. *Journal of Contemporary Asia, 9*(4), 434–54.

Shamsul, A. B. (1986). *From British to Bumiputera rule: Local politics and rural development in Peninsular Malaysia*. Singapore: Institute of Southeast Asian Studies.

Shamsul, A. B. (1994). Religion and ethnic politics in Malaysia: The significance of the Islamic resurgent phenomenon. In C. Keyes, L. Kendall, & H. Hardacre (Eds.), *Asian visions of authority: Religion and the modern states of East and Southeast Asia* (pp. 99–116). Honolulu: University of Hawaii Press.

Shamsul, A. B. (1996a). Malaysia's nation-of-intent. In Stein Tonnessson & Hans Antlov (Eds.), *Asian forms of the nation* (pp. 323–347). London: Curzon.

Shamsul, A. B. (1996b). The construction and transformation of a social identity: Malayness and Bumiputeraness re-examined. *Journal of African and Asian Studies, 52,* 15–34.

Shamsul, A. B. (1998a). Ethnicity, class, culture or identity? Competing paradigms in Malaysian studies. *Akademika, 55,* 33–59.

Shamsul, A. B. (1998b). Debating about identity in Malaysia: A discourse analysis. In Z. Ibrahim (Ed.), *Cultural contestations: Mediating identities in a changing Malaysian society* (pp. 8–31). London: ASEAN Academic Press.
Shamsul, A. B. (2000a). Redefining cultural nationalism in multiethnic Malaysia: A recent observation. *Inter-Asia Cultural Studies, 1*(1), 169–171.
Shamsul, A. B. (2000b). Colonial knowledge and identity formation: Literature and the construction of Malay and Malayness. *Asian Culture Quarterly, 28*(1), 49–64.
Shamsul, A. B. (2000c). Ilmu Kolonial Tunjang Pembinaan Ilmu Sains Sosial: Satu Tinjauan Kritis. *Jurnal Pengajian Umum l.*
Shamsul, A. B. (2000d). Ilmu Kolonial dan Pembinaan Fakta Mengenai Malaysia. In R. Aziz & Mohamed Yusoff Istnail (Eds.), *Masyarakat, Budaya dan Perubahan*. Bangi: Penerbit Univesiti Kebangsaan Malaysia.
Shamsul, A. B. (2002a). The European—American—Asian knowledge complex: A critical commentary. In K. S. Nathan (Ed.), *The European Union, United States and ASEAN: Challenges and prospects for cooperative engagement in the 21st century* (pp. 139–155). London: ASEAN Academic Press.
Shamsul, A. B. (2002b). Globalization and democratic developments in Southeast Asia: Articulation and social responses. In C. Kinnvall & K. Jönsson (Eds.), *Globalization and democratization in Asia: The construction of identity* (pp. 193–209). London: Routledge.
Shamsul, A. B. (2003a). Adat Perpatih and Malay ethnicity: A report from the field in Jempol, Negeri Sembilan, Malaysia. In T. Goda (Ed.), *Postcolonialism and local politics in Southeast Asia* (pp. 1–29). New Day: Quezon City.
Shamsul, A. B. (2003b). Introduction: Reputation lives on: Michael swift remembered. In A. B. Shamsul (Ed.), *Social anthropology of the Malays: Collected essays of M. G. Swift*. Bangi: Penerbit Universiti Kebangsaan Malaysia.
Shamsul, A. B. (2004). Anthropology, identity, and nation formation in Malaysia. In Shinji Yamashita, Joseph Bosco and J. S. Eades (Eds.), *The making of anthropology in East and Southeast Asia* (pp. 286–306). Oxford: Berghahn.
Shamsul, A. B. (2005). A question of identity: Knowledge and the formation of post-colonial nation-states in Asia. In R. Hassan (Ed.), *Local and global: Social transformation in Southeast Asia. Essays in honour of professor Syed Hussein Alatas* (pp. 31–44). Leiden: Brill.
Shanin, T. (Ed.). (1971). *Peasant and peasant societies: Selected readings*. London: Penguin.
Smith, L. T. (1999). *Decolonising methodologies: Research and indigenous peoples*. Dunedin: Zed Books and University of Otago Press.
Snodgrass, D. (1980). *Inequality and economic development in Malaysia*. Kuala Lumpur: Oxford University Press.
Swettenham, F. (1895). *Malay sketches*. London: John Lane.
Swettenham, F. (1900). *The real Malay: Pen pictures*. London: John Lane.

Swift, M. (1965). *Malay peasant society in Jelebu*. London: Athlone Press.
Swift, M. (1967). Economic Concentration and Malay Peasant Society. In M. Freedman (Ed.), *Social organisation: Essays presented to Raymond Firth* (pp. 241–69). London: Cass.
Swift, M. (2003). *Social anthropology of the Malays: Collected essays of M.G. Swift*, ed. A. B. Shamsul. Bangi: Penerbit Universiti Kebangsaan Malaysia.
Taylor, J. (1979). *From modernisation to modes of production: A critique of the sociologies of development and underdevelopment*. London: Macmillan.
Terray, E. (1975). Classes and class consciousness in the Abron Kingdom of Gyaman. In M. Bloch (Ed.), *Marxist analyses and social anthropology* (pp. 85–136). London: Malaby Press.
Ungku, A. A. (1957). Facts and fallacies about the Malay economy. *Straits Times*, 28 February–5 March.
Ungku, A. A. (1964). Poverty and rural development in Malaya. *Kajian Ekonomi Malaysia, 1*(1): 70–105.
Hashim, Wan. (1988). *Peasants under peripheral capitalism*. Bangi: Penerbit Universiti Kebangsaan Malaysia.
Wolf, E. (1966). *Peasants*. Englewood Cliffs NJ: Prentice-Hall.
Wolpe, H. (1972). Capital and cheap labour in South Africa: From segregation to apartheid. *Economy and Society, 1*(4), 425–56.
Yamashita, S., Bosco, J., & Eades, J. S. (2004). Asian anthropologies: Foreign, native and indigenous. In S. Yamashita, J. Bosco, & J. S. Eades (Eds.), *The making of anthropology in East and Southeast Asia* (pp. 1–34). Oxford: Berghahn.
Zahid, E. (1992). *Malay labourers: Work and the moral economy of a post peasant village*. Ph.D. thesis, Cornell University.
Zahid, E. (2003). Changing occupations as a strategy for survival: case study of a Malay village in Peninsular Malaysia. In D. Storey, J. Overton, & B. Nowak, (Eds.), *Contesting development: Pathways to better practice*. Proceedings of the Third Biennial Conference of the International Development Studies Network of Aotearoa New Zealand. Palmerston North: Massey University.
Zawawi, I. (1982). Perspectives on capitalist penetration and the reconstitution of the Malay peasantry. *Jurnal Ekonomi Malaysia, 5*, 60–105.
Zawawi, I. (1983). Perspectives towards investigating Malay peasant ideology and the bases of its production in contemporary Malaysia. *Journal of Contemporary Asia, 13*(2), 198–209.
Zawawi, I. (1984). Investigating peasant consciousness in contemporary Malaysia. In A. Turton & S. Tanabe (Eds.), *History and consciousness in South East Asia* (pp. 135–157). Osaka: National Museum of Ethnology.
Zawawi, I. (1990). Rural Malays and tobacco: A study of organisation, response and changing values. In *Issues and challenges for national development: Selected*

papers presented during the 21st Anniversary Conference, December 1987. Kuala Lumpur: Faculty of Economics and Administration, University of Malaya.

Zawawi, I. (1998a). Orang Asli identity in the nation-state. *Journal of Malaysian and Comparative Law, 28*, 1–15.

Zawawi, I. (1998b). The making of a Subaltern discourse in the Malaysian nation-state: New subjectivities and the poetics of Orang Asli sispossession and identity. In I. Zawawi (Ed.), *Cultural contestations: Mediating identities in a changing Malaysian society*. London: ASEAN Academic Press.

Zawawi, I. (1998c). *The Malay labourer: By the window of capitalism*. Singapore: Institute of Southeast Asian Studies.

Zawawi, I. (2000). Regional development in rural Malaysia and the 'tribal question'. *Modern Asian Studies, 34*(1), 99–137.

Zawawi, I. (2003a). The search for a 'new cinema' in post-colonial Malaysia: The films of U-Wei bin Haji Saari as counter-narrations of national identity. *Inter-Asia Cultural Studies, 4*(1), 145–154.

Zawawi, I. (2003b). Globalization and national identity: Managing ethnicity and cultural pluralism in Malaysia. In Y. Sato (Ed.), *Growth and governance in Asia*. Honolulu: Asia Pacific Center for Security Studies.

Zawawi, I. (2004). On Erma Fatima's 'The Last Malay Woman' *(Perempuan Melayu Terakhir)*: Gendering discourses in reclaiming Malayness in the New Malaysian cinema. *Spectator*. Special Issue: *Screening Southeast Asia, 24*(2), 27–38.

Zawawi, I. (2005). Return of the lazy native: Explaining Malay/immigrant labour transition in Terengganu plantation society. In Riaz Hasssan (Ed.), *Local and global: Social transformation in Southeast Asia: Essays in honour of professor Syed Hussein Alatas*. Brill: Leiden.

Zawawi, I. (2007). The beginning of neo-realist imaginings in Malaysian Cinema: A critical appraisal of Malay modernity and representation of Malayness in Rahim Razali's films. *Asian Journal of Social Science, 35*(4–5), 511–527.

Zawawi, I. (Ed.). (1996). *Kami Bukan Anti-Pembangunan: Bicara Orang Asli Menuju Wawasan 2020*. Bangi: Persatuan Sains Sosial.

Zawawi, I. (Ed.). (2008). *Representation, identity and multiculturalism in Sarawak*. Kuching: Dayak Cultural Foundation and Kajang: Persatuan Sains Sosial Malaysia.

CHAPTER 4

Colonial Knowledge and the Construction of Malay and Malayness: Exploring the Literary Component

Shamsul Amri Baharuddin

In Lieu of an Introduction

The late Professor Shaharil Talib Roberts, a historian, in 1979, introduced and guided me during my archival research at the Malaysian Archive, then located at Petaling Jaya, for my Ph.D. in the field of social anthropology. He had just returned from Monash University, Melbourne, Australia after the completion of his Ph.D. in 1978. One major point of epistemological convergence in our discussion was on the global peasantry, in general, and the Malaysian peasantry, in particular, his from the viewpoint of history and mine from an anthropological perspective. But both of us were fascinated by the brilliance of sociologist Barrington Moor, *Social Origins of Dictatorship and Democracy: Lord and Peasant in the Making of the Modern World* (1966) in which he sought to explain in broad historical sweep the developmental transition that transformed peasant agrarian

S. A. Baharuddin (✉)
National Institute of Ethnic Studies, Universiti Kebangsaan Malaysia, Bangi, Malaysia

R. Rasiah et al. (eds.), *Contesting Malaysia's Integration into the World Economy*, https://doi.org/10.1007/978-981-16-0650-2_4

societies into modern industrial ones by drawing empirical material from England, China, France, Germany, Japan, the United States, and Russia.

Barrington Moore argued that there are three historical routes from agrarianism to the modern industrial world: first a "capitalist democratic route"; second, a "capitalist reactionary route"; and third, "the communist route". Which one is the Malaysian route, we asked? We thought the Malaysian case doesn't really fit into any of the routes. How should we start exploring, epistemologically and ontologically, the parts from each of the routes that Malaysia has had experienced? In this context, we were drawn into another area of discussion, namely, colonialism. The countries from where Barrington Moore drew empirical evidence from, namely, England, China, France, Germany, Japan, the United States, and Russia, were colonizers and not colonized.

In this discourse we had, I have had an opportunity to introduce to Prof Shaharil the works of the late Bernard Cohn, who was a Professor of Anthropology and History at Chicago University whose essays and books, redefined the field of the sociology of knowledge through his research on the colonial forms of power and its representation much before Michel Foucault enter the realm of South Asian and Southeast Asian studies. Cohn's two books, compilation of essays over twenty years, are *An anthropologist among Historians and Other Essays* (1987), and *Colonialism and its Forms of Knowledge: The British in India* (1996). Essentially, he was interested in the historical and anthropological making of the British colonial state in India. His focus was on the modes in which "colonial" culture and practices were enforced through multiple regulatory mechanism. He ably demonstrated that the colonial state and its historical anthropology were inseparable from the ideology of power and the political character of the state. His work retains immense relevance even today.

Prof Shaharil recognized the lacuna in Malaysian historiography regarding colonial knowledge. We discussed this at length and he encouraged me to explore the theme in more detail and in a critical manner utilizing the archive as much as I could. Indeed, for the last two decades (1988–2008) I have been pursuing this mission encouraged by Prof Shaharil and have eventually published a few essays related to colonial knowledge (Shamsul 1999, 2001, 2008, 2011, 2012, 2015).

The present chapter is a revised version of my first article on colonial knowledge and its impact on Malaysian society. I am truly indebted to Prof Shaharil Talib for all his encouragement and assistance in my endeavor to discover colonial knowledge and how it shaped the society, history, and territory of Malaysia.

Since 1988, I have been analyzing the process of identity construction in Malaysia. An aspect of it touches upon the role of "colonialism" and "colonial knowledge" and how categories and classifications introduced and used during the colonial era have become naturalized into the social life of Malaysians, both at the authority-defined and everyday-defined levels. The empirical focus has been on the Malays as a community. The choice is both personal and academic. As a person, I wish to know more about the community that I have been born into, not only knowing it in the popular sense, but I strongly feel there is still a lot more to be done in the latter sense. This is one such attempt, indeed a modest and exploratory one, too.

I wound argue that colonial conquest was not just the result of the power of superior arms, military organization, political power, or economic wealth, it was also the result of a cultural invasion in the form of a conquest of the native "epistemological space", or, put simply, the dismantling of native thought system, hence disempowering it of its ability to define things and subsequently replacing it with a foreign one, through a systematic application of a series of colonial investigative modalities. It is this "cultural technologies of rule" employed successfully by the British that has not been discussed in-depth by historians of Malaysian society. In Malaysia, it seems to be analytically convenient, almost routinized, for historians and others to accept an unproblematized "colonial knowledge", both as the basis and the accepted form of Malaysian and Malay history. This is despite the fact that there exists the politico-academic attempt, until today, to "indigenize" Malaysian history by privileging the native-Malay viewpoint.

Indeed, it is an admired effort; but the emphasis has clearly been motivated by the perceived conceptual and "cultural-nationalistic" need to reinterpret history rather than to problematize and question the construction of historical knowledge, in this case, the colonial knowledge, which, in fact, is the basis of identity formation in modern Malaysia. The lack of analytical attention, especially in Malaysia, on the problematic origin, development, and nature of colonial knowledge has also been the result of viewpoints that have emphasized either the good or bad side of the paternalism which informed colonialism, but have nothing to say about colonial knowledge itself (Omar 1993). This is sadly true as evident in a contribution on the state of Malaysian historiography made by no less than Cheah Boon Kheng (1997), a retired history professor from Universiti Sains Malaysia, Penang.

This deafening silence on colonial knowledge, something which has been taken as given, or taken-for-granted or as something natural, both among historians and non-historians, is a cause for intellectual and ideological concern, especially in the context of the present development of Malaysian studies and society. My basic concern here is clearly about the "identity of knowledge", one which has even escaped the mind of many scholars and analysts who themselves are deeply involved in the general study of (people's) identity.

For instance, in the discourse on Malay identity in Malaysia, one could argue that colonial methods of knowledge accumulation and the resultant corpus of knowledge gathered have been critical in providing not only substance, but also sustenance to the whole exercise. The sheer amount of "facts" accumulated and amassed by the British, be it on traditional Malay literature or modern history of Malaya, establishes, without doubt, the hegemony of colonial knowledge in Malaysia's intellectual realm. Thus, a sustainable discussion on Malay identity, whether in the past or at present is made possible by the rich colonial knowledge. Milner (1995) demonstrated convincingly that even the discourse on "politics" (or should I say 'identity') among the pre-war Malay writers-cum-nationalists was informed mainly by or conducted within a framework of colonial knowledge.

In the first part of this chapter, I would present an argument that the history of the much discussed contemporary Malay identity and Malayness, largely a colonial-orientalist construction, reflects very much the identity of the overall history of Malaya and then Malaysia, one that was dominated, shaped, and "factualised", culturally, by colonial knowledge. In short, colonial knowledge has not only enabled conquest of British Malaya and the Malays as well as the immigrant population, but also was produced by it, as much as by the more obvious and brutal modes of conquest that first established colonial power in the Straits Settlements and later in the Malay states. The first half of the second part of the chapter takes a brief look at how Malay and Malayness was constructed, namely, the creation of the three pillars of Malayness—*bahasa, raja dan agama* (lit. language/Malay, sultan/Malay, and religion/Islam), through the implementation of a host of colonial policies directly affecting the Malays, all of which came to be officialized and instituted during the colonial period within the framework of colonial knowledge. This in turn has given rise to the modern idea of a Malay "race" (kaum) and "nation" (bangsa) as strongly reflected in its nationalist and anti-colonial movement, but embellished and localized by the British for its immediate ideological and materialist interests in British Malaya. The second half deals directly with matters relating to the contribution of the literary component to colonial knowledge and the construction of the ethnic category Malay and Malayness, through an examination of the contributions of three major colonial administrator-scholar figures, Raffles, Wilkinson, and Winstedt.

Colonial Knowledge, the Methodology and Modern Identity Formation

What is relevant here is for us to examine further the methods of knowledge accumulation that were responsible for creating an impressive corpus of colonial knowledge. I find the approach introduced and applied by the anthropologist Bernard Cohn (1996), based on his longitudinal research on British rule in India extremely useful.

He argues that what enabled the British to classify, categorize, and bind the vast social world that was India (by implication in Malaysia, too) so that it could be controlled was its all-important "investigative modalities" devised to collect and amass "facts". These "facts" and translation works made it possible for the British to conquer the "epistemological space" that he mentioned. According to Cohn, "an investigative modality includes the definition of a body or information that is needed, the procedures by which appropriate knowledge is gathered, is ordering and classification, and the how it is transformed into usable forms such as published reports, statistical returns, histories, gazetteers, legal codes, and encyclopedias" (1996: 5).

Cohn also shows that some of the investigative modalities are general in nature, such as historiography and museology. The survey and census modalities are more highly defined and closely related to administrative needs. These modalities are constructed and tailored to specific institutional or "departmental" agenda and become routinized in the day-to-day colonial bureaucratic practices. Some are even transformed into "sciences" such as economics, ethnology, tropical medicine, comparative law, or cartography, and their practitioners became professionals (Cohn 1996: 5). Obviously, this was an activity of not only the British, but also other colonial power, including the Dutch, as explored by Pyenson (1989) and the French (Mamdani 1996).

There are six major investigative modalities employed by the British and they are as follows. First, there is the "historiographic modality" that has three important components: (1) the production of settlement reports, which are produced on a district-by-district basis, and it usually consists of a detailed account of how revenue is assessed and collected by the different local indigenous regimes and a collection of local customs, histories, and land tenure systems; (2) the ideological construction regarding the nature of indigenous civilizations which eventually provided the space for the formation of a legitimizing discourse about British civilizing mission in the colony; and (3) constructing the histories of Great Britain in the colony through such methods as the creation of "emblematic heroes" concretized in the form of memorials and sacred spaces in various parts of the colony. The second modality is the "survey modality." It encompasses a wide range of practices, from mapping to collecting botanical specimens, to recording architectural and archeological sites of historic significance, or the most minute measuring of peasant's field. When the British came to India, and later Malaysia, through systematic surveys, they were able not only to describe and classify both countries' zoology, geology, botany, ethnography, economic products, history, and sociology, but also created an imaginary nationwide grid and could locate any site in both countries for economic, social, and political purposes. In short, the concept of "survey" came to cover any systematic and official investigation of the natural and social feature of indigenous society through which vast amounts of knowledge were transformed into textual forms, such as encyclopedias and extensive archives.

The third is the "enumerative modality", particularly in the form of official census, that enabled the British to construct social categories by which the indigenous society was ordered for administrative purpose. In fact, census was assumed to reflect the basic sociological facts, such as race, ethnic groups, culture, and language. It thus objectified social, cultural, and linguistic differences among the indigenous peoples and the migrant population that led to the reification of Malaya as polity in which conflict could only be controlled, from the colonialist's viewpoint, by the strong hands of their bureaucracy and armed forces (Hirschman 1986, 1987). This control was effected through "the surveillance modality", the fourth in the modality list. Through this modality, detailed information was gathered on "peripheral" or "minority" groups and categories of people whose activities were perceived as a threat to social order were closely observed and contained, often using methods such as fingerprinting.

The museological modality is the fifth. It begins with the perception that the colony is a vast museum, thus its countryside is assumed to be filled with ruins and it is a source of collectibles and curiosities, or artifacts, to fill local as well as European museums, botanical gardens, and zoos. This modality became an exercise of macro open representation of the indigenous antiquity, culture, and society to both local and European public. The sixth and final modality, which is the travel modality, complements the museological one. If the latter provides concrete representations of the natives, the former helps to create a repertoire of images and typifications, even stereotypes, that determine what is significant to the European eyes, something usually considered as aesthetic—"romantic", "exotic", "picturesque"—such as architecture, costume, cuisine, ritual performances, historical sites, and even bare-breasted females. These images and typifications are often found in paintings and prints as well as novels and short stories, written by the colonial scholar-administrators or their wives and friends. The tradition of coffee table books, for instance, emerged from such a context.

These modalities represent, according to Cohn (1996: 1), a set of "officialising procedures" upon which the British established and extended their capacity into numerous areas controlled by defining and classifying space, making separations between public and private spheres, by recording transactions such as sale of property, by counting and classifying populations, replacing religious institutions as the registrar of births, marriages, and deaths, and by standardizing languages and scripts. The colonial state, therefore, introduced policies and rules that helped frame the people's mind and action within a pre-decided epistemological and practical grid.

For instance, the famous Malay Reservation Enactment of 1913 first defines who is a Malay and second defines the scope of the use of land categorized as such and eventually sets the public commercial value of the land. Since this Enactment is instituted in eleven different *negeri* (province) in Malaya, each, according to the *negeri* constitutions, offers a slightly different definition of who is a Malay. So someone of an Arab descent is a Malay in Kedah but not in Johor, or someone of a Siamese descent is a Malay in Kelantan but not in Negeri Sembilan. It could be said that Malay and Malayness is not only created and represented but contested through a single legal document such as the Malay Reservation Enactment 1913.

In a different circumstance, the growth of public education and its rituals fosters official beliefs in how many things are and how they ought to be because the schools are crucial "civilizing" institutions and seeks to produce moral and productive citizens. Through schools much of the "facts" amassed through the officializing procedures or investigative modalities are channeled to the younger population, thus shaping their own perception of what social reality is, most of which are constructed by colonial knowledge anyway. More than that, with the existence of Chinese, Malay, Tamil, and English schools, ethnic boundaries become real and ethnic identities become essentialized and ossified through elements such as language and cultural practices. Mandarin, as a language, for instance, is never the mother tongue of the Chinese, instead, their respective dialects are (Dikotter 1992).

The bigger and more lasting sociological implication that colonial knowledge has impacted upon the colonized is the idea that "nation-state" is the natural embodiment of history, territory, and society. Thus nation-state becomes dependent on colonial knowledge in determining, codifying, controlling, and representing the past as well as documenting and normalizing a vast amount of information that forms the basis of its capacity to govern. We are too familiar with "facts" provided by reports and statistical data on commerce and trade, health, demography, crime, transportation, industry, and so on, all of which are taken as self-evident in an unquestioning manner.

We rarely question the identity of these "facts", at least in the Malaysian case. These facts and its collection, conducted in the steep tradition of colonial knowledge, lay at the foundation of the modern post-colonial nation-state, such as Malaysia. The whole Westernization process, and the onset of the modernization project, through which the nation-state concept is introduced and practiced, is indeed founded on such knowledge which is rooted in the European world of social theories, belief and thought system and classificatory schema that subsequently shape and reshape the lives of the subjects.

What I have briefly described above is basically the identity of a history, most if not all of the Malaysian one. It is within this history that modern identities in Malaysia, such as Malay and Malayness, have emerged, consolidated, and reified. Against such a background, I shall now proceed to examine the experience of identity formation and contestation in Malaysia, in particular the contestation about Malayness, both in the past and at present, and the role of literature.

The Construction of Malay and Malayness: The Literary Component

Historical Backdrop

In a recent important contribution, framed within Anthony D. Smith's empiricist concept of *ethnie*, Reid (1997) sketches the different meanings and applications of the term Malay and Malayness in the history of the Malay archipelago; first, as self-referent categories among the peoples inhabiting the archipelago; second as a social label used by the peoples of South Asian and China, who were mainly traders, and third, by the Europeans, namely, the Portuguese, the Spanish, the Dutch, and the British, as travelers, traders, and eventually colonizers.

In the first and second instances, arguable a non-European context, Malay and Malayness, by the sixteenth and seventeeenth centuries, were associated with two major elements, namely, (1) "a line of kingship acknowledging descent from Sriwijaya and Melaka and (2) a commercial diaspora which retained some of the customs, language and trade practices in the emporium of Melaka" (Reid 1997: 7). The kingship (read ***kerajaan*** and the royal family), as a pillar of Malayness, was more prominent in the area around the Straits of Malacca. Islam was also considered as another pillar of Malayness because the kingship had Islam as the provider of its core values. The commercial diaspora constituted peoples from outside the Straits of Melaka area, such as from Borneo, Makassar, and Jawa. They defined their Malayness in terms of language and customs, thus adding two more pillars of Malayness.

Sociologically speaking, the way the label Malay or Malayness was used by indigenous inhabitants of the archipelago during the pre-European era was both objective and subjective in nature. The kingship was used as an objective measure. The use of Islam was both objective and subjective, in the sense that it was an objective criterion to define the kingship and his subjects (Muslim and non-Muslim). However, subjectively, anyone who embraced Islam could be counted as Malay. Equally, those who were non-Muslim or non-Malay could be labeled as Malays as long as they lived the

Malay way of life, speak and write Malay, put in Malay costumes, cooked Malay cuisine and became an integral part of the Malay trading network.

Interestingly, this was not dissimilar to the way the Portuguese, Spanish, and the Dutch were using both the labels, Malay and Malayness. Both, being merchants first and rulers second, their main concerns were materialistic. Ideologically, at home, unlike the French and the German, they were not propagators of the concept of nation-state, but more inclined to frame their approach towards "civilising" the natives (perceived at first as non-human) within a vigorously religious orientation. This is confirmed emphatically by Norman Davies, in his brilliant *Europe: A History* (1997), when describing the activities and behavior orientation of European overseas, including in the "East Indies", in mid-fifteenth century. He said:

> European sailed overseas… for reasons of trade, of loot, of conquest, and increasingly of religion. For many, it provided the first meeting with people of different races. To validate their claim over the inhabitants of the conquered lands, the Spanish monarchs, for instance, had to first establish that non-European were human… and were ordered to read out to all natives peoples: 'The Lord our God, Living and Eternal, created Heaven and Earth, and one man and woman, of whom you and I, and all the men of the world, were and are descendants'. To confirm the point, Pope Paul III decreed in 1537 that 'all Indians are truly men, not only capable of understanding the Catholic faith, but…. Exceeding desirous to receive it. (1997: 510–511)

Like all merchants and sailors trading across oceans, compiling detailed inventory lists of people and things, including the cargoes, carried in their ships, was a mandatory exercise for the Portuguese and Dutch merchants, not only for the reason of general accountability, but also for the sake of safety. Therefore, they had to devise ways and means of classifying and categorizing the content of the ship, including the sailors and officers. It is in these records that it was found that captains of ships were identified and recorded by Dutch harbor masters as Chinese, Javanese, Bugis-Makassar, Balinese, Madurese, Arab and Malay captains and sailors, too. They were mainly adopting the local labels without any conscious attempt to reconstitute and redefine according to a preconceived European notion. Therefore, both the objective and subjective local notions embedded in the social labels "Malay" or "Malayness" remained unchanged. Based on these evidences, Reid (1997: 8) argues that the subjective aspect of Malay and Malayness, as observed in the sixteenth and seventeenth centuries, allowed plurality in the subsequent composition of the social category Malay because it was "exceptionally open to new recruits from any background." He thus postulates that "it (Malayness) can be seen to have evolved towards the idea of *orang Melayu* as a distinct *ethnie*", indeed a helpful analytical construct to tie together the historical evidences available to him. However, using the same evidences, one could still offer alternative analytical construct because they could be read in many different ways. The fact that the British reconstituted the whole meaning of Malay and Malayness, almost ignoring its *ethnie* sense, as described by Reid (1997: 10) himself, is instructive.

Not unlike in India, as described by Cohn (1996), the British in Malaya developed an entirely different approach toward acquiring an understanding of the natives, especially the Malays. It began during the East India Company era, especially from the early sixteenth to mid-nineteenth century, after direct British intervention, it was the crop of colonial officers who became the "administrator-scholars", who, not unlike anthropologist and antiquarians, diligently and painstakingly studied the Malays and the other natives. Both sets of scholars were not only interested in "socialscape" (the laws, language, culture, and economy), but also the "environscape" (flora-fauna and the environment in general). They have at their disposal a set of investigative modalities informed by a Scottish Enlightenment idea that human beings should be classified in a scientific manner not dissimilar to the way Carl Von Linne (Linnaeus) and Charles Darwin classified all living things. In the social scientific sense, these modalities became more refined and were further informed by a notion of cultural relativism that clearly exhibited, in Edward Said's term, "orientalism". Hence, through various ideas and methods within each of the investigative modalities (namely, historiography, survey, museological, enumerative, travel, and surveillance) and through colonial knowledge, the British was able to construct, with supporting "facts", and introduced many names and categories which many in Malaysia today think as something natural and have existed since time immemorial. It is in this context literature plays an important role to give content and substance to the colonial construction of Malay identity.

The Literary Component

The literary component of colonial knowledge is often neglected because it has always been discussed under the broader theme of "language and culture", in particular, how the native language and knowledge of local culture become standardized by the colonialist for both the general administrative purpose of official communication and interaction with the indigenes. The language in particular became the medium of instruction in vernacular schools or teachers' colleges set up for the locals. Literature thus became an integral component of the schools or teachers' college curriculum. For that reason, language, more than literature, has often been seen as directly related to the construction of an ethnic identity. In fact, in the context of Malayness, the Malay language or *Bahasa Melayu*, is seen as one of its pillars, not Malay literature.

However, if we examine closely, it is not too difficult to discern the critical role of the literary component, and activities related to it, in constituting and establishing the "Malay language" as a critical element in constructing Malayness. In the following pages, we shall explore briefly the role and contribution of three well-known British scholars—one "merchant-scholar" and the other two "administrator-scholars"—in the construction of Malay and Malayness through their individual efforts in studying and writing on various aspects of Malay literature and on the general topic of Malay culture; they are Stamford Raffles (1782–1826), R.J. Wilkinson (1867–1941) and R.O. Winstedt (1887–1966).

Giving the Malay a Nation and History: Stamford Raffles the "Merchant-Scholar". The single most important British "merchant-scholar" that has been responsible for developing what could be called "Malay colonial knowledge" was Stamford Raffles, who was once the Governor-General of Batavia and subsequently became the founder of Singapore. He was a scholar in his own right. Besides being greatly informed by the Scottish Enlightenment tradition in his general orientation, he seemed to have been deeply influenced by the German Romanticist movement in Europe, especially the ideas of Johann Herder (1744–1803) who emphasized common language, blood, and soil as constitutive elements of *Volk*. This influence was amply articulated in his finest and defining essay, entitled "On the Malayu Nation, with a Translation of its Maritime Institution" in the journal Asiatic Researches

(Vol. 12, 1816, original 1809: 140-160) that set the tone for the subsequent discourse on Malay and Malayness among the European as well as amongst the Malays much later. He wrote:

> I cannot but consider the Malayu nation as one people, speaking one language, though spread over so wide a space, and preserving their character and customs, in all the maritime state lying between the Sulu Seas and the Southern Oceans, and bounded longitudinally by Sumatra and the western side of Papuan or New Guinea. (Raffles 1816: 103)

Raffles thus became the first scholar who not only introduced the concept of "Malay nation", but also elaborated on the concept of the "Malay race", the "Malay world", and the "Malay language".

What was more significant was the fact that he also gave the Malays a history. Together with his friend Dr. John Leyden, who was then residing in Penang, Raffles renamed a Malay chronicle, originally called *Sulalatus-Salatin* (lit. Royal Protocol), translated into English by his friend Dr. John Leyden, as *Sejarah Melayu* or the *Malay Annals*. This Raffles did in his "Introduction" to the Leyden's translation, the full title of which is *Malay Annals: translated from the Malay language by the late Dr. John Leyden, with an introduction by Sir Thomas Stamford Raffles* (London: Longman, 1921). What Raffles effectively did at once was not only to claim that "here it is, the book on the history of the Malays" but also denied the fact that there were a number of other palace-centric Malay chronicles of the same gender which collectively could be categorized as the history of the Malays, too. Instead of claiming the rest as such, he chose one and claimed it as the history of the Malays as if to support further his contention in the "Introduction" that the Malays not only a race and a nation, it also has a history.

In short, Raffles provided an epistemology for Malay colonial knowledge based upon European classificatory schema and social theory of the Enlightenment and Romanticist kind. Such an orientation was also informed by a kind of "free trade and the civilizing mission" approach that often occupied Raffles' mind then. In a sense, he provided critical input into the making of a "Malay literate civilization" more than many scholars of Malay studies would be willing to, with the exception of Alatas (1976). Thus, the "Raffles paradigm" on the Malays was established, particularly through the *Malay Annals*. It later came into used and was popularized as a text for the study of the Malays, hence a critical contribution to the creation of "Malay studies".

Constituting a 'Malay Literature, Ethnography and Malay Studies': Richard James Wilkinson and Richard Olof Winstedt, the 'Administrator-Scholar'. Wilkinson was a British administrator who studied Malay during his student days. After a brief stint as a district officer, he became a school inspector for the colonial Department of Education. Later, he rose in the ranks rather quickly in the colonial administration in British Malaya to reach the position of Colonial Secretary, based in Singapore. In 1916, he was posted to West Africa to become the Governor of Sierra Leone from 1916 to 1922, after which he retired.

When he was in Malaya, his major pre-occupation was compiling a two-volume *Malay-English Dictionary* (1903). It is useful to note that a large proportion of the Malay entries was drawn from Malay literary sources. Important as it may be the dictionary and his other contribution in constituting a corpus of knowledge that could be broadly categorized as 'Malay literature and ethnography' were equally significant. However, the most important contribution of Wilkinson was his research, documentation and writing on various aspects of Malay culture and ethnography, between 1907 and 1927, which was compiled in a volume called *Papers on Malay Subjects*. The research and publication of the volume were mooted by no less than the Council of British Residents, who in 1906, agreed to set aside some funds for that purpose. The themes that were researched into included history, government and law, art and craft, social life, culture and literature. Wilkinson was appointed as the general editor of these series of *Papers*. It is also useful to point out that in one of the essays, "Malay History and Literature", Wilkinson offered for the first time not only a categorization of Malay literary genres, but also traced the origins of Malays to West Sumatra. Under the section "History" in the same volume of *Papers*, Wilkinson also wrote a "History of the Peninsular Malays".

This compilation of papers became important not only to trainee colonial administrators but also to those who were interested in understanding the finer points of culture, literature, belief system, etiquette and history. Indeed for a long time, it became the "authentic" authority on the "Malay subjects", used by academicians and others. It became an integral part of colonial knowledge in constituting the Malay identity. All in all, Wilkinson could be considered as a pioneer in the construction of 'Malay literature and ethnography'.

What is more significant is the fact that he was a member of a small group of British officers who was considered as being "pro-Malay" or had "real love for and sympathy with the Malay people" (Roff 1994: 130). However, his pro-Malay position was informed by what could be termed as "exotic and paternalistic concerns", namely, the need for the protection and preservation of the Malays and its culture.

Winstedt, on the other hand, a former assistant to Wilkinson, was well-known for his study on Malay literature, particularly Malay classical literature. In fact, his famous book is entitled *A History of Classical Malay Literature*, first published in 1940 and later a revised edition was published in 1960. Prior to the publication of this book, Winstedt had been a regular contributor to the *Journal of the Straits Branch of the Royal Asiatic Society* (JSBRAS) and *Journal of the Malayan Branch of the Royal Asiatic Society* (JMBRAS). Indeed, his book consisted of materials culled from essays which had appeared in JSBRAS and JMBRAS. These essays and eventually the book were based on his painstaking research and documentation over a period of some forty years. Even until today, he is still considered the pioneer in the study of Malay classical literature (Braginsky 1993).

Indeed, Winstedt was a prolific writer, having written more than fifteen books and scores of articles on Malay language, history, literature, customs, laws and arts, very much in the mould of Sir Edward Tylor, a famous British social anthropologist. In this sense, he is more influential than his mentor, Wilkinson, in consolidating the corpus of material that was to become the basis of "Malay studies". This contribution is further enhanced by the fact that he also published textbooks to be used at Malay Teacher's Training College, such as *Kitab Tawarikh Melayu* (lit. A Malay History Book) co-authored with Daing Abdul Hamid Tengku Muhammad Salleh, published in 1918. In the same year, Winstedt also published a geography textbook entitled *Ilmu Alam Melayu* (lit. Malay Geography). It was meant for teachers and students in the teachers' college as well as Malay schools.

Along with contributions from other colonial administrator-scholars, such as Swettenham, Skeat, Maxwell and others, Malay colonial knowledge became the main source of what came to be known as "Malay studies", that eventually was instituted as one of the academic programmes, called the Department of Malay Studies of the Faculty of Arts at the University of Malaya that was established in 1949. The department grouped its courses into three, namely, language, literature and culture.

Some of the academic staff were indeed former colonial administrators whose contributions in the study of the Malays were important and they were supported by academicians from the Netherlands. The department played a critical role in producing graduates, most of whom were Malays themselves, who later became administrators in the Malayan civil service, both before and after the Independence. In fact, many ended up as politicians and cabinet ministers.

The department has continued to play an important ideological role in providing Malay leadership, political and others, with research and publications that have contributed to further strengthening of "Malayness" as a ethno-political ideology, not only for the Malays, but also for the so-called "national culture" policy which proclaimed "Malay culture" as the basis of that policy. In this context, colonial knowledge remains the main pillar of Malay ethnicity and Malayness in Malaysia even until today, of course with some reconfigurations owing to political and social changes.

Conclusion

At the beginning of the chapter, I stated that the nature of the present analytic endeavour is an exploratory one. It promises to explore the role of the literary component (literary meant in the broader intellectual sense), as part of colonial knowledge, in the construction of "Malay" as ethnic category and "Malayness". Admittedly, in strict empirical terms, what I have presented as evidence is brief and sketchy. However, my intention is to prove three rather simple points: first, that literary component is an integral part of each of the colonial investigative modality, more obvious in the historiographic, survey, enumerative and travelogue modalities but less so in the rest; second, that combined with other facts, data, ethnographic and material culture artifact, knowledge on native literature classify, categorize, consolidate and objectify a particular social group (?) and give it an identity, in this case, an ethnic one and third, such invented social groups become naturalized through the implementation of colonial policies that manipulate their existence. For these reasons, "colonial knowledge" shall continue to be the most powerful form of knowledge that ever existed, but increasingly less and less recognized because it never has been or will be systematically analyzed or questioned as long as it is the source of power and legitimacy for the post-colonial state, particularly those surviving on post-nationalism of the ethnic kind. This brief exploratory chapter, therefore, provides an empirical example of the Malaysia case and thus invites debate and criticism.

References

Alatas, S. H. (1976). *Stamford Raffles: Schemer or reformer?* Sydney: Angus & Robertson.

Andaya, B., & Andaya, L. 198. *A history of Malaysia*. London. Macmillan.

Braginsky, V. I. (1993). *The system of classical Malay literature*. Leiden: KITLV Press.

Cohn, B. (1987). *An anthropologist among historians and other Essays*. New Delhi: Oxford University Press.

Cohn, B. (1996). *Colonialism and its forms of knowledge: The British rule in India*. Princeton: Princeton University Press.

Davies, N. (1997). *Europe: A history*. London: Pimlico.

Dikotter, F. (1992). *The discourse of race in modern China*. Stanford: Stanford University Press.

Hirschman, C. (1986). The making of race in colonial Malaya: Political economy and racial category. *Sociological Forum, 1*(2) (Spring), 330–361.

Hirschman, C. (1987). The meaning and measurement of ethnicity in Malaysia: An analysis of census classification. *Journal of Asian Studies, 46*(3), 555–582.

Kheng, C. B. (1997). Writing indigenous history in Malaysia: A survey on approaches and problems. *Crossroads: An Interdisciplinary Journal of Southeast Asian Studies, 10*(2), 33–81.

Mamdani, M. (1996). *Define and rule: Native as political identity*. Boston: Harvard University Press.

Milner, A. (1995). *The invention of politics in colonial Malaya: Contesting nationalism and the expansion of the public sphere*. Cambridge, UK: Cambridge University Press.

Omar, Ariffin. (1993). *Bangsa Melayu: Malay concepts of democracy and community 1945–1950*. Kuala Lumpur: Oxford University Press.

Pyenson, L. (1989). *Empire of reasons: Exact sciences in Indonesia 1840–1940*. Leiden: E.J. Brill.

Reid, A. (1997, September). Malayness and the forging of national cultures in Southeast Asia. In *Paper at international seminar on external challenge and local response: Modern southeast asia in historical perspectives* (pp. 20–22). Brunei: Universiti Brunei Darussalem.

Roff, W. (1994). *Origins of Malay Nationalism*. 2nd Ed. Kuala Lumpur: Oxford University Press

Shamsul, A. B. (1999). Colonial knowledge and the construction of Malay and Malayness. *Sari, 15*(2), 3–17.

Shamsul, A. B. (2001). A history of identity, identity of history. *Journal of Southeast Asian Studies, 32*(3), 355–366

Shamsul, A. B. (2008). Colonial knowledge and the deepening or Orientalism. In A. Baharuddin et al. (Ed.), *Orientalism and occidentlism: Reflections of the East, perceptions of the West* (pp. 1–16). Universiti Malaya: Centre for Civilizational Dialogue.

Shamsul, A. B. (2011). Ilmu Kolonial dalam Pembentukan Sejarah Intelektual Malaysia. Siri Kertas Kajian Etnik, No. 17, Bangi: Institut Kajian Etnik, UKM.

Shamsul, A. B. (2012). When knowledge invents boundaries: From colonial knowledge to multiculturalism. In S. Nair Venugopal (Ed.), *The gaze of the West, framings of the East* (pp. 107–122). London: Palgrave Macmillan.

Shamsul, A. B. (2015). Ethnicity and identity formation: Colonial knowledge, colonial structures and the transition. In M. Weiss (Ed.), *Routledge handbook of contemporary Malaysia* (pp. 267–278). London: Routledge.

Shamsul, A. B., & Aziz, A. (2011). Colonial knowledge and the Reshaping of Islam, The Muslim and Islamic Education in Malaysia. In K. B. Ahmad & P. Joy (Eds.), *Islamic studies and Islamic education in contemporary Southeast Asia* (pp. 113–135). Kuala Lumpur: Yayasan Ilmuan.

CHAPTER 5

Analysing Pre-modern Malay Political Systems: From Raffles to Shaharil Talib

Anthony Milner

Introduction

Shaharil Talib was an innovator among historians of Malaysia. He wrote on pre-colonial Malay political life in new ways. Every analyst, of course, employs one framework or another in examining a distant society—a social "other", remote in time or culture. Historians and anthropologists possess their own different "horizons" as they engage their subject of study (Gadamer, 2004: part 2, chapter 4). Sometimes critics write about whether an historian has "got at the truth" or not—but things are not so simple. What we researchers find when interrogating

I am grateful to Peter Borschberg and Gareth Knapman for advice on this essay.

A. Milner (✉)
Australian National University, Canberra, ACT, Australia
e-mail: Anthony.Milner@anu.edu.au

University of Melbourne, Melbourne, VIC, Australia

University of Malaya, Kuala Lumpur, Malaysia

R. Rasiah et al. (eds.), *Contesting Malaysia's Integration into the World Economy*, https://doi.org/10.1007/978-981-16-0650-2_5

source material—whether written or interview documentation—depends, as often observed, on the questions we ask. At times our questions—our frameworks—vary so radically that the reader is left wondering whether different analysts are addressing the same or different societies. Those hoping to discover some form of objective reality beneath all the methodological experimentation are time and again frustrated.

To survey the way specific perspectives and methodologies shape analysis can be rewarding—certainly in the case of writing on the pre-modern Malay polity. In the context of this volume, it helps to assess Shaharil's achievement—and reminds us as well that debates in Malay studies, as in other historical fields, are not merely about the quality of archival research. Historians—just as much as the historical protagonists they study—are influenced by one prevailing ideology or another. That is, their analyses are grounded not outside but within the history of ideas—and in some cases, as James Boon has suggested, Western observers can seem as "exotic" as the people they seek to describe (Boon, 1987: 45).

In the pre-modern era, Malays themselves produced manuscripts of different types that reflected on past developments in their polities—and on the institutions and value structures within which they continued to live.[1] My concern here, however, is with how outsiders analysed Malay political arrangements—beginning in the early nineteenth century. Some important work has been done on this topic, particularly for the early nineteenth century[2]—and my hope is that an overview survey, reaching from Raffles to Shaharil, might provoke others to investigate significant shifts and contests in the historiography of the Malay world.

Early Nineteenth Century

To start with the most famous English official in Southeast Asia, Thomas Stamford Raffles—who served in the Malayan civil service from 1805 to 1824 (holding a number of high offices)—was influenced by the contemporary concern for ranking the different human communities in the world (Robertson, 1777; Marsden, 1966; Carroll, 2019: 26–48). He observed

[1] I have considered the way Malay writings do this in Milner (1982).

[2] (Carroll, 2005; Maier, 1988; Quilty, 1998, 2001). *F*or a superb study in another field, which examines an investigator in the context of the scholarly discourse and debates of his time, see Hill (2003).

in 1815 that the "Malays are a people by no means advanced in civilization". He then immediately compared their society—in its prevailing "habits and notions" with "some of the borderers in North Britain, not many centuries ago". The "generally wandering and predatory life" of the Malays, he said, induced them "to follow the fortunes of a favourite Chief, and to form themselves into a variety of separate clans". [3]Malay life was in one sense highly structured. According to Raffles, "the Malay" was "the most correctly polite of all savages..." (Raffles, 1991: 236). Although the chiefs were "jealous and punctilious in a high degree about their own titles", he pointed out that they were able to work in hierarchies—accepting (in earlier centuries), for instance, the ruler (or Betara) of Majapahit as a "superior, or Suzerain" (Raffles, 1991: 71).

Raffles admitted that some observers claimed Malays were "a people devoid of all regular government and principle...." He admitted that they did not have "efficient government"; nevertheless, in the past, before the introduction of Islam, Malays "occupied a high and commanding political station in these seas". Also, when the Portuguese arrived in the region in the late fifteenth century, Melaka as an "emporium embraced the largest portion of the commerce between Eastern and Western nations". In describing the "government of these [Malay] states", Raffles said it was "founded on principles entirely feudal". He stressed that a "high respect" was paid "to the person and family of the prince"; also, the nobles were "Chiefs at the head of a numerous train of dependants whose services they command" (Raffles, 1991: appendix, 25–27). With respect to economic matters, these "Malay chiefs" tended to seek to monopolise trade (Raffles, 1991: 81). The "civil institutions and internal policy" of these states, were a mixture of "the Mohomedan with their own more ancient and peculiar customs and usages"—and the latter, which in some states were collected in a law code, tended to predominate (Raffles, 1991: appendix, 27).

The political system—as Raffles saw matters—was by no means static. A deep social change was underway. In the pre-Muslim era, the Malays had possessed "regular institutions of their own", which were "generally derived from Indian nations...." The old Malay codes—what came to be referred to as "the Undang Undang and Addat Malayu"—were

[3]Raffles (1991: 81). For Raffles's attitude to Islam, see Aljuneid (2005). Quilty stresses the role of the Romantic movement in encouraging Raffles's sense of loss when considering the decline of ancient institutions—and, in the case of Java, of ancient buildings; Quilty (1998: 68).

the "systems of national law among the Malays", and they differed from "Mahomedan law". At the time Raffles wrote, he found that there was in "almost every state", a "constant struggle between the adherents of the old Malay usages and the Hajies, and other religious persons, who are desirous of introducing the laws of the Arabs..." (Raffles, 1991: 80, 562). What Raffles advocated was a British policy of resistance to the growing Islamic influence—he wanted a "revisal of [the Malay] general system of laws and usages."[4]

In portraying what we might today call the pre-colonial Malay political system, therefore, Raffles wrote in terms of European feudalism and Scottish chieftains. He was concerned to make a judgement about the level of civilisation the system represented—and here compared Malays unfavourably with Javanese (Raffles, 1991: 179, 479), and insisted as well that Malay government would have been more deserving of respect in the period before the impact of Islamic doctrines. Malay society, he suggested, was in motion—but heading backward.

Moving from Raffles to other observers, John Anderson—an East India Company official based in Penang from 1813 to 1829—wrote about a range of Malay states both on the Peninsula and on Sumatra. With respect to the Peninsula, he was mainly concerned with inter-state relations, in particular, the rights of Malay states vis-à-vis Siam. Here he turned to the eighteenth-century Swiss specialist on international law in Europe, Emer de Vattel, to find support for the idea that in unequal or even tributary relations the weaker state nevertheless retained its sovereignty (Anderson, 1965: 42–44). In the case of Sumatra, Anderson concentrated on the pepper-producing principalities on the East Coast. He led a mission to the region in 1823—and the published version of his report appeared in 1826. The historian, Farish Noor, has suggested recently that Anderson was only concerned about economics, producing essentially an "economic map..." (Farish, 2016: 120). He "wasn't really interested in human beings but was more interested in what these humans were eating, buying, selling and producing instead" (Farish, 2016: 115).

Anderson was certainly interested in trade, but his concerns actually went beyond economics. He employed a broader "analytical framework"

[4] Raffles (1991: 81). For Raffles's attitude to Islam, see Aljuneid (2005). Quilty stresses the role of the Romantic movement in encouraging Raffles's sense of loss when considering the decline of ancient institutions—and, in the case of Java, of ancient buildings; Quilty (1998: 68).

(Farish, 2016: 119). His writing conveys at times a respect for the "otherness" of the societies he had encountered. Like Raffles, he viewed Malay sultanates in terms of pre-modern Scotland. Having grown up in Dumfriesshire, Southwest Scotland, he drew upon his own memories. He recalled the "old Scotch hospitality to which I was accustomed in my boyish days, among my native hills" when describing the way he was entertained by a chief in the state of Batu Bara. (Anderson, 1971: 116–117). He also drew on the writings of Walter Scott—so fashionable in the early nineteenth century, including among the British community (including Raffles) in Penang (Wurtzburg, 1954: 47; Quilty, 1998: 63–64)—to describe the people and societies he encountered.[5] One great "rajah" of the state of Siak reminded Anderson of a pre-modern Scottish chieftain. Dressed in a "superb suit of gold thread cloth", his chiefs were all gathered around him—and with slaves holding a sword of state, spears and a "seree box"—he wore a "most magnificent *pinding*", or brooch. The *pinding* reminded Anderson of the "Brooch of Lorn" described in a poem by Walter Scott—a poem, *Lord of the Isles*, which Anderson proceeded to quote, beginning with the lines "Whence the brooch of burning gold, that clasps the chieftain's mantle fold" (Anderson, 1971: 173).[6]

A contemporary of Anderson, John Crawfurd (who worked for the East India Company in Southeast Asia from 1808 to 1827) was a more prominent official, and also more scholarly. Not only did he have extensive experience right across the region—having had official duties in Burma, Siam and Cochin China (Vietnam), as well as in Java and among the Peninsular Malays—he was also widely read in the theoretical literature of his time.[7] When focusing on the Malays, he did not express a particular interest in how they viewed their own history and social condition:

[5] See his reference to a character in Scott's novel, *Guy Mannering;* Anderson (1971: 45).

[6] Anderson also quotes lines from John Gibson Lockhart, Walter Scott's son-in-law (Anderson, 1971: 85). For Scott's influence on Charles Hose—who wrote about Sarawak—see Boon, 1990: 13. Quilty has noted that Anderson uses lines from William Wordsworth to portray the Sumatran jungle (Quilty, 1998: 36).

[7] Thomas Carlyle, one of the leading thinkers of the age, was an admirer of John Crawfurd's writings—a reminder that nineteenth-century Southeast Asianists did not write only for one another but were in dialogue with mainstream intellectual developments (Knapman, 2017: 242). For an introduction to the theoretical context in which Crawfurd wrote, see, for example, Burrow (2009: chapters 21–24).

he considered the classic text about the Melaka sultanate, the Malay Annals, to be "worthless"—"a wild tissue of fable" (Crawfurd, 1856: 250). He examined the social organisation of Malay and other Southeast Asian societies partly in terms of the developing theory of race (and race attributes)—but also with respect to fashionable thinking about environmental determinism. By the opening of the nineteenth century the category of "race" was being deployed in the quest to achieve "the whole 'map of mankind'" (Bayly, 2004: 110). Different races were said to exhibit their own particular "state of society", as Crawfurd put it. For instance, even that class of "the Malay nation" which Crawfurd called the "civilised Malays"—as alluded to above—possessed "no true history"(Crawfurd, 1856: 250).[8] Like Raffles, Crawfurd did not rank the Malays very high among the different civilisations of the world.

Race, however, was not the only consideration for Crawfurd in analysing a society. The racial hierarchy was not static—a people could rise civilisationally, given the right circumstances (Knapman, 2017: 113). One consideration was the role of environmental factors, so much discussed by Enlightenment thinkers (Knapman, 2017: 108). The Malays whom Crawfurd believed migrated to Minangkabau in the centre of Sumatra achieved a higher form of civilisation—acquired "a degree of power which the same people have certainly nowhere else reached"—because of environmental factors. They lived "among the fertile valleys of volcanic mountains" and their region became "as populous and well cultivated as any part of Java" (Crawfurd, 1856: 252)—which itself (possessing "volcanic soil of great fertility") hosted "the highest civilization which has been reached in the Indian islands…." (Crawfurd, 1856: 260). Crawfurd took the view that it was because the Malay Peninsula possessed "the most stubborn and intractable soil of all the large countries of the Archipelago", that it possessed a small population—and one that could "hold no very respectable position in the social scale" (Crawfurd, 1856: 260).

As for "forms of political association", these were determined—in Crawfurd's view—by a community's position in the "scale of social improvement". As people "advance in civilization" so their freedom "abridged"—until, "at the top of the scale" they were "subjected to a

[8] The physical attributes of the Malay and other Archipelago races are discussed in Crawfurd (1967: Vol. 1, chapter 1). I am grateful to Gareth Knapman for his advice on Crawfurd's approach. On the influence on Crawfurd of Scottish thinking about the different stages of social development, see Quilty (1998: 44).

tyranny where not a vestige of liberty is discoverable" (Crawfurd, 1967: Vol. 3, 4). Drawing on the writings of Alexander von Humboldt, Crawfurd suggested that it was especially where people happened to be devoted to agricultural industry that they became "more tame, and more at the mercy of power than wandering tribes"—and thus more likely to be "living under absolute government" (Crawfurd, 1967: Vol. 3, 4). For a "picture of absolute government" Crawfurd turned to Java, but also presented some observations on Malay states. The Javanese government, he said, was "hereditary despotism" and there was "no hereditary nobility to control or limit" the ruler's authority. It was the case as well that the ruler himself was "the first minister of religion". Every word which related to the monarch proclaimed "his unbounded authority"—just as the language and sumptuary laws in a Malay court announced the slave-like obedience of the Malay subject, even when that subject was a high official (Crawfurd, 1967: Vol. 3, 16–17).

The High Colonial Period

Few later scholar-officials were as self-consciously alert to so-called scientific theory as Crawfurd. Their observations on Malay societies, however, were always shaped by analytical perspectives developed outside the Malay world. In the late nineteenth century—when Britain was taking over much of the government in Peninsular states, and thus had a growing practical need to understand Malay society—some administrator pioneers again began to view Malay society through a pre-modern, especially Scottish framework. Two of the early British advisors (or Residents) most concerned to acquire knowledge of Malay society, Frank Swettenham and Hugh Clifford, likened the relationship between chief and people to that between members of "an old Scottish clan". The observation was: "they will do his bidding and take harsh treatment from him more contentedly than from anybody else" (Sadka, 1968: 13).

Clifford described Malays as "living in the Middle Ages" and "under a complete Feudal System"; Malay society, he said, was "a curiously close parallel to that which we face in Medieval Europe" (Goh, 2007: 330; Wicks, 1979: 67; Clifford, 1903: 5). The Malay storyteller, the *Penglipor Lara*, had much in common with the "wandering bards" who wandered around Europe in the Middle Ages (Clifford, 1903: 153–154). The Malay's "proper place", so Clifford concluded, was "amidst the conditions of the Thirteenth Century" (quoted in Allen; Holden, 2000:

20–21). And he advised that in dealing with Malay rulers British officials needed to adopt "what I can only describe as a certain chivalry of manner" (Holden, 2000: 36).

Such comments today read as patronising—but they do not convey the type of superiority defined specifically by race which was common in Victorian England. Even the much-admired Charles Darwin saw "savages" as necessarily inferior in intellectual and moral terms—talking of the "inferior vitality of mulattoes"—and at times seemed untroubled when they suffered discrimination or brutality in European hands (Wilson, 2003: 375–376). James Hunt, who co-founded the Anthropological Society of London in 1863, was one of those who believed in the "*natural* inferiority of the 'lower' races" (Lienhardt, 1966: 6, 9).[9] Swettenham and Clifford saw Malays as being in a sense "backward", but did not deny that their society could "progress" as European societies had done—for instance, since the thirteenth century. Recalling our earlier discussion, John Crawfurd was explicit about the potential of all societies to progress. As a Scottish Highlander he had experienced a "society undergoing social and economic change"—and assumed that other peoples could also move forward (Knapman, 2017: 21–22, 74).

Swettenham was a competent painter and his written portrayals of individual Malays and their physical and social surroundings—often perceptive and sympathetic—seem to be executed with a painter's eye. The title of one of his books, "Malay sketches" (Swettenham, 1903; on his painting, see Lim & Barlow, 1988) captures this style. "I will try to draw the man as he was at this time"—is the way Swettenham begins his analysis of a particular Malay ruler, and then he commences with a detailed (and elegant) description of the man's physical appearance (Swettenham, 1903: 162). Clifford's writings—perhaps influenced by his enthusiasm for the work of the psychological novelist, Joseph Conrad, as well as the racial stereotyping fashionable at the time—are more concerned to explore Malay mentality, the concepts that shaped Malay behaviour. His purpose, he said, was "to appreciate the native point of view…" (Clifford, 1903: ix).[10]Like Swettenham, Clifford appears to have been committed

[9] Crawfurd was a critic of Hunt, and less inclined to stress inferiority (Knapman, 2017: 220).

[10] For the Conrad connection, see Gailey (1982: 39); also, Hampson (2000: chapter 3). A.R.Wallace's *The Malay Archipelago* (1869) influenced Conrad, and probably Clifford, and certainly included racial stereotyping (Hampson, 2000: 76).

to understanding Malay society not only to assist the task of the colonial administrator—but also for its own interest.

One concept Clifford identified was the Malay concern for what is "fitting"—for acting according to what is "fitting or not fitting" ("*patut*" or "*ta'patut*") not in accordance with what is "right" or "wrong" (Mohamad Rashidi Pakri, 2014: 26–31). Other aspects of Malay thinking—or of that of any "Asiatic race" (Clifford, 1898: 225)—were the tendency to see "no steps between the inception of an idea and its realisation" (Clifford, 1898: 224); and also the preference, when dissatisfied with "the Present", to fix one's eyes not on "What Ought To Be" but on "What Has Been" (Clifford, 1898: 225). A further element in the Malay perspective was the belief that "technically, the whole country was [the ruler's] property, and all its inhabitants his slaves" (Clifford, 1903: 4). Along with this was the assumption that the peasant possessed "no rights either of person or of property" (Clifford, 1927: xi). The implications of this perspective—for instance, with respect to understanding private ownership of land, or the capacity of the royal subject to effect change—are all too obvious (Mohamad Rashidi Pakri, 2014: 47).

When Clifford and others described Malays as living "in the Middle Ages", it should be remembered that in the mid- and late-nineteenth century Gothic Revivalism was influential and "resonated with" medievalism (Goh, 2007: 325). Hugh Clifford had certainly been immersed in Thomas Carlyle's writings (Holden, 2000: 40)[11]—and would have been aware of Carlyle's respect for medieval organic societies when compared to the narrow economic reductionism of modern industrialising England (Carlyle, 1965). Though Clifford was a colonialist with the task of reforming a subject society, bringing it into the modern world, there was always ambiguity in his judgements. At times, perhaps in the spirit of Carlyle, he admitted to being drawn to Malay medievalism—to the manners and style of social interaction in this *ancien regime* (Wicks, 1979: 67; Allen, 1964: 58–60, 71–72). He seemed almost to regret that British rule had reduced Malay society to a "dead monotony of order and peace" with a "high-class, triple-action automatic revenue-producing administration" (quoted in Allen, 1964: 59). He recalled that "until British interference"—which Clifford himself helped to implement—the

[11] See footnote 8 above on how Carlyle, on his part, admired Crawfurd's work. Crawfurd's view of the European Middle Ages, however, was not positive (Quilty, 1998: 8).

state of Pahang "was the best type of an independent Malay State in the Peninsula" and much could be "seen and learned" there which "cannot now be experienced anywhere else" (Clifford, 1903: 16).

Later Scholar-Officials

In the early years of the twentieth century, R. J. Wilkinson and R.O. Winstedt were the leading third-generation scholar-officials—if we think of Raffles, Crawfurd and Anderson as the first generation. Wilkinson and Winstedt were both dedicated to research into Malay history and culture but were also well aware of the colonial impetus behind the gathering of Malay knowledge. When he had become one of the most senior colonial governors in the empire, Clifford put the point with characteristic clarity. In Nigeria as in the Malay states, he insisted, a British official had the duty to study "every native custom, every native conventionality, every one of the ten thousand ceremonial observances to which the natives, among themselves, attach so much importance" (Kirk-Greene, 1965: 179–180).

Wilkinson, who served as an official from 1889 to 1916, sought to write a "history of the Peninsular Malays" for the emerging British-administered entity which some were beginning to call "British Malaya". To this end, he focused only on those Malay states that were part of the British sphere, and not under Dutch or Thai domination (Wilkinson, 1971: 26). His official concerns were also apparent when, in introducing an essay on the Negri Sembilan state of Sri Menanti, he called "Malay *adat* [custom]" a "dull subject"—but insisted that it "enters so largely into the work of a Negri Sembilan District Officer that Government cannot afford to ignore it" (Wilkinson, 1971: 363). With the objective of investigating Malay history and Malay perspectives, Wilkinson also took a more positive view of pre-modern Malay writings than Crawfurd had expressed.[12] *The Malay Annals* he considered an "invaluable source of information" (Wilkinson, 1971: 78); and he called the Malay text, the *Misa Melayu*, "Perak's fine XVIII century history" (Wilkinson, 1971: 80). Wilkinson was keen to offer an overview history of the states he was covering and noted that Malay tradition (recorded in Malay texts), though "inaccurate in detail", tended to be "truthful in its drift" (Wilkinson, 1971: 34).

[12] Crawfurd's private views may have been different. Gareth Knapman tells me that Crawfurd read aloud Javanese texts to his family.

Wilkinson, of course, was concerned with much more than narrative. He had somewhat anthropological concerns, influenced perhaps by his friendship with Walter Skeat and also the increasing interest in this new discipline in the late nineteenth century (Gullick, 2001: 22).[13] Wilkinson noted, for instance, the "strange sentiment" of loyalty among the people (or rather the "old Malays"). A "man might murder a hero or a saint, or betray a relative or friend, or abduct an innocent girl"—but if this was done "in the interest of a royal intrigue" it was considered "a noble act of self-sacrifice according to his ethical code" (Wilkinson, 1971: 39). Wilkinson also said that the Malay writings revealed "the curiously personal character of Malay sovereignty". In Europe, he remarked, there was "no place for a fallen king except as a subject". In the thinly populated Malay world, "so long as a fugitive prince could induce a few followers to share his lot he might always hope to find some unoccupied valley or river in which to maintain an empty title and a miniature court" (Wilkinson, 1971: 59). Wilkinson concluded that "royal rank" was "a great thing in Malay eyes and explains the faked pedigrees, the insistence on petty family details, and the long discussion on trivial issues of court etiquette" (Wilkinson, 1971: 60). Such observations—drawn largely, one assumes from classical Malay writings as well as personal experience—certainly have an ethnographic tone. In the manner of the cultural anthropologist (see below), Wilkinson was exploring with care some of the cultural categories which shaped the way pre-modern Malays may have perceived the world (Wilkinson, 1932: 67–137; 1957: 1–87).

In Wilkinson's writing, however, Malay society was far from static. Like Raffles and others from an earlier era, he highlighted the importance of foreign influences—for instance, the impact of Indian religions and languages, and also of Islam (Wilkinson, 1971: 29–30). But it was Winstedt (serving in "British Malaya" from 1902 to 1935) who concentrated on the issue where specific phenomena or cultural traits in Malay society may have originated. Diffusionism was increasingly fashionable at the end of the nineteenth century, when Winstedt was at university, and this may have influenced his analytic priorities. In its extreme form, diffusionism argued for human society having a single civilisational source—in G. Elliot Smith's view, Egypt. For others, diffusionism involved merely

[13] He certainly cited Skeat's work – and also, for instance, that of the cultural anthropologist, Edward Burnett Tylor. See Wilkinson (1932: 135–137); see also Lienhardt (1966: chapter 1).

a stress on cultural diffusion (and migration) rather than evolution, or independent (autochthonous) invention.[14]

Winstedt had joined Wilkinson in writing histories of the different Malay states. They carried out documentary research on Malay, Portuguese and Dutch records—establishing the genealogies of rulers and noting other key figures and events in the state. They wrote notes on the ceremonies and customs as well—and on relations between one sultanate and another, and with the Thais as well as European powers (Winstedt & Wilkinson, 1934). All this would have been important for British officials to know. They might have benefitted too from the insight that it was only "ceremony that made life tolerable for the Perak peasant"—and that for "his masters" too, ceremonies were "their only amusement" (Winstedt & Wilkinson, 1934: 93).

In Winstedt's case, however, it is his particular concern about origins that is striking. It is fundamental in the "horizon" through which he came to Malay studies. He analysed institutions and customs in terms of where they came from. In the context of the state of Perak, the chief herald at the Kuala Kangsar court was said to be a descendent of Batala, "the mythical incarnation of Siva's bull, Nandi". At the coronation of the Perak ruler, the coronation address was in Sanskrit (Winstedt & Wilkinson, 1934: 11).[15] In the sixteenth and seventeenth centuries, Perak came under Aceh's influence, and Winstedt attempted to list the different ways Aceh had a continuing influence on Perak dress and ceremony (Winstedt & Wilkinson, 1934: 23).

When Winstedt offered a chapter on "Political System" in his general text, *The Malays: A Cultural History*, it opened with the statement that the "Malay State" (negeri) is "itself a Hindu concept…." The chapter then suggests that the "conception of the power of Malay kings" will have come from "Babylon or some other centre in the Middle East". Following this, Winstedt noted the pre-Hindu idea of the ruler as shaman, mentioned a connection with kingship in Japan, and then highlighted many types of Indian influence in these supposedly Muslim political

[14] An influential essay in Southeast Asian studies, influenced by Diffusionism (though not unicentric Diffusionism), is Heine-Geldern (2018). I am grateful to Wilbert Wong for drawing my attention to evidence of Winstedt's interest in Heine-Geldern's work. On the influence of diffusionism, see Kuper (1973: 15–16).

[15] See also, Winstedt (1947b) on the cultural origins of different features of Malay rulership.

systems (Winstedt, 1947a: 53–79). To take one further example from a Winstedt publication, the concluding chapter in his pioneering overview volume, *A History of Malaya*, commences with: "The Malays have experienced many foreign influences, incomparably the greatest being that from India..." (Winstedt, 1968: 267).

What is not delivered in Winstedt's writings is a serious analysis of the way Malay society was changed as a result of the encounter with foreign ideas. Although he listed numerous events—often relating to Aceh, the Dutch, the Bugis (from Sulawesi) or Siam, as well as to early interaction with India—we get little sense of the way the political structure may have been transformed over time. There is, for instance, no detailed examination of the social impact of the adoption of Islam, or the way inter-state behaviour may have altered as a result of engaging with European powers.

Functionalist Approaches—And Some Marxist Influences

Focusing on the West coast states, confronted with British intervention in the nineteenth century, Winstedt—like several later historians—(Parkinson, 1960; Khoo, 1972; Thio, 1969) was more concerned to present a narrative than to attempt an analysis of how pre-Malay sultanates operated. C.D. Cowan, Professor of the History of South East Asia at the University of London, was to some extent an exception. When he paused to examine Malay political systems, he emphasised the concept of power. He commenced his analysis by explaining that "rivers provided the key to this wild and roadless country." The "majority of the population" lived along the rivers, and "in the main" rivers were the "only practicable highways for the trader bringing in his wares and for the tin-miner sending his produce out". In these circumstances, the ruler "established at the river mouth" was "able to control the hinterland" and to draw income from "tolls on the traffic passing up and down the river" (Cowan, 1961: 35).

Cowan observed, however, that—just as in tenth and eleventh century France—the Malay ruler was in fact "virtually powerless" vis-a-vis the territorial chiefs of his province. The Malay system was not, in fact, precisely feudal—because "all political relationships were personal relationships", not relationships based on the holding of land (Cowan, 1961: 43, note 38). In analysing a Malay polity—and Perak was his main focus—Cowan was concerned to identify exactly where power lay among the chiefs (Cowan, 1961: 50–51). In terms of stability, the failure of the rulers to control chiefs meant that most of the Peninsular states did not possess "a government able to offer stable conditions..." (Cowan, 1961: 26). This conclusion, one might observe, helped to justify British intervention in the administration of such Malay states. It is consistent with Sir Frank Swettenham's observation, and justification—made in his influential text of 1907, *British Malaya*—that on the eve of British intervention "the western states of the Peninsula, from Perak to the borders of Johore" were "given up to native warfare, with all the evils and miseries that follow in its train" (Swettenham, 1907: 132).

A study of great importance which countered this line of analysis was John Gullick's *Indigenous Political Systems of Western Malaya*. Gullick, who served in the Malayan Civil Service from 1945 to 1956, was—like John Crawfurd—one of the most scholarly officials ever to write about Malay society. Writing after the end of the colonial period, Gullick had no official need to advance a justification for British intervention. He also took a postgraduate diploma in social anthropology at London University under Raymond Firth, and was a pioneer in anthropology/history research—writing even before this particular interdisciplinary analysis became fashionable in English history writing (Burrow, 2009: 494–495). At London he was introduced to functionalism, which was positioned against the earlier diffusionism, and gave no particular causal role to race—assuming that "any society can be studied as an organic whole of which the parts are functionally interdependent ..." (Lienhardt, 1966: 28).[16] Unlike most anthropologists, Gullick worked with documentary sources not living people—but, in the functionalist tradition, he took for granted that he was analysing "a working system of social control and leadership" (Gullick, 1965: 1). He highlighted institutions, not merely personal relations.

Gullick examined the "indigenous political systems" of the Malays at a moment in time—the mid 19th century—and focused on what he termed the "essential functions of a political system" (Gullick, 1965: 113), "political institutions" (Gullick, 1965: 113) and the distribution of "real power" (Gullick, 1965: 49). With this framework, he concluded that the "key institution in the [Malay] political system" was the "district chief" not the Sultan (Gullick, 1965: 96). He also pointed to material wealth as being "the basis of power because it provided the means to

[16]For the contest between functionalism and the earlier diffusionism (and evolutionism), see for example, Boon (1987: 10–20).

attract a following" (Gullick, 1965: 96). Employing such a functionalist perspective, Gullick moved away from the view that these Malay polities were simply anarchical. His perspective, however, provoked debate—as well as a good deal of imitation.

Like Gullick, the historian, Sharom Ahmat (former Dean of Humanities at Universiti Sains Malaysia), in his study of a "Malay state during its traditional phase", wrote in terms of the "economic and political system" (Sharom, 1984: 173). The state he focused on was Kedah, and he argued that it differed from the states Gullick examined. In Kedah, "the Sultan was the real master of his house. The control exercised by him over his chiefs was real" (Sharom, 1984: 173). Given the importance of material wealth in the accumulation of power, the Sultan's control of taxing in Kedah was vital (Sharom, 1984: 87–88); also, the village headmen in this state were always appointed by the ruler not by district chiefs (Sharom, 1984: 82). Sharom's observations on Kedah's government are also more positive than many other accounts of Malay states. This may have been because Kedah itself was different—but we must remember as well that Sharom did not have the same agenda as that of the colonial officials whose observations on Perak and Selangor were often cited by Gullick.

To take an example, there may have been some truth in Swettenham's observation that "few commoners accumulated any wealth" because they knew the "Raja would rob them" or oblige them to lend [their wealth] without any prospect of payment" (Gullick, 1965: 30). What is certain, however, is that such statements put the British imperial project in a more favourable light. They present the new British administrators as saving the people from their tyrannical rulers. By contrast, writing of Kedah, Sharom argued that the "*raayat*"—the common people—were not so submissive. They sent petitions to the Sultan, some being complaints against headmen. Also, there were signs that the people were reasonably content—choosing to live under the Sultan's rule even when they had the opportunity to move into British-governed territories (Sharom, 1984: 84). Sharom stressed the stability of Kedah, and attributed this in particular to the "centralizing of political power in the Sultan..." (Sharom, 1984: 85, 88). The "centralization of economic resources in the hands of the Sultan in Kedah was absolute" (Sharom, 1984: 88).

Gullick's approach to the pre-modern polity influenced numerous other researchers as well as Sharom (e.g. Ileto, 1971) but it also attracted criticism. One line of attack—to which I contributed (Milner, 1982)—came from specialists on political culture. Cornell University researchers, the prominent American Anthropologist, Clifford Geertz, and the Malaysian sociologist, Syed Hussein Alatas, were important influences here (e.g. Wolters, 1979; Anderson, 1972; Errington, 1989; Andaya, 1979; Drakard, 1999; Geertz, 1980; Syed Hussein Alatas, 1972; Chandra Muzaffar, 1974). This approach—also tending to be synchronic—sought to understand pre-modern Malay political life from the perspective of the people themselves. It focused not on institutions and movements of power but on defining the categories of experience influential in a society—in this case, the different "meaningful structures" (Geertz, 1973: 364) by means of which Malays, in one situation or another, perceived their political condition.

This style of analysis—anticipated to some extent by the observations on cultural phenomena developed by such colonial writers as Clifford and Wilkinson—requires a close interrogation of historical sources, with the identification of key terms or concepts. Colonial records provide abundant evidence regarding many historical developments, but it is difficult—though not impossible (Guha, 1983, and see below)—to use them to gain insights into the consciousness of subject peoples. Political culture studies have often concentrated on the writings of Malays (rather than Europeans), noting that although they may be unreliable regarding chronological and other so-called factual matters, they often contain critical evidence of value and conceptual structures. In my own work, I focused sharply on exactly how Malay writings defined the key terms, *kerajaan* (government or kingdom) and *nama* (reputation)— and argued that this offered a basis for reconstructing how Malay people may have perceived their "political condition" (as we today might term it). This examination of perceptions generated a model of the Malay polity significantly different from that offered by Gullick's study of institutions and power, particularly in the significance attributed to the Ruler in Malay society. Again, however, this political culture approach itself stimulated criticism.

A second line of criticism of Gullick's functionalism—and to some extent of the political culture approach as well—called for a diachronic rather than synchronic analysis, stressing processes of change. The point was also made that both Gullick's analysis and the political culture approach are elite perspectives—and what was needed was bottom-up not top-down methodology.

Patrick Sullivan, for instance, analysed the pre-colonial Malay state of Perak through the identification of hierarchical "social relations"—and his study was informed by Marxist-influenced methodology. He saw Gullick's functionalist methodology as "necessarily synchronic" and conservative—the "only purpose" of the "social structure", as Gullick portrayed things, had to be "its own perpetuation" (Sullivan, 1982: xvi). Gullick's account, suggested Sullivan, was "ruling class history" and celebrated "the given social order, however much that order may adversely affect certain social groups" (Sullivan, 1982: xvi). In contrast to Gullick, what Sullivan determined to investigate was "conflicts between classes ... within and between modes of production" (Sullivan, 1982: xviii).[17] To this end, he wrote a monograph that concentrates on slavery and debt slavery in Perak—harnessing as much evidence as possible about the lives and treatment of different groups of slaves (Sullivan, 1982: chapter 3). Sullivan was concerned also to develop a diachronic as well as a synchronic analysis. Others, of course, had observed that pre-colonial political arrangements were not unchanging: Raffles, for instance, had pointed to the way proponents of Islamic law were forcing far-reaching change. In the Marxist tradition, Sullivan sought to identify economics-driven processes of change. He suggested that "Perak social formation" was in "a process of transition from kin-based to class-based" (Sullivan, 1982: xx, 75)—and this could be seen in the growing importance of debt slavery.

Labour was needed for the burgeoning tin industry, Sullivan said, but European pressure in the nineteenth century made it difficult to purchase foreign slaves. Malays, he pointed out, could be made debt slaves as a result of real or fictitious debts incurred with members of the Malay ruling class. By the latter half of the nineteenth century many "Malay debtors had been reduced to the status of chattel slaves" (Sullivan, 1982: 50–51, 65–68, 69). This situation was altered when the British assumed authority over Perak in the 1870s and 1880s—but the earlier growth of a "class-based" society, as Sullivan portrayed it, is an example of real diachronic development within a pre-colonial Malay polity.

[17] Sullivan cites the methodological approaches of C. Meillassoux, M. Godelier and E.P.Thompson, as well as B.Hindess and P.Hirst.

Shaharil Talib

Let me now return to Shaharil Talib. The Marxist-influenced concern about the economic dynamics of change is certainly a feature of Shaharil Talib's writing. In his major book, *After Its Own Image: The Trengganu Experience 1881–1941* (Shaharil, 1984), he too sought to identify diachronic processes in pre-modern Malay society. This does not mean he neglected functionalist objectives.

A starting point for Western scholarship on Terengganu was the short history written by M.C.ff. Sheppard—like Gullick, one of the last scholar-officials in British Malaya. Terengganu, according to Sheppard, possessed "the time-honoured feudal system, common to all Malay states…." Adopting the "feudal" framework, Sheppard stressed territory rather than personal relations. He described the "country" as being "divided into a number of territorial divisions, each of which was held in fief from the Sultan by a Dato". The chiefs had the task of supplying "levies of able-bodied fighting men" when requested by the Sultan and were also expected to obtain taxes and "free labour" from their people (Sheppard, 1949: 34–35).[18] Sheppard did not suggest, however, that the system was unchanging. In the time of the ruler Baginda Omar (1806–1876) a degree of centralisation had taken place. This lively ruler refused to appoint successors to district chiefs who had died—and instead appointed headmen (or *penghulus*) who would be "in charge of one or more villages" and would report directly to Baginda Omar himself (Sheppard, 1949: 35).

Shaharil also focused on the Terengganu elite—making the strategies which this elite adopted the main concern of his book. He was by no means, however, blind to non-elite perspectives. In Terengganu he highlighted the "overwhelming odds" against the peasantry class—including the burden of taxation and the lack of personal rights (Shaharil, 1984: 34–35). In an earlier study on early twentieth-century Kelantan he had employed innovatory methodology to examine "the peasant's story" (Shaharil, 1983: 177). As Patrick Sullivan was to do a few years later, he read colonial records against the grain, focusing not on the official perspective and official policymaking, but rather on singling out sources that seemed to access indigenous, non-elite voices. Shaharil provided

[18] On Terengganu history, see also Mohamed Anwar Omar Din and Nik Anuar Nik Mahmud (2009), Abdul Rahman Embong (2112), Muhammad Abu Bakar (ed), (2018).

quotations from petitions submitted to colonial officials expressing, for example, "grief" caused by the introduction of the Torrens land system (which changed land from being a "natural resource" to a "commodity", which had a value in itself). There were also petitions containing threats to migrate if the petitioner was prevented from using fish traps—or from growing rice. Migration, it should be recalled, was the established sanction against bad government. Complaints about specific government officials were another element which Shaharil singled out in these petitions (Shaharil, 1983: 179–180).

Such documents from beyond the elite, in Shaharil's view, offered insights into "that subjective area of verbal human action which embodies feelings, attitudes, thoughts and perceptions…" (Shaharil, 1983: 177). In exploring peasant perspectives in this way—on the basis of a close reading of government documents—Shaharil can be said to have contributed to what the Indian historian, Ranajit Guha, called "Subaltern Studies", a style of research that became highly influential in the 1980s (Guha, 1997).

Turning to Shaharil's more ambitious investigations concerning Terengganu, his analysis of the "Indigenous Ruling Class" is impressively detailed. He examined four elite groups: the royalty, the aristocracy, the religious class (*ulama*) and the most favoured commoner officials (who had served the Sultanate in some special way). Shaharil concluded his careful description with the intriguing comment that "these ruling class elements, whose roots go back to the inception of the present Sultanate in Terengganu, survived the onslaught of British political control". Also "the group structure as such was basically retained unchanged" (Shaharil, 1977: 46; Shaharil, 1984: chapter 2).

In describing the ruling class, however, Shaharil was in fact setting the scene for an investigation into the dynamics of change. The book, *After Its Own Image*, was based on a doctoral thesis written at Monash University under the supervision of J.D. Legge—a leading Marxist-influenced historian of Indonesia, always concerned to highlight and examine processes of change (Mackie & Milner, 1986). Shaharil was an innovative scholar—as his investigation of "voices from the Kelantan desa" demonstrates—and took seriously theoretical developments in the wider academic world. If we compare his Terengganu volume with his much earlier work on Kelantan—eventually published as *History of Kelantan 1890–1940*—we gain an indication of how he could respond to new historiographical approaches.

The Kelantan history provides a useful narrative of the transition of government, starting in 1890 and following through the period of the Siamese (1903–1909) and then the British advisory system (starting 1909). Shaharil concentrated on administrative issues, particularly on the fortunes of the elite. Religious developments and the political culture of Kelantan received less attention. Members of this elite, in Shaharil's account, lost power and privileges during the periods of Siamese and British intervention—but they found opportunities, working in the government administration. Some in the elite also joined Europeans in exploiting state resources—for instance, in building the rubber industry. Shaharil's book is an important study of a period of transition in Kelantan, but it does not have the sharp focus on a process of change which his Terengganu book employs—in particular, there is not the same concern to examine closely the specific strategies of a particular social grouping. *After Its Own Image* is a more theoretically informed work—written with an eye to contributing to the discipline of history or "the mainstream of social science enquiry" (Shaharil, 1984) (to use Shaharil's words), and not merely to the field of Malaysian studies.

In his Terengganu study, Shaharil acknowledged the way Gullick's functionalist analysis demonstrates the "interdependence of political and economic power" (Shaharil, 1984: 4) in a number of Malay states. But Shaharil was determined to write a more dynamic account, focusing on the way the Terengganu ruling class sought to adapt to the changing economy—how that class "used the traditional state apparatus to tap different sectors of the changing economy" (5). These efforts, he said, were to the "detriment of the peasants' interest and well-being"—and ultimately the British succeeded in breaking "the ruling class grip on the economy and the political system…." The elite was compensated, however, by being made "salaried members of the colonial administration" (6).

This was the long-term fate of the elite. What Shaharil was concerned about in this book—and what he called "the most significant development" in the late nineteenth and early twentieth centuries—was the "response of members of the ruling class to the expansion of capital" (36). In the case of every Malay state, according to Shaharil, the period "immediately prior to British political advance" was "marked by a rapid economic expansion"—and in Terengganu this offered the ruling class a "breathing space and an opportunity" (3). In examining what occurred in Terengganu, Shaharil noted a distinction (he quotes the American political scientist, James C. Scott) between a "politically oriented capitalist system" and a "market-oriented capitalist system". The first type of capitalism—which entailed the "granting by the state to members of the ruling class, privileged opportunities for private profit"—was the "more dominant" form in Terengganu (36).

In Shaharil's account, therefore, members of the ruling class are the key protagonists—harnessing the "state apparatus" to their benefit. Their "economic moves" took the form of "three initiatives" to "absorb the new wealth flowing into Trengganu" (36). The first involved the extension of the revenue farming (*pajak*) system to gain advantage from increased trading activity in the state; the second was the elaboration of concession activity in planting and mining and the third was the "revival of ancient state rights to extract surplus produce" from the peasant economy (36). Shaharil provided examples of the way in which the *pajak* system was made to be a "lucrative source of income" for the ruling class (64). He noted as well how foreign companies were given concessions to develop the tin and coconut production in the state, and how giving concessions to ruling class members—episodes in the commodification of land—itself brought "royalties, premiums, ground rents..." (74–75, 80). Even in the first decade or so of British administration in the state, this elite group "used the concession system to capitalize on the penetration of production capital in the plantation and mining economy..." (80).

In the case of the third initiative, the "ancient state rights", the elite revived the *cap kurnia*, or "deed of Royal gift". It was "revived" in the sense that it was based on a "hitherto unenforced Malay principle – that all land belonged to the ruler ..." (115). In fact, until the late nineteenth century the peasant had paid no tax on the self-sufficient production in which he was engaged. At the end of the century, however, members of the ruling class wereobtained from the ruler *cap kurnia*—which delivered them property rights over an area of land, giving them the authority to extract tithes from the peasants working there. At one point, Shaharil's book calls this a "new claim" rather than a "revived" one (115). Certainly, it had the effect of creating "a new landlord class" (116), and Shaharil gave examples of situations in which peasants (possibly 30,000 by the late 1920s) "lost their customary tenure rights and were forced to become tenants virtually overnight..." (128).

In case studies on individual members of the ruling class—people such as Tengku Abdul Rahim, Tengku Maimunah and Tengku Osman—Shaharil revealed the different ways in which this class sought to control "peasant commodity production" (128). Far from conveying the sense of a static political system, Shaharil presented a diachronic account of an aristocracy in action—asserting their agency and ingenuity in a time of change and opportunity. Employing diligent archival research and a rigorous methodology, Shaharil gave Malaysian studies a landmark work. Like Patrick Sullivan, he conveyed dissatisfaction with the limits of Gullick's functionalism, but Shaharil dug deeper—seeking to show the reader the real people who were driving change in the years leading up to and following British intervention. Following Shaharil, we can never take for granted that individuals in pre-modern Malay societies were somehow programmed against initiating innovation.

This said, like any fine research volume, *After Its Own Image* not only offers a fresh interpretation but also raises questions—one of which (of particular interest to me) concerns the way in which Shaharil presented his Terengganu protagonists as *homo economicus*. For Shaharil, it was the ruling class' exploitation of economic opportunity that was the "most significant development" in Terengganu in the period under study. True, he highlighted the creativity of members of the ruling elite—but, in his account, their concern seems always to have been about material welfare. The problem is that even Shaharil's own account includes data that makes one wonder whether material gain was always the key driver of action.

In the case study on Tengku Osman, mentioned above, it is clear that he and his sons made no economic use of the *cap kurnia* which they had obtained. They seem to have had no interest in *harta*, or "property". They wanted no one else to exploit the area and, in this sense, they were conscious of their rights. But they made little attempt to collect dues from the cultivators, and in later years their visits to the area were remembered by many for the *makyong* theatre which they brought to the region (126–128).

Just what other considerations influenced aristocrats such as Tengku Osman is an important question. Shaharil referred to the quest for power—and insisted at one point that "by far, the most important foundation of political power was the control of revenue" (116). At another point, however, he indicated the reverse—that it was power that was the foundation for acquiring wealth. It was "easier", he wrote, "for a man of power to acquire wealth than for a man of wealth to acquire power" (9). It might be asked, therefore, in what other ways someone could gain power—apart from through the possession of wealth?

Some in Terengganu held high office on hereditary grounds—but there were also "low-born leaders" who gained a high position on the basis of their service to the ruler (13–14). The ruler would bestow "gifts" on loyal subjects, giving them land or at least rights over people who happened to be working a particular area of land (31–32). Loyalty and service to the ruler, presumably, brought enhanced status and, in turn, was a consideration when decisions were made in the royal distribution of revenue farms, concessions and *cap kurnia*. Assuming a significant link between power and status, another observation which Shaharil made was that the "social status" of a member of the ruling class depended not on his wealth but on the "number of debt-slave retainers he possessed" (15). Debt slaves, one assumes, were especially valuable because they did not have the freedom to shift loyalty from one ruler to another—which is a prominent feature of the fluid politics of the pre-modern Malay world.

There can be no doubt about the importance of the quest for status. Members of the aristocracy, Shaharil pointed out, "all aspired to move up the status ladder" (12–13). They also valued the titles which the ruler bestowed on his favourites—because these "gave them a status and distinguished them from the *rakyat*" (38, note 20). Although Shaharil insisted on the priority of economic drivers, therefore, *After Its Own Image* presents data that demands further investigation of the way the quest for wealth relates to the accumulation of status, and power—and also to claims of hereditary.

Another factor raised but not strongly developed by Shaharil was the role of religion. He noted, for instance, that in the cases of three important rulers—Sultan Mansur (1741–1795), Baginda Omar (1839–1876) and Zainal Abidin III (1881–1918)—their "appointments" to the office of Sultan were all influenced by religious officials, that is to say the "Ulama" (41, note 62, 22). The role of the "leading Ulama" in the state, he explained, was "not merely confined to religious teaching ...They were ministers, state councillors, and district chiefs of Sultans" (26). As to local government in Terengganu, Shaharil suggested the Imam and other "functionaries of the village mosques" were "the undisputed leaders of rural Trengganu" (27). In the field of education, not surprisingly, the role of religion was pronounced. In fact, the centres of Islamic teaching in Terengganu attracted students "from all quarters of the state and even from other states" (27).

The part played by the Islamic religion in the life of the Terengganu community was not unchanging. Raffles had highlighted the way a struggle over religious obligation was bringing political change in the Malay world. Shaharil cited evidence that tends to confirm the presence of such a development in Terengganu. A British visitor to Terengganu in the 1830s, George Earl, wrote about the efforts of *ulama* in the state to impose the Islamic *Shari'a* law—struggling against the proponents of the local Terengganu customary or *adat* law (28). Also, Shaharil pointed to another sign of change, in noting that the first Terengganu *Mufti* (Juri-consult) was only appointed in the early nineteenth century (27). Also, in the later years of that century, Sultan Zainal Abidin III was outstanding as a supporter of the Islamic code (27). By that time as well, the institution of *penghulu* or headman had declined—and the "role of the village religious functionaries in rural politics" was "strengthened" (25).

When *After Its Own Image* turns to investigate the famous 1928 peasant uprising in Terengganu (in chapter 6), Shaharil's observations again provoke queries about the role of Islamic commitment as a driver of action. He insisted that religious leaders in the uprising were "mainly local property owners and they had good reasons for resenting the exaction of land rents and survey fees by the government" (145). He admitted, it is true, that peasant protests were "expressed primarily in religious terms" (143)—but stressed that the revolt was ultimately a "manifestation of deeper social tensions as the agrarian society became increasingly absorbed into the colonial economy (163)". Following the theoretical work of James Scott, Ben Kerkvliet and others, Shaharil saw such uprisings as "symptoms of agrarian societies undergoing major changes" (143).

Time and again for Shaharil, the "really real" was economic—but as a careful historian who mined the archives, he offered evidence for an alternative explanation. The peasants struggle, he noted, was directed against "all those who had not followed the Hukum Syariah" [Islamic Law] (143). They listened to *Ulama* who told them that the land regulations being introduced in the period of British intervention "were those of the kafir [the unbeliever] and that anyone who paid rent was thus a kafir" (154). To determine whether the peasant complaints were fundamentally economic and merely expressed in religious terms (or language) is a formidable task. Since Shaharil wrote this book, however, I think there has been growing recognition that religious commitment can itself be a critical driver.

Conclusion

There is then plenty of room for debate around Shaharil's *After Its Own Image*.[19] That is partly why it is one of the most important books on Malay history. Shaharil did not write a colonial history, focusing on British policy and action, and its consequences. He sought to get inside Terengganu society—to read the official sources against the grain in order to reveal a pre-modern society in motion. He endeavoured to present developments in a transitional period from a Malay perspective—to understand the preoccupations and strategies of the Terengganu elite, the considerations which motivated them. To some extent influenced by his theoretical reading, Shaharil portrayed the elite of Terengganu as *homo economicus*—as historical protagonists driven by the quest for wealth. In presenting such a bold, interpretive analysis, he was a skilful innovator—advancing the historiography of the Malay world.

Looking back over two centuries of writing on political and social life in the pre-modern Malay world, Shaharil—like the many scholars before him—approached the task of analysis through his own particular horizon. He responded not only to historical documentation but also to the possibilities flowing from a foreign theoretical framework—in his case, one which appears to have been influenced by the Marxist and other social theory promoted at Monash University.

Historical scholarship (as Hans-Georg Gadamer helps us to understand) is typically a process of "fusion"—between the horizons of the researcher on the one hand and those of historical protagonists, the historical documentation, on the other (Gadamer, 2004: 305–306). In the nineteenthcentury, Walter Scott's particular way of portraying pre-modern Scottish society helped shape British perceptions of Malay sultanates, as did the then fashionable ranking of different races in civilisational terms; then the institutions of medieval Europe (and the debate about whether they had anything to offer to industrialising Britain) affected the analytical and moral responses of British scholar-officials. By the early twentieth century, the preoccupation with diffusionism—with identifying the particular origins of one or another feature of a social

[19] Among the positive reviews of the book, see especially those by John Gullick (*Journal of Southeast Asian Studies,* 18, 2, 1987, 335–337) and Carl Trocki (*Journal of Asian Studies*, 46, 1, 1987, 220–221). See also my review: Milner (1986). 'Capitalism, the dominant classes and the peasantry in Trengganu: a review article', *Review of Indonesian and Malaysian Studies,* 20, 1, 1986, 129–140.

formation—had become influential. Later that century, the specific operations of power drew the most attention. Then there was the profound influence of anthropological functionalism, always seeking to portray a society in synchronic terms as a "working system of social control". And partly in resistance to this approach, some analysts shifted their attention away from institutions (and the flow of "real power") to the investigation of key terms and categories in political culture. Shaharil contributed to a later development, a determination to analyse these Malay states diachronically, as societies in motion—driven forward (so this social theory insists) by a quest for wealth.

What might be given greater attention in a more comprehensive survey than I have attempted is intertextuality—the manner in which one observer's text on pre-modern Malay polities responds to another's. At times I have noted this taking place both in nineteenth-century and more modern scholarship, but in general, I have been concerned mainly to identify different phases and styles of analysis.

I will not deny my preference for the political culture approach—seeking to understand the "meaningful structures" through which members of pre-modern Malay polities may have comprehended their political condition. This approach more than any, it seems to me, pays close attention to actual testimony from the past. In working towards a "fusion of horizons" between historian and historical subject, the political culture methodology appears to offer a more balanced conversation.

Shaharil might not have agreed. He would possibly have accused me of being preoccupied with false consciousness rather than with the investigation of deeper forces. I suspect, however, that he would have approved the project in this chapter. Like Gadamer, Shaharil would see the point of examining how different historical researchers, investigating pre-modern Malay political systems, were "defined and limited" (Gadamer, 2004: 211). Joining me in a survey of types of historical writing over almost two centuries, I think he would have agreed that "real historical thinking must take account of its own historicity" (Gadamer, 2004: 299).

References

Abdul Rahman, E. (ed.). (2112). *Terengganu merentasi tiga abad: Kesultanan, Politik, Ekonomi, Agama dan Budaya*. Kuala Terennganu: Yayasan Diraja Sultan Mizan.

Alatas, S. H. (1972). *Modernization and social change: Studies in modernization, religion, social change and development in South-East Asia*. Sydney: Angus & Robertson.

Aljuneid, K. (2005). *Rethinking Raffles: A study of Stamford Raffles' Discourse on Religions Amongst Malays*. Singapore: Marshall Cavendish.

Allen, J. D. V. (1964). Two imperialists: A study of Sir Frank Swettenham and Sir Hugh Clifford. *JMBRAS, 37*(1), 41–73.

Andaya, B. W. (1979). *Perak: The abode of grace*. Kuala Lumpur: Oxford University Press.

Anderson, B. R. O. G. (1972). The idea of power in Javanese culture. In Claire Holt (Ed.), *Culture and politics in Indonesia* (pp. 1–69). Ithaca: Cornell University Press.

Anderson, J. (1965). *Political and commercial considerations relative to the Malayan Peninsula and the British settlements in the Straits of Malacca* (p. 1824). Singapore: MBRAS; orig.pub.

Anderson, J. (1971). *Mission to the East Coast of Sumatra in 1823* (p. 1823). Kuala Lumpur: Oxford University Press; orig. pub.

Bakar, M. A. (Ed.). (2018). *Orang Terengganu: Asal Usul*. Arus Hidup dan Aras Tuju (Kuala Terengganu: Perbanan Perpustakaan Awam Terengganu.

Bayly, C. A. (2004). *The birth of the modern world 1780–1914*. Malden: Blackwell.

Boon, J. A. (1987). *Other tribes, other scribes: Symbolic anthropology in the comparative study of cultures, histories, religions and texts*. Cambridge: Cambridge University Press.

Boon, J. A. (1990). *Affinities and extremes*. Chicago and London: University of Chicago Press.

Burrow, J. (2009). *A history of histories*. London: Penguin.

Carlyle, T. (1965). *Past and present* (p. 1843). Boston: Houghton Mifflin Company; orig. pub.

Carroll, D. J. (2005). *William Marsden and his Malayo-Polynesian legacy*. Ph.D. thesis, Australian National University.

Carroll, D. J. (2019). Before liberalism: William Marsden's late enlightenment imperial critique. In G. Knapman, A. Milner, & M. Quilty (Eds.), *Liberalism and the British Empire in Southeast Asia*. London and New York: Routledge.

Chandra, M. (1974). *Protector? An analysis of the concept and practice of loyalty and leader-led relationships within Malay Society*. Penang: Aliran.

Clifford, H. (1898). *Studies in Brown humanity*. London: Grant Richards.

Clifford, H. (1903). *In Court & Kampong*. London: Grant Richards.

Clifford, H. (1927). *The further side of silence*. New York: Doubleday.

Cowan, C. D. (1961). *Nineteenth-century Malaya: The origins of British political control*. London: Oxford University Press.

Crawfurd, J. (1856). *A descriptive Dictionary of the Indian Islands and adjacent countries*. London: Bradbury & Evans.

Crawfurd, J. (1967). *History of the Indian Archipelago*. London: Frank Cass.
Drakard, J. (1999). *A kingdom of words: Language and power in Sumatra*. Shah Alam: Oxford University Press.
Errington, S. (1989). *Meaning and power in a Southeast Asian Realm*. Princeton: Princeton University Press.
Farish, A. N. (2016). *The discursive construction of Southeast Asia in the 19th century colonial-capitalist discourse*. Amsterdam: Amsterdam University Press.
Gadamer, H.-G. (2004). *Truth and method*. London: Continuum.
Gailey, H. A. (1982). *Clifford: Imperial consul*. London: Rex Collings.
Geertz, C. (1973). *The interpretation of cultures*. New York: Basic Books.
Geertz, C. (1980). *Negara: The theatre state in nineteenth-century Bali*. Princeton: Princeton University Press.
Goh, D. P. S. (2007). Imperialism and 'medieval natives: The Malay image in Anglo-American travelogues and colonialism in Malaya and the Philippines. *International Journal of Cultural Studies, 10*, 3.
Guha, R. (1983). *Elementary aspects of peasant insurgency in colonial India*. Delhi: Oxford University Press.
Guha (ed), R. (1997). *A Subaltern studies reader, 1986–1995*. Minneapolis: University of Minnesota Press.
Gullick, J. M. (1965). *Indigenous political systems of Western Malaya*. London: Athlone Press.
Gullick, J. M. (2001). Richard James Wilkinson (1867–1941): A man of parts. *JMBRAS, 74*(1), 19–42.
Hampson, R. (2000). *Cross-cultural encounters in Joseph Conrad's Malay Fiction*. Basingstoke: Palgrave.
Heine-Geldern, R. (2018). *Conceptions of state and kingship in Southeast Asia* (p. 1942). Ithaca: Cornell University Press; orig.pub.
Hill, B. (2003). *Broken song: T.G.H. Stehlow and aboriginal possession*. Sydney: Vintage.
Holden, P. (2000). *Modern subjects/colonial texts. Hugh Clifford and the discipline of English literature in the straits settlements and Malaya 1895–1907*. Greensboro: ELT Press.
Ileto, R. (1971). *Magindanao, 1860–1888: The Career of Dato Uto of Buayan*. Ithaca: Cornell University.
Khoo, K. K. (1972). *The Western Malay States 1850–1873: The effects of commercial development on Malay politics*. Kuala Lumpur: Oxford University Press.
Kirk-Greene, A. H. M. (ed). (1965). *The principles of native administration in Nigeria*. London: Oxford University Press.
Knapman, G. (2017). *Race and British Colonialism in South-East Asia: John Crawfurd and the politics of equality*. New York: Routledge.

Kuper, A. (1973). *Anthropologists and anthropology: The British School*. New York: Pica Press.
Lienhardt, G. (1966). *Social anthropology*. London: Oxford University Press.
Lim, C. K., & Barlow, H. (1988). *Frank Swettenham & George Giles Watercolours & Sketches of Malaya 1880–1894*. Kuala Lumpur: The Malaysia-British Society.
Mackie, J.A.C., & Milner, A. (1986). John Legge as a historian. In D. P. Chandler & M. C. Ricklefs. *Nineteenth and twentieth century Indonesia: Essays in honour of Professor J.D. Legge* (pp. 163–176). Clayton: Centre of Southeast Asian Studies, Monash University.
Maier, H. M. J. (1988). *In the center of authority: The Malay Hikayat Merong Mahawangsa*. Ithaca: Cornell University Southeast Asia Program.
Marsden, W. (1966). *The history of Sumatra* (p. 1811). Kuala Lumpur: Oxford University Press; orig.pub.
Milner, A. (1982). *Kerajaan: Malay political culture on the eve of colonial rule.* Tucson: Association of Asian Studies Monograph, 1982. Second edition: Petaling Jaya: Strategic Information and Research Development Centre, 2016.
Milner, A. (1986). Capitalism, the dominant classes and the peasantry in Trengganu: A review article. *Review of Indonesian and Malaysian Studies, 20*(1), 129–140.
Mohamed Anwar Omar Din and Nik Anuar Nik Mahmud. 2009. *Dirgahayu Tuanku: Sejarah Kesultanan Terengganu 1708–2008,* Kuala Terengganu: Yayasan Diraja Sultan Mizanm.
Pakri, M. R. (2014). *The fiction of colonial Malaya*. Pulau Pinang: Universiti Sains Malaysia Press.
Parkinson, C. N. (1960). *British intervention in the Malay States, 1867–1877.* Kuala Lumpur: University of Malaya Press.
Quilty, M. (1998). *Textual empires: A reading of early British histories of Southeast Asia*. Melbourne: Monash Asia Institute.
Quilty, M. (2001). *British economic thought and colonization in Southeast Asia, 1776–1850*. Ph.D. thesis. Sydney: University of Sydney.
Raffles, S. (1991). *Memoir of the life and public services of Sir Thomas Stamford Raffles* (p. 1830). Oxford: Oxford University Press; orig.pub.
Robertson, W. (1777). *The History of America*. London: Cadell and Davies.
Sadka, E. (1968). *The protected Malay States 1874–1895*. Kuala Lumpur: University of Malaya Press.
Shaharil, T. (1977). The Terengganu ruling class in the late nineteenth century. *JMBRASL, l*(2), 25–47.
Shaharil, T. (1983). Voices from the Kelantan Desa 1900–1940. *Modern Asian Studies, 17*(2), 177–195.
Shaharil, T. (1984). *After its own image: The Trengganu experience 1881–1941*. Singapore: Oxford University Press.
Sheppard, M Cff. (1949). A short history of Trengganu. *JMBRAS, 22*(3), 1–74.

Sharom, A. (1984). *Kedah. Tradition and change in a Malay state: A study of the economic and political development*. Kuala Lumpur: MBRAS.
Sullivan, P. (1982). *Social relations of dependence in a Malay state: Nineteenth-century Perak*. Kuala Lumpur: Malaysian Branch of the Royal Asiatic Society.
Swettenham, F. (1903). *Malay sketches*. London: John Lane, The Bodley Head.
Swettenham, F. (1907). *British Malaya. An account of the origin and progress of British influence in Malaya*. London: John Lane the Bodley Head.
Thio, E. (1969). *British policy in the Malay Peninsula 1880–1910*. Singapore: University of Malaya Press.
Wicks, P. C. (1979). Images of Malaya in the stories of Sir Hugh Clifford. *JMBRAS, 52,* 1.
Wilkinson, R. J. (1932). Some Malay studies. *JMBRAS, X, 1,* 67–137.
Wilkinson, R. J. (1957). Malay customs and beliefs. *JMBRAS, 3*(4), 1–87.
Wilkinson, R. J. (1971). *Papers on Malay subjects*. Kuala Lumpur: Oxford University Press.
Wilson, A. N. (2003). *The victorians*. London: Arrow.
Winstedt, R. O. (1947a). *The Malays: A cultural history*. Singapore: Kelly & Walsh.
Winstedt, R. O. (1947b). Kingship and enthronement in Malaya. *JMBRAS, XX*(1), 129–139.
Winstedt, R. O. (1968). *A history of Malaya*. Kuala Lumpur: Marican & Sons.
Winstedt, R. O., & Wilkinson, R. J. (1934). History of Perak. *JMBRAS, 12,* 1.
Wolters, O. W. (1979). Khmer "Hinduism" in the seventh century. In R. B. Smith & W. Watson (Eds.), *Early South East Asia: Essays in archaeology, history and historical geography* (pp. 427–442). Oxford: Oxford University Press.
Wurtzburg, C. E. (1954). *Raffles of the Eastern Isles*. London: Hodder and Stoughton.

CHAPTER 6

Homage to Shaharil Talib and His Question of Divide in Malay Society: Merchants, Weavers and Specialists as the 'Middle-Class' of an Old Malay World

Maznah Mohamad

Abbreviations for Files from Archival Sources

ART	Annual Report of Terengganu
BAK	British Adviser of Kelantan
ARP	Annual Report of Pahang
DOP	District Office of Pekan
BAT	British Adviser of Terengganu
STT	State Treasurer of Terengganu

M. Mohamad (✉)
The National University of Singapore, Kent Ridge
Crescent, Singapore
e-mail: mlsmm@nus.edu.sg

R. Rasiah et al. (eds.), *Contesting Malaysia's Integration into the World Economy*, https://doi.org/10.1007/978-981-16-0650-2_6

Introduction

Honouring the memory of Shaharil Talib would be to appreciate the force of his scholarship on nineteenth-century Malay society. Shaharil passionately writes about the intricacies of intra-ruling class layering as much as he would emphatically ensure that the desperate voices of the peasant would leap out from the pages of his scholarly tome. Having had the honour of being supervised by him from 1983 to 1990 for my dissertation at the University of Malaya, we exchanged many thoughts and ideas on how to uncover the stories of people long dead but whose legacies have lived on, albeit in uncertain forms and for the most part, untold. Shaharil was adept at equally capturing the quintessence of those who ruled and those who were ruled. He had just published his highly regarded *After Its Own Image* (Shaharil 1984) by the time I started on my doctoral studies with the Southeast Asian Studies Department, which he had earlier founded. Shaharil was full of energy and brimming with many innovative ideas on how best to tell the story of people who inhabited our space of study. The east coast states of Terengganu and Kelantan were our common study sites. His work was rich and written with much zest, containing many delightful, if not powerful turn of phrases. His rendition of the ruling class was luxuriant and multi-layered and his conveyance of peasant angst against the establishment was lucid in as much as it was crushing. Reading his words on paper would be almost like listening to him gesticulating in body and form, while commanding your undivided attention to his point of view, and new revelations of the human condition.

Shaharil wrote as though he was always on the path of uncovering something new, and true enough he did, even in detailing a seemingly small but poignant point of a peasant's anguish. He writes of how, in 1922, a woman complained through a letter penned to the Sultan of Kelantan about how, 'neighbouring trees overshadowed a part of her land. Their shadow, she contended, adversely affected the growth of her padi, causing much loss', but, "henceforth she suffered in silence' after being told to pay a money deposit for the case to be brought forward to the authorities (Shaharil, 1983: 178). It was this spirit which sustained me throughout my doctoral studies as I delved into the world of the handloom weavers, always with the intention of discovering new scholarly truths on the one side, and doing justice to those denied the splendour and glory of history, on the other.

In this chapter I reflect on and revisit my work on the handloom weavers (Maznah, 1996) a project which I shared closely with Shaharil, who imparted his intellectual vigour into it, and for which I am forever indebted. Uncovering the history of the handloom industry and its assemblage and classes of working people, opened up a narrative and a concept of the plural Malay society, which went beyond just the *Raja* versus the *Rakyat* duality. Within their interstices were the industrious 'middle-class' which were part of an intertwining world of producers, merchants, markets, consumers and interveners. In the ensuing passages of this chapter, I describe how I developed a hunch that most works on the pre-colonial and colonized 'Malay' society seemed to have missed some crucial details in their construction of the 'feudal' or pre-colonial Malay world. Although my work had only focussed on the handloom weavers, the generalization from the thesis could be applied to the study of brass-ware makers, silversmiths, boat-builders, woodcarvers and all manner of 'craftspeople' whose significance was often overlooked when considering the question of class divides in Malay society. The second part of the chapter details how these group of people did not function in isolation within their 'cottage industries' but were all part of an assemblage, a network and a web of specialists and productive workers with ties beyond the shores of their 'feudal' enclosure. The chapter ends by discussing how this 'world' was affected by British colonial governance and the onslaught of industrial capitalism which inevitably and ultimately led to its demise.

Engaging with Shaharil's Dichotomization of Malay Society

My engagement with the class question with Shaharil was to challenge his presumptions. Perhaps a tad too critical of his work I had mildly berated him in my thesis and later book (Maznah, 1996: 58–59) for not giving enough attention to a specific class. In an earlier article, he had pronounced rather emphatically that power duality pervaded in Malay society which,

> *[] was essentially a division of two classes. The ruling class and the subject class formed the main elements in the Malay social system...The social ramifications of the ruling class in Terengganu were complex and there is some difficulty in drawing a demarcating line between it and the subject class. Nevertheless the dichotomous model was essentially accurate...There was*

> *however, a further class which can be identified. This was the merchant class whose members, with the exception of the Chinese Kapitan China and the Chinese Jurubahasa (translator), did not have official status, but who also belonged by wealth and standing to the upper levels of society. They were too feeble and dependent upon the patronage of the ruling class to be described as a "middle class" and their presence did not therefore alter the two-class division to which reference has been made.* (Shaharil, 1977: 25–26).

We had a healthy debate on this, and I proceeded with my thesis that there had to be more than the two-side divide, that there had to be something in the middle in nineteenth-century Terengganu and Kelantan society, before land wealth became the lynchpin in bolstering the relationship between Malay rulers and British capitalists. Since trading activities contributed to a large share of the surplus extracted by the ruling class in Terengganu, there had to be important actors within its space. It was already quite established, even in his own work that Terengganu had a trading economy which was based on manufactured commodity rather than primary products. Who then constituted the backbone of this economy? Shaharil's insistence on his 'dichotomous model' was useful in bringing out the clash of the two divides within society in a more intense way. However, a binary class war would not explain the missing thread which connected rulers to their source of revenue and wealth.

I felt that Shaharil's study was less vivid in outlining the role of many other classes which sustained this trading economy. My thesis wanted answers to a question such as this—who were the producers, the brokers, retailers and sellers of these manufactured commodities? The role of the revenue farmers who leased or paid for use of strategic tributaries (riverways, mainly) in exchange for tax revenues was overemphasized at the expense of other probable and crucial players in the economy. The revenue farmers' source of revenue was from taxation, and not from profits of sale, or capital at its circulation level. There were also monopoly traders who were granted the sole rights to the price of particular commodities. However, the monopoly farms in which these monopoly traders operated were restricted to mainly primary commodities such as jungle produce, crops and essential items such as kerosene (Shaharil, 1984: 51–59). I thought about all the other products such as processed goods in the form of dried fish or pepper, and manufactured ones as in textiles and brassware. The extant of trading activities or the *pajak* system described by Shaharil suggests all the more reason for the crucial presence of a merchant class, contrary to his pronouncement that they were 'feeble'. In a book review of *After Its Own Image,* J. M. Gullick did hint at the puzzlement of Shaharil's reference to a 'feeble' class which seemed important enough in many ways. The reign of an earlier ruler, Baginda Omar (1839–76), had opened up much economic activity in the state, religious leaders had become wealthy through trade, while the aristocratic class was far from being entrepreneurial (Gullick, 1987: 337). Such was the challenge, as well as the inspiration which Shaharil and his works provided me in the course of completing the dissertation.

Contesting Shaharil's Thesis

The work by R. D. Hill (1977) on the geography of rice cultivation surprisingly gave me the breakthrough to convince Shaharil that more unconventional questions needed to be posed about the state of the Terengganu economy. Hill had surveyed the status of rice production in the various states of the peninsula and highlighted that agrarianization may have been a fairly recent process in Terengganu, which began probably at the turn of the century and completed by the 1930s. Hill pointed out that Terengganu, until that period, was substantially urbanized with about half of its population residing in the town of Kuala Terengganu. The town supported an extensive manufacturing industry. The proceeds from these exported manufactures were in fact used to support staples like rice. There was also the availability of commercialized grazing land and pastoral farming for the production of *ghee* (clarified butter) for export to Singapore (Hill, 1977: 69). Among the probable reasons suggested by Hill to explain the later-day shift to agrarianization and Terengganu's subsequent impoverishment was the loss of manufacturing skills and markets. Furthermore, population growth may have necessitated the conversion of grazing lands to rice farms.

In order to seek for more clues about an earlier Terengganu, I also drew upon earlier works such as the much-acclaimed chronicles of Abdullah Munshi (Kassim, 1966) which contain extensive information of the pre-colonial *negeri*. Even though Abdullah's pro-European influence and his disdain for the ways of the locals are often overbearing, his writings on the eastern Malay states provide us with insights into the kind of society that existed then. For instance, while not primarily attempting to describe the eastern states' economic system, he had carefully listed the kind of products that were produced locally, including those that were exported as well as imported. In 1838, the year Abdullah made his visit to Kelantan, Terengganu, and Pahang, the production of silk sarongs was described as a thriving, if not a critical industry, as silk sarongs constituted one of the more important export items from these *negeri* (Abdullah Munsyi in Kassim, 1966: 33, 34, 52, 87, 88).

All these left me with an intriguing question to pursue—what were the events which led to such a dramatic change in demographic, economic and social trends of the east coast states? Shaharil was convinced that a deeper examination of the 'in-between' classes would be worth pursuing. Aspects of everyday life not captured in epic renditions of 'dichotomous' class wars, the industrious and bustling, but ironically quiet networks of merchants, brokers, traders and specialist army of producers of the handloom textile were to be given more voice and visibility.

By the early twentieth century, there was greater impoverishment and the proportion of agriculturalists rose in Terengganu, indicating that food supplies were limited despite population reduction. R. D. Hill suggests that this had to do with the declining importance of the industrial craft sector (particularly the metal-working, ship-building and transportation of sailing vessels) (Hill, 1977: 190). The decline of the manufacturing industry occurred between 1890 and 1910 which was accompanied by impoverishment and emigration (Hill, 1977: 169–170). As the local industries could not expand either in terms of the enlargement of the putting-out base or the formation of factories, labour was left unutilized leading to immiserization, emigration and the switch to less profitable agricultural work. Features of the industry's 'ebb' can be discerned by several indications. Firstly, production relations and structure within the industry were not able to provide the necessary basis for the transformation of the enterprise into industrial capitalism. Instead, the production relations and structure merely adapted to reduce production cost per unit and maintained the putting-out system. Secondly, the putting-out system was flexible and able to accommodate economic fluctuations experienced by the industry without incurring great costs to either owners of production or dependent producers. The third indication of decline was when handloom-manufactured textiles became progressively insignificant in Malaysian export trade. The volume of handloom textile production as well as the variety of textile products was reduced even though the local market was retained. The industry was forced to diversify into specific products that required lower-skills input to reduce production costs. Fourthly, the decline became even more acute when ancillary industries were wiped out as a result of the displacement and the erosion of work skills. The industry also declined when its dependency upon the global demand and supply chain was intensified. Handloom products progressed from being dependent on only imported raw materials, such as silk and cotton yarn, to becoming dependent on imported gold threads and chemical dyes, especially after it had diversified into *songket*. The dependence was intensified when the textile community began to consume ready-made cloths that were then used for the batik printing industry. This whole gamut of dependency features subjected the industry to global fluctuations in trade and impaired its ability to expand independently. Finally, the features of decline were compounded when the industry became open to the total intervention of the state. After independence, the Malaysian handloom industry became dependent on the state at almost all levels of production, from procurement of raw materials to final marketing of finished products, including defining a national identity for the industry.

Handloom Textiles as Craft or Commodity?

Handloom production was frequently overlooked as an important economic sector even in the eastern Malay states because artisans, unlike the peasantry, did not require colonial policy intervention until much later. However, going by the above accounts by Hill and Abdullah Munshi, we could place the existence of an active handloom industry as part of an urbanized economy in the states of Terengganu and Kelantan. In 1895, Hugh Clifford had already bestowed upon Kuala Terengganu the title, 'Birmingham of the Peninsula', having described the nature of work involved among the artisan community of weavers, boat-builders, wood-workers and metal-smiths (Clifford, 1961: 91–95). He was nevertheless guarded and condescending about this, downgrading the artisans' ingenuity to their imitative skills rather than originality (ibid., 95). A few years after Clifford's report, W. W. Skeat and F. F. Laidlaw who were part of the Cambridge University expedition team to the northeastern states and upper Perak from 1899 to 1900 wrote an account of their confirming the conditions described by Clifford of Kelantan and Terengganu. They described the existence of handicraft manufacturers from pottery to tiles to boats to textiles to metalware (Skeat, 1953: 31, 41, and Laidlaw, 1953: 122). They were 'truly astonished at the range of activities, and in part at the high quality of the work' (Skeat, 1953: 122). Nevertheless by the time W. A. Graham, a Siamese Adviser to the state of Kelantan, came to the state at the beginning of the twentieth century, boat-building was among the principal industries there but on the decline due to the introduction of steamers (Graham, 1907: 65).

However, most of the available reports on the production of local commodities were either written by or for the anthropologists (of the British school), the practical craft enthusiasts, or the art collectors (Roth, 1910). The most comprehensive information on locally manufactured objects (dubbed 'Malay handicrafts') are in the collection of *Papers on Malay Subjects* compiled by R. J. Wilkinson (1925). R. O. Winstedt, writing in the second part of this report on 'Malay Industries' divides his discussion on Malay industries into two parts. The first was on 'Arts and Crafts' and the second on 'Fishing, Hunting and Trapping'. Industries such as boat-building, carpentry (including house-building), metalsmithing and textile weaving are all categorized under the designation of 'Arts and Crafts'. This naturally leads to a conception that even large-scale economic activities such as the construction of boats and houses are merely leisure-time pursuits of Malay 'peasants'. Winstedt reports that boats of two hundred tons were built for long distance journeys between Singapore and Siamese ports. Although the report's intention was far from presenting a socio-economic picture of the boat industry, details like this suggest that there must have been a considerable volume of seafaring trade conducted by the population for such an industry to thrive (Winstedt, 1925: 8–17). Winstedt's appraisal of Malay boat-building techniques is focussed only on the artistic value of these boats. To him, the Malay boat is just another cultural artefact rather than a representation of the Malay economy of that time. He also underestimates the role of the Malay silversmith whom he paints as not being of 'professional intent only on his art, but rather a gifted amateur pursuing his craft by fits and starts and at leisure'. (ibid.: 46–47). This despite his own description of the laborious process involved in churning out silverware. To begin with, raw silver had to be obtained from outside the confines of the village. Then the so-called 'rice-planter-cum-amateur-craftsman' had to invest in many specialized implements and raw materials such as the melting crucible, hammer, anvil, chisels, resin and polishing chemicals (ibid.: 50–53). Given all of this how could silversmithing then be a leisure-time activity?

Winstedt's rendition of spinning, weaving and dyeing is also discussed in the same tonal inclination as the above, although again, perhaps inadvertently, a picture of the economic organization of the industry is made obvious. Winstedt praises the handloom industry as the 'the most beautiful, unique and valuable of the industries considered' (ibid., 38). He then makes a vague reference to the existence of some form of division of labour in the production of a type of printed fabric in Terengganu. It is described that at one stage in the production process for the dyers (another group of workers)(missing word/s?). The cloth was prepared by the earlier group of women by stitching the appropriate portions or by tying pieces of banana leaf on them. Then these cloths were passed on to the dyers, and then subsequently returned to yet another group of people for the cloths to be sold (ibid.: 67). What is described is the process of making a type of tie-and-dye cloth or the ***kain pelangi***. Going by such a description, production at that time was certainly based on the putting-out system and wage labour was clearly being used.

These occupations were not considered a form of manufacture as the above colonial administrative-scholars were officers of the Federated Malay states and were more familiar with the western Malay states where agricultural occupations tied to the land were more predominant. This conception of the Malays was then transposed onto other situations, even when large-scale agrarianization was absent, or that silversmiths and weavers did not own any plot of land. For these colonial scholars, any activity not connected to rice-farming or agriculture could only be understood as a 'past-time' vocation.

Handloom Merchants, Weavers and Specialist Others: 'Peasants' or 'Middle-Class'?

My study of the handloom industry followed Shaharil's calling to wander 'off the beaten path' (Shaharil 1983: 195) so that other voices can be heard. The production of Malay handloom textiles was in actual fact based on an extensive division and differentiation of labour. What went into the production of finished handmade textiles were in fact multiple divisions and distribution of work skills. These were broken up into many tasks performed in a serial and successive manner. Furthermore, the detachable nature of weaving accessories and implements made it possible for these tasks and assembly to be completed in different households. The variety of implements and tools for production could also in turn be owned by many different specialists and individuals. The laborious and tedious stage of 'weaving' as represented by the ubiquitous image of women sitting at their looms is only one of these sets of work. Almost all of the work in producing handmade textiles were done on a putting-out basis whereby the implements and nature of tasks were transportable from one physical site to another. Outside of these directly relatable weaving processes were several upstream specializations particularly yarn dyeing and construction of weaving implements. Further on, a pool of brokers, middlemen and merchants would make up the full assemblage of an urbanized and industrious labouring class producing a manufactured commodity within a proto-industrial setting. Deservingly they should be classified as the 'middle-class' of this once thriving Malay world. Nevertheless the grouping of this 'middle-class' must also take note of the hierarchy of power relations within it.

In Terengganu, for example, weaving labourers were bound to specific merchants who controlled almost every aspect of the production process. Merchants played a strategic role in the production chain as they were responsible for sourcing raw materials, specifically, silk and cotton yarn, including gold and silver threads from abroad, as well as the marketing of the finished products to places outside of Terengganu. British agents posted in Terengganu during the period 1910–1919 made several references to the status of local industries, especially on the role of women:

> *The standard of living is extremely low throughout the state, and economic pressure keeps men and women engaged in ceaseless industry. The latter make mats and weave silk or cotton cloth; there are very few houses in which one or more handlooms are not continuously at work.* (ART, 1916: 8)

There was evidence of the presence of big merchants who profited from this condition of cheap labour and lucrative markets:

> *The payment for weaving a single sarong (the work of four seven-hour days) is 60 cents. Large profits are made by the middlemen who export the local products for sale in Singapore and the FMS.* (ART, 1919: 9)

Although industrial capitalism had not set in by the turn of the twentieth century, a form of early industrialization or 'proto-industrialization' (Mendels, 1972) or simply, 'industrialization before industrialization' (Kriedte et al., 1981) was being observed inTerengganu of the early 1900s. There, when merchants entered the area of production, they did so by investing in yarn and fixed capital in terms of the implements. The most expensive part of the loom, the *jentera*, was never usually owned by putting-out workers but by those who have the greatest control over production. A piece-rate wage was common in places like Terengganu—this indicated the existence of 'merchant-capitalists' in handloom production who may be classified as occupying the top-tier of the middle-class.

When interviewed in the mid-1980s, weavers in their fifties did not remember a time when weaving was only done for household consumption. All the sarongs that they or their ancestors wove were all for sale. Most of them started weaving by helping their mothers to do so, or did so for a wage under a relative or a *toke* (term used to denote a master weaver, merchant, commission agent or broker from whom raw materials or implements were obtained or a wage paid out). The preparation of the warp and weft yarn for the loom was usually done by skilled master weavers who sometimes worked under a merchant or who themselves graduated to become the *toke* themselves. Unlike the 'coldness' or business-like relations in a production factory, the putting-out system practised for handloom weaving had the *toke* cultivating a measure of cordiality among the weavers. A woman interviewed then remembered how it was like in the olden days when she as a *toke* valued the good rapport between the weavers and herself. She had to travel far into the villages to deliver her warp beams (pre-prepared for attachment to the looms). The weavers in turn gave her offerings of new rice, fruits and other village produce. Maintaining cordiality and mutual respect under the putting-out system was important as under the putting-out system weavers could choose under which *toke* they would accept the work from. Due to this, rivalries among the *toke* were some of the features of the system. Weavers recounted a bitter fight between a Chinese and a Malay *toke* over the control of weavers within a certain *kampong* in Kuala Terengganu.

The whole differentiation and division of labour in the handloom production process actually defies the simple dichotomous and unequal relationship between *toke* and weavers. There were at least three groups of specialists involved from the start to the finish in production, (1) the ancillary process, (2) primary weaving preparation process and (3) the loom-weaving process. Within each of the three processes, there was a further division of sub-specializations. For example, under the preparation process there could be up to eight different workers performing distinct tasks such as dyeing, spinning, warping, stringing of heddle frames and patterning.

Under ancillary production, men predominated in these occupations, especially in dye-making. An 1895 account by Hugh Clifford on specializations within the weaving industry observed a gender-based division of labour:

> *The weaving is done exclusively by the women. The men confining themselves to aiding in procuring the ingredients from which the numerous vegetable dyes are prepared, devising the patterns, making and setting up the loom, and disposing of the silks and cottons when ready for sale.* (Gullick, 1952: 138)

By the 1900, natural dyes were gradually being replaced by chemical or aniline dyes from Germany and Britain. By 1923, the colonial government was not even able to get the services of a skilled natural dye-maker for its Art School in Kuala Kangsar (BAK 313/1923). By 1927, Kelantan weavers were only using three shades of vegetable dyes in the colours of black, red and yellow (BAK 1436/1927). The switch to cheaper chemical dyes displaced men from participating in the ancillary stages of the handloom industry. When this happened the role of the merchants was boosted with the additional trade in imported dyes.

Men were also the skilful designers of textiles as this could have been due to their role as traders who were able to gauge the tastes of consumers. On the other hand the range of motifs on traditional textiles was limited and had to follow restrictive rules that are sacred, spiritual and religious in nature. Hence, only specialized master weavers and designers, who were aligned to the royal court, could possess such knowledge. This is the cultural dimension in which many women weavers were not predisposed to. Changing patterns and motifs had to be decided by others higher in the hierarchy of production.

Wood-working was another ancillary task in which men dominated, which involved the construction of implements such as the handloom and its associated parts. Some of these distinctive specializations included the making of the *jentera* or the warp reeds and comb, and the loom-frame. The best constructed loom frames would incorporate artistic adornments on them, such as in the exquisite carvings. A superior loom must be sturdy and heavy in order to produce better quality weaves.

Another ancillary process in handloom weaving included printing and finishing work. Batik is one example of a printing technique on textiles. However, before the adoption of batik-making there were other printing techniques used on handmade textiles. Woven cloths could be block-printed or gilded with gold leaf. Printing of textiles by means of the tie-and-dye technique to produce the ***kain pelangi*** and the gilding technique for ***kain telepuk*** were some of the specializations which formed the supportive occupations of the handloom industry. The finishing process in textiles also included calendering, or 'polishing' the cloth with cowrie shells, whose expert was known as the ***tukang gerus*** (Winstedt, 1925: 65).

For work within the primary weaving preparation process, more women would be involved. The preparation process could be divided between the preparation of the yarn, the preparation of the loom and the setting for the design. The most specialized of skills within these would be the preparation of the loom with warping threads. After this was done the warp yarns would then be transferred onto warp beams or the ***papan loseng***, a task which needed to be done with several people. When the ***papan loseng*** was completed, they were then transported to another locality, if need be for other subsequent preparations to be done. This would usually involve threading of the warp yarns through fine reed combs, which required exceptional dexterity. Heddle-stringing was the subsequent task, which enabled the setting up of a template for the textile design.

Relative to all the other processes before it, weaving would be considered least demanding in terms of skills, precision and dexterity. However, it was not an entirely unskilled job as the weaver must be adept enough to be able to manipulate the accessories of the loom, which included the warp, weft and supplementary yarns.

With such a fragmented division of labour, even a simple piece of sarong would be produced by the labours of numerous persons and travelling through long distances before it reached the consumer. Thus, even though handloom weaving was done entirely by home-based workers, the level of differentiation was extremely elaborate and advanced, likening the whole process to a home-based assembly plant of the modern factory. The complexity, together with the 'invisible' nature of work involved in making handloom textiles, had most of the time escaped the scrutiny of studies and policy formulations affecting the industry.

Costs of producing high-quality handmade textiles gradually but ultimately led to the deterioration of the industry. Cheaper imported chemical dyes displaced the skills and contribution of natural dye-makers which in turned lowered the quality of the handloom products. On the other end, costs of silk and metallic yarns escalated which forced weavers to find cheaper substitutes in poorer quality silk yarns or even cotton in place of traditional silk sarongs. The debasement (as a survival strategy) was manifested in the lowered yarn weightage in each piece of textile, in the narrowing of sarong widths, the loosening of weaves to save on yarn-use, and limiting the use of gold or other metallic yarn which compromised on the design. All these added to the progressive decline in the quality of a once-well regarded handmade commodity, and with these also the de-skilling process. Ultimately of course, the mechanization of textile production and its machine-made products overwhelmed what could ever be produced by the handmade tradition.

By the turn of the twentieth century, the structure of handloom production undoubtedly contained capitalistic elements with the presence of owners of capital and waged labour. Although the point about them being the middle-class of an old Malay world was not propounded in my dissertation and subsequent book, the revisitation of my work in the present context, clearly defined the character of merchants, weavers and other specialists who constituted the industry as belonging to a class distinct from the peasants. In paying homage to Shaharil's own mapping of the class question, it is thus fitting that merchants, weavers and others within their midst be recognized as constituting a 'middle-class' who were not 'feeble', but in fact key to the prosperity of nineteenth-century Malay states.

Death by Dependency Rather Than Revolt: Colonial State Intervention in the Industry

Colonial government intervention in the textile industries of Kelantan, Terengganu and Pahang in the early twentieth century can be read variously—either as being disruptive or benign. Merchants, weavers and trade specialists appeared to be shielded from the rupture of discontentment over the loss of entitlement to natural resource, particularly land. Peasants were not, and as a result culminated in the 1928 Terengganu peasant revolt, a study of which, was one of Shaharil's finest contributions to scholarship on anticolonial dissent. Why was the 'middle-class' of the handloom industry not led to the same route? Land, in the case of the peasant, was subjected to new regulations on taxation and other unfair concession deals. On the other hand, merchants and weavers did not own any natural resource, and by virtue of this lack, were less subjected to capitalist exploitation. The colonial state could only play its role either as merchant middleman, as in the Pekan industry, or as investors in the Kuala Terengganu case. The autonomous nature of handloom production was nevertheless an insufficient condition to save it from the onslaught of industrial capitalism.

The Pekan Case

In 1920, this was how the Pekan District Annual District Report summed up the situation of the weaving industry:

> *While the demand for Pekan sarongs remained great as ever, it is regretted that it was found more and more difficult to fill the orders. The truth is that a critical stage has been reached when the weavers should be expected to have found their feet and to be in a position to carry on with a minimum of government interference. From the small beginnings of four years ago, a regular business has grown up, and as times have changed considerably, it is now not possible to give the association the attention that it then received.* (ARP 1920, in DOP496/1920).

Referring to some failed efforts on the part of the District Office to help out with obtaining silk yarn supplies for the weavers, the District Officer (DO) then did not have kind words for the weavers who were accused of being 'thriftless, shortsighted and ready to take advantage of any assistance extended to them' (ibid). Nevertheless, the weaving industry appeared to have a new lease of life about a few years after that when the Pekan Weavers Cooperative Society (PWCS) was formed in 1923 under the auspices of the District Office (DOP14/1923).

This relationship between the District Office and the PWCS paved the way for other imperialistic European industrial powers in marketing their new products. Germany, for example, succeeded in marketing its chemical dyestuffs among Pekan weavers by the later 1920s (DOP 1185/1930). By 1931, a British company, the Imperial Chemical Industries (ICI), was also keen on capturing the same market.

> *We shall be very pleased to have your assistance in establishing the use of English dyes in this territory which in the past has been supplied exclusively by dyes of foreign manufacture* (DOP 1185/1930).

However the switch to less time-consuming and easily available dyestuffs, marketed by a growing chemical industry from the West, inevitably led to the deterioration of the hand-woven sarongs. It also put these sarongs almost on par with other imported sarongs with its loss of exclusivity. Pekan sarongs were no longer unique then and the price of these sarongs fell. By 1932, debts outstanding for silk sarongs sold and borne by the District Office amounted to a considerable amount (DOP 621/1932). These debts were unpaid and the government was unable to replenish the silk stocks. A new scheme was rolled out whereby weavers were compelled to switch to cotton weaving instead. Various government departments were encouraged to purchase hand-woven cotton sarongs as uniforms for their peons and lower-ranking Malay staff (DOP 63/1937). While outwardly and from an administrative viewpoint, the Pekan District Office was earnest in trying to resuscitate the industry as well as extend maximum assistance to weavers, it was not able to stop the trend towards an impending decline of the industry. Production did not expand, the quality of handloom products deteriorated and the size of the weaving community eventually shrunk. With their displacement it was thus not surprising that many former weavers turned to agriculture, hence the onset of 'agriaranization' as implied by Hill (1977).

The Kuala Terengganu Case

The Terengganu colonial government's intervention in the weaving industry was kept to a minimum until the late 1930s. There was little reason for the state to intercede due to the already extensive and established commercial network supporting the industry. The state merely played its role in regulating and adjusting tariffs to suit the demands of concerned groups. For example, import duties on raw silk and cotton were lifted following cloth traders' requests (BAT 417/1938). However, by the late 1930s, signs of the industry's decline were being felt. In 1938 a proposal was submitted by J. D. Dalley, who was the Honorary Secretary to the Terengganu Arts and Crafts Society (TACS), for the government to invest in a dyeing facility. The justification was that in order to expand the handloom textile trade all fabrics exported from Terengganu must be of high quality and dyed with good fast dyes. Government intervention was considered necessary to safeguard a growing industry which was increasingly being led into using cheaper and lower-quality dyes. Dalley proposed that the colonial government invest in a factory for dyeing raw silk, which would be managed by a specialist dyer. A further expansion of the trade would involve training girls of school-leaving age who can be employed in a possible weaving factory (BAK 621/1938).

There would also be a management committee to oversee the direction of the factory. It was envisaged that when the trained young women marry they would be able to augment their family incomes by continuing to weave in their homes. A list of the more expert of the weavers among them would be kept, so that they can undertake orders to weave textiles using the high-quality factory-dyed yarns, while payment would be made on a piece-rate basis. Dalley was confident that,

> *With judicious, guaranteed dyes (each piece of fabric to be stamped "Made in Terengganu"), the establishment of selling agencies, the trade will in time expand until it embraces the whole of the East in addition to filling part of the luxury trade of Europe.* (BAK 621/1938)

The proposal impressed the British Adviser of Terengganu then, as well as the Secretary to the High Commissioner, R. Irvine, who informed the Governor, Sir Thomas Shenton, about the nature of the above proposal. Irvine remarked that,

> *This industry is clearly of great value to Terengganu and I think it is in every way desirable for the government to assist in its development...Mr McKerron tells me he took a great interest in the industry while he was in Terengganu and that the proposals now put forward were worked out jointly by himself and Mr Dalley. I knew cloth weaving was an important cottage industry in Terengganu, but I had no idea it had developed to such an extent, nearly $1/2 million of exports last year. I feel sure the scheme has Y. E's strong support.* (BAK 621/1938)

Governor Shenton approved this proposal (BAK 62/1938). The British company, ICI was finally given the contract despite the detailed and seemingly viable proposal drawn up by its Dutch competitor, the N. V. Straits Java Trading Company (BAK 621/1938). By June 1938, Che Dol was already undergoing training at the Malayan Weaving Works and taking a course with ICI. In 1940, a sum of money was advanced to Mr N. Rees, the Chief Inspector of Schools, towards the setting up of the Textile and Dyeing Factory (STT316/1946). Unfortunately, the establishment of this potentially vibrant industry occurred too close to the breakout of the Second World War. When the war broke out around 1942 the whole project was disrupted. After the end of the war the attempt to re-establish the enterprise did not take on the same momentum as that before the war period. There were no records traceable indicating whether J. D. Dalley continued with his involvement in the Terengganu weaving and dyeing industries during the post-war period. Hence, as time and circumstances had shown the colonial government was not able to arrest the declining trend of handloom textile production, despite the fact that there were efforts to promote, aid and provide a lifeline to the industry.

By Way of a Conclusion: 'Breaking the Myth of Silence'

This chapter has tried to bring alive Shaharil's legacy in sharpening our understanding of the concept of social class, its features in local society, and the colonial state within its midst. Colonial records together with a decolonizing framework could be used to deconstruct unacknowledged aspects of the past. These would have remained untold if not for persistence and passion to the craft of archival mining, which Shaharil was most adept at, and his deep curiosity about unearthing more than meets the eye:

> *This rich corpus of material embedded in the archives breaks the myth of silence that is often ascribed to people living in the countryside.* (Shaharil, 1983: 178)

I learnt to pick up all of these from the interactive supervision which Shaharil provided for my research and eventual dissertation. The chapter pays homage to how Shaharil's own work had stimulated my re-questioning of his categorization of Malay society, and that colonial records can always, and should be read against the grain.

> *An examination of these sources allows the student of history who wanders off the beaten track to hear voices from the desa.* (Shaharil, 1983: 195)

I am grateful to Shaharil for the opportunity to debate and discover the existence of classes of people who reside within the interstices of the all-powerful *Raja* on one side and the down-trodden *Rakyat* on the other. The middle-class of merchants, weavers and specialist others had carved up a vibrant space of globally interconnected production, commodities and markets. The handloom industry was a complex and interlocking world of multiple specializations, which crumbled by the twentieth century due to the onslaught of new competing economic systems. Did the colonial state hasten it? I am circumspect about pronouncing any definitive answers to such a question. Colonial policies were paternalistic in nature, but ultimately prioritized the interests of the Empire. In the end, the juggernaut of industrialization and mechanization swept most things along its way, despite the best of intentions of some colonial officers to prolong the lifespan of the industry. The handloom weaving industry of Terengganu, Kelantan and Pahang did not survive the glory of its heyday, but a window to its past must acknowledge that a form of industrialization did define its character, while an urban-based 'middle-class' of an old Malay world, was its lifeblood.

References

Clifford, H. (1961). Report of an expedition to Terengganu and Kelantan. *Journal of the Malaysian Branch of the Royal Asiatic Society, 34*(1), 1–162.

Graham, W. A. (1907). *Kelantan: A state of the Malay peninsula*. Glasgow: J. Maclehose and Sons.

Gullick, J. M. (1952). A survey of the Malay weavers and silversmiths in Kelantan in 1951. *Journal of the Malaysian Branch of the Royal Asiatic Society, 25*(1), 134–148.

Gullick, J. M. (1987). After its own image: The Trengganu experience 1881–1941 (Book Review). *Journal of Southeast Asian Studies, 18*(2), 335–337.

Hill, R. D. (1977). *Rice in Malaya: A study in historical geography*. Kuala Lumpur: Oxford University Press.

Kassim, A. (1966). *Kisah Pelayaran Abdullah ke Kelantan dan ke Judah (pengenalan dan annotasi)*. Pulau Pinang: Penerbit Fajar Bakti.

Kriedte, P., Medick, H., & Schlumbohm, J. (1981). *Industrialization before industrialization*. Cambridge: Cambridge University Press.

Laidlaw, F. F. (1953). Travels in Kelantan, Terengganu & upper Perak: A personal narrative. *Journal of the Malaysian Branch of the Royal Asiatic Society, 26*(4), 148–165.

Maznah, M. (1996). *The Malay handloom weavers: A study of the rise and decline of traditional manufacture*. Singapore: Institute of Southeast Asian Studies.

Mendels, F. (1972). Proto-industrialization: The first phase of the industrialization process. *Journal of Economic History, 32*(1), 241–261.

Roth, H. L. (1910). *Oriental silverwork, Malay and Chinese: A handbook for connoisseurs, collectors, students and silversmiths*. London: Truslove and Hanson.

Shaharil, T. (1983). Voices from the Kelantan Desa 1900–1940. *Modern Asian Studies, 17*(2), 177–195.

Shaharil, T. (1984). *After its own image: The Trengganu experience 1881–1941.* Kuala Lumpur: Oxford University Press.

Shaharil, T. R. (1977). The Trengganu ruling class in the late nineteenth century. *Journal of the Malaysian Branch of the Royal Asiatic Society, 50*(2), 25–47.

Skeat, W. W. (1953). Reminiscences of the Cambridge university expedition to the northeastern states, 1899–1900. *Journal of the Malaysian Branch of the Royal Asiatic Society, 26*(4), 9–147.

Wilkinson, R. J. (Ed.). (1925). *Papers on Malay subjects*. Kuala Lumpur: Government of the Federated Malay States Press.

Winstedt, R. O. (1925). Malay industries. In R. J. Wilkinson (Ed.), *Papers on Malay subjects*. Kuala Lumpur: Government of the Federated Malay States Press.

CHAPTER 7

Malay Aristocrats' Participation in Business in Colonial Malaya

Sivachandralingam Sundara Raja

Introduction

One of Shaharil Talib's main preoccupations was his study on the extent to which the capitalist world economic system had affected traditional Malays during the British colonial rule in the late nineteenth and twentieth centuries. Considerable attention was devoted to the sensitivity of the Malay ruling class toward the creation of a colonial economic order and the rapid penetration of foreign capital. In fact, that was the central theme of Shaharil's (1984) work, *After Its Own Image: The Trengganu Experience 1881–1941*, in which he concluded that the Malay ruling elites not only adjusted to, but also adapted parts of the evolving capitalist instruments to appropriate personal profits. This chapter follows such an enquiry to shed more light on how the traditional ruling class integrated itself into capitalist business.

S. S. Raja (✉)
Faculty of Arts and Social Sciences, University of Malaya,
Kuala Lumpur, Malaysia
e-mail: siva@um.edu.my

R. Rasiah et al. (eds.), *Contesting Malaysia's Integration into the World Economy*, https://doi.org/10.1007/978-981-16-0650-2_7

It is widely acknowledged that during the late nineteenth and twentieth centuries the British pursued their economic interests in the Malay states, which was explicitly reflected in the mining and agricultural sectors in which Asians of different classes were treated differently and, in some cases, in a discriminatory manner. For example, in July 1904, the United Planters Association of the Federated Malay States (FMS) requested the High Commissioner to restrict Asian holdings to two or three miles apart in order to avoid their occupation of too much road frontage so as not to make the land behind owned by European planters less attractive (Drabble, 1972/1973: 25). Accordingly, in 1905, H. C. Belfield, the Selangor Resident, had instructed that land with road frontage shall not be sold to smallholders (Drabble, 1972/1973: 25). The decision undoubtedly demonstrates the FMS administration's policy of discouraging local Asian smallholders from negatively affecting the interests of European investors. In fact, several laws were enacted prohibiting Malay peasants from becoming capitalists. Most significant among them were the Malay Reservations Enactment (1913) and the FMS Rice Land Enactment (1917), which were applied largely on Malay and Asian commoners. The Malay aristocrats were among the Asian classes that the British administration did not handle in a negligent manner.[1] Indeed, the two groups seemed to have established cordial business ties, particularly in the agricultural and mining sectors.

Using a number of case studies, this chapter seeks to explore the relations that the British established with the Malay aristocrats, how both parties gained from such relationships, and how the aristocrats managed to uphold their business demands. By deconstructing the capitalist ventures of the Malay aristocrats, the study will attempt to identify the primary benefactors, sources of capital, and those who benefited from such relationships. In doing so, the chapter attempts to shed light on the extent to which capitalism took root among traditional ruling classes in Britain's evolving colonial economic structure in Malaya over the colonial period until 1941.

[1] Aristocrats refer to the rulers and chiefs of the Malay states.

Malay Aristocrats' Business Dealings in the Malay States

Active Malay rulers' participation in business activities in the Malay states can be traced back to the second half of the nineteenth century, which is also known as the age of New Imperialism when efforts were made by the British administrators to assist their participation in agricultural and mining ventures.[2] In some states, the aristocrats engaged Chettiar money lenders to obtain financial services for the cultivation of rubber, paddy, and the leasing of mining land. While the Malays were not encouraged to pursue capitalist ventures, special consideration was allocated to the Malay aristocrats by the FMS administration in order to ensure un-resisted indirect control over the protectorate-fashioned Malay states. Consequently, this chapter examines a number of case studies in the Malay states from the time of British intervention to the Japanese occupation in 1941 to establish the thesis that the Malay aristocrats were encouraged by the British to engage in business.

The extant literature on Malay rulers deals mainly with their role during colonial decentralization in the 1920s and 1930s, the constitutional changes during the formation of the Malayan Union and the Federation of Malaya, which primarily deal with how the rulers responded to British colonialism, the establishment of the Malayan Union, the Malay protest, and their position thereafter. In fact, Gullick (1985: 64) wrote extensively on the subject of the Malay rulers, stating expressly that:

> It is much more difficult to trace the story of Malay trade and mining through this period [British Rule] since British administrators were much less concerned with it and say little of it in their records.

Also, it is generally believed that the ruling class of Malaya had adjusted to a new position in the civil service of the colonial administration and that very few had gone into the business sector. In contrast, many Malay aristocrats had the penchant to be successful in business, especially jointly with Chinese entrepreneurs and Chettiars. The evidence I provide from

[2] see Loh (2002) for an understanding on the policy environment of the colonial state in Malaya with regard to business between 1874 and 1945, and Bach (1976) on the historical patterns of capital penetration.

the Federated Malay States and in the Unfederated Malay state of Kedah in the subsequent sections will show that business ventures involving the Malay aristocrats did grow in colonial Malaya.

Business Activities Before Intervention

Some studies on the history of Malay economic activities prior to British intervention depict the Malays as a subsistence population, primarily focused on planting paddy, without any inclination to engage in commercial activities (e.g., Kaur, 1989; Lim, 1977; Winstedt, 1981; Shaharil 1981, 1985; Wan Hashim, 1988). However, other researchers have shown that this is not the case as there were instances of aristocrats and even ordinary Malays participating in business ventures. Gullick (1985) and Azmi (1996) have shown in their works that Malays engaged in business before British intervention, which became clear when Singapore was developed as a free port, and products from the Malay States were exported to other parts of the world. For example, Khoo (1972) examined the importance of these developments. Also, Cant (1973) indicated how the Malay subsistence economy collapsed when Singapore's demand for jungle produce and alluvial gold rose. Furthermore, Gullick (1987) found Malaya's economy to be only partly self-sufficient as colonialization witnessed the introduction of Western capitalism, and thus, the integration of the Southeast Asian economy into the trading links of the global economy (see also Azmi, 1996: 229). From then onwards, Malay economic life, including that of aristocrats and peasants, experienced a steady but radical change toward commercialization.

Before intervention by the British in 1874, several studies show that Malays were involved in large-scale business activities. For example, Winstedt (1981) believed that Malays were engaged in mining activities in the states of Malacca, Pahang, Johor, Klang, Perak, and Sungai Ujong in the fifteenth century (Winstedt, 1981). This was especially true during Dutch rule, when the Malay rulers signed treaties with the Dutch to sell their tin only to them and not to the English or other traders. In 1642, for example, a treaty was signed between the Dutch and the Sultan of Kedah stipulating that tin could only be sold to the Dutch at the price decided by the Dutch (Arasaratnam, 1979: 483). In the same year, the Dutch signed a treaty with Johore (Kathirithamby-Wells, 1980: 50). In Perak, Sultan Muzaffar Shah III (1728–1756) and Sultan Muhammad Shah (1764–1773) were forced to sign treaties with the Dutch whereby the Sultan agreed to sell tin at the price decided by the Dutch. In 1758, through a treaty, the ruler of Rembau was compelled to sell tin to the Dutch in Malacca. Although the Dutch forced the Malay rulers to sell the tin at prices dictated by them, there were many occasions when the latter sold it to British country traders/private traders who offered higher prices.[3] The business activities of the Malay aristocrats in the state of Selangor could be seen in the 1840s when Sultan Abdul Samad of Selangor (1857–1898) and Raja Abdullah (1874–1877) opened mines in the Klang Valley by borrowing $30,000 from Chinese financiers in Malacca (Gullick, 1953: 93). Sultan Abdul Samad was said to have a tin hoard worth $100,000, while he also invested in new tin mines in Ulu Langat and a tapioca estate owned by Yap Ah Loy.

Business Activities After Intervention

British intervention that began in Perak in 1874 saw changes in the structure of state administration (Nonini, 1992: 48). Prior to intervention, the Malay rulers enjoyed absolute authority, but had to share power with their chiefs, who controlled fiefdoms and the right to impose taxes, *corvee* and military service on the Malay peasants (Cheah, 1994). In some cases, the territorial chiefs were wealthier than the Sultan, and the Sultan controlled only the royal district where he resided (Bach, 1976: 469). With the appointment of the British Resident, the system changed dramatically as the District Officer he appointed acted on internal matters, including that of the state's revenue, which is to be collected in the name of Sultan. This was in contrast to the earlier practice where the chiefs collected and kept the revenues obtained in their respective districts (Smith, 1994: 85). An European District Officer, that emerged as a new layer of state administration, oversaw the appointment of the village *penghulu* and acted as their supervisor. Under the new system, the ruler and the *penghulu* remained Malay, but British officers now replaced the once powerful district chiefs. The sudden changes were, at some point, considered too invasive with the

[3] According to Arasaratnam (1979: 160), "A great deal of energy was expended in the second half of the seventeenth century in entering into trading contracts with rulers of various tin producing states of the region requiring the sale, at fixed prices, of all, or a stipulated share of produce of tin in each state. But it had been clearly established by recent studies that these treaties produced little results and were often breached soon after they were signed." According to Bassett (1965: 95), between 1786 and 1874, every Malay Ruler tried to establish friendship with the East India Company.

potential of undermining the British colonial administration, which relied primarily on the political support of the Malay ruling class. That is why the British tried to train the Malay aristocrats into the junior arm of colonial service and attach them to land offices with the duty of demarcating land, collecting rent, and inspecting mines, paddy fields, and orchards (Sadka, 1968: 279). When the British were able to win the confidence of the Malay aristocrats, they passed laws governing land use, creating tenure, and registering land titles. Specialist departments (surveys, lands and mines, customs, treasury, etc.) were also established to undertake these activities, which contributed to the bureaucratization of the Malay aristocracy (Amoroso, 2014: 64).

To administer the government, State Councils were formed, first in Selangor and in 1887 in Perak and later in the other protected Malay States to introduce the ruling class to the process of consultation and governance (Gullick, 1991: 4). This helped to retain the traditional authority of the Malay rulers. The councils also had a Chinese and European representative to promote their interests and advise the government on developments on the ground. In short, the British set up an administration in which the Malay rulers were able to pursue their needs and retain their traditional authority.

However, the Sultans and Chiefs had to comply with the advice of the Resident, while the British determined their incomes with some fixed allowances, which limited the autonomy they had enjoyed prior to British intervention as they had then collected taxes on their subjects, the Chinese and capital investors. In order to avert potential reactions from the loss of power, the British encouraged the Malayan aristocrats to participate in business ventures. Allowances were a sensitive issue for the Malay aristocrats whose way of life was significantly altered by the introduction of Victorian ideals following British intervention. They had several demands, including, to have more than one household, several dependents, several wives and dependents, to support their subjects. They needed at least $100,000 (Straits dollars) annually, but this was not forthcoming (Amoroso, 2014: 74). Their revenue prior to intervention was through import duties on opium and spirits, as well as export duties on paddy and tin. Upon the appointment of a British Resident, the aristocrats lost this source of income, except from privately held businesses (Amoroso, 2014: 75) as state revenues were now distinguished from the personal allowances of the ruler. This was the reason why the Malay rulers frequently petitioned for their allowances to be increased, which they regarded as reasonable because they needed more money to carry out new activities and lifestyles under British rule. The new functions included entertaining British dignitaries, official trips to the center of British administration in Singapore and London, as well as the need to educate their children in English schools. In addition, they had to entertain foreign guests, equip their *istana* (palace) with European furniture, use new modes of transport, such as steamships, yachts, and horse-drawn carriages. Additionally, they had to be active in religious events and make charitable contributions. Rulers also had to take charge of the upkeep of their children, palace officials, guards, servants, and watchmen.

In Perak, the British granted the chiefs and *penghulus* the right to draw up a 10% tax (*chabut*) on duty paid on all goods exported from their districts (Sadka, 1968: 281), which provided the opportunity for the Malay chiefs and *penghulus* to generate wealth from the economic expansion of the Kinta district. The huge tax revenue collected from mining by the Malay chiefs and *penghulus* in the Kuala Kangsar, Batang Padang, and Kinta districts offered them massive wealth to invest in large-scale mining and real estate trading. State laws stipulated that the Malay owners of ancestral mines were entitled to royalties (*hasil tanah*) on tin obtained from the mines. In 1899, the royalty on tin from ancestral mines was estimated at $5500 and the *chabut* to *penghulus* was valued at $40,398 ($33,940 from the Kinta district alone). The royalty enjoyed by private mines was estimated at $2400 in 1893, but the *penghulus*' *chabut* was valued at $74,000 ($70,000 from Kinta alone). In 1894, the *chabut* paid to each individual was limited (the largest allowance of $900 a month was allocated to Dato Panglima Kinta, To Muda Wahab and the assistant penghulu of Ulu Kinta). The total amount was estimated at $48,360 (Sadka, 1968: 281). The amount paid in Kinta alone added up to $30,252 in 1888 and $41,264 in 1889. There were ten recipients: the Sultan, the Panglima Kinta, the *penghulus* of Sungei Raya, Papan, Sungai Trap, Kuala Teja, Teja and Kampar; the assistant *Penghulu*, Ulu Kinta, and Raja Drahman. In 1889, the largest sums were paid to the *penghulus* of Papan ($7332) and Sungai Trap ($7560) (Sadka, 1968: 281).

From the wealth acquired from mining ventures, the chiefs and *penghulus* built large villas in Ipoh and other mining townships, invested in houses and shops, and engaged in mining operations in partnership with Chinese miners. They also tried to exploit the transport difficulties of the Kinta miners by renting out elephants at exorbitant prices (Sadka, 1968: 282).

There were also other Malay aristocrats active in business activities in the nineteenth century. Gullick (1985) highlighted a few individuals who were involved in large-scale business following the colonial intervention. Sultan Abdul Samad of Selangor was said to have held tin ingots and silver dollars in his palace in Kuala Langat, which were used as resources to support paddy planters in his state. There were 400 ancestral mines in the Kinta Valley in 1888 (Gullick, 1985: 64), which suggests that Malay aristocrats must have owned them, and that they were very much involved in mining activities.

Azmi (1996) revealed that when Hugh Low, the first British Resident of Perak visited Selama, Perak from 4 to 6, May 1877, he granted Abdul Karim bin Ibrahim, a retired clerk of Che Long Jaafar and Ngah Ibrahim, a tin mining concession. In February 1874, around 1000 Chinese workers were recorded to have worked at that mine. Karim was given a monopoly on the import and sale of opium, though it was under Chinese control before 1877. Hugh Low was appreciative of Karim's initiative, stating that

> … his enterprise is very unusual and very praiseworthy in a Malay state and on the whole his settlement is a flourishing as could be expected under the adverse circumstances caused by the fall of price in tin.[4]

Among the evidence in the state of Perak on the participation of Malay aristocrats in plantation and mining enterprises was *penghulu* Syed Musa of Chigar Galah, who in 1880 obtained a loan of $8000 from the government of Perak to plant 16 acres of pepper using Achinese and Javanese labour (Gullick, 1985: 65). He also traveled to Penang to sell his products. It was said that this was a move by Hugh Low to draw foreign investors to Perak. He felt that by demonstrating that the locals were successful, he would be able to draw European investors (Gullick, 1985: 65).

In the 1860s, Kulop Rheo was said to have owned two tin mines in Gopeng, Perak, which were run by Chinese and Malay miners. Apparently, he received one tenth of the output of tin from each of the mines. He was also reported to have worked at Sultan Ismail's mine in Papan with 400 Malay miners (Burns, 1986: 64). In 1884, 500 mines were opened in the Kinta Valley and the Malay aristocracy owned 350 of them (Hale, 1885: 35). Ngah Ibrahim was another individual who was very

[4] Azmi (1996; cited from Sadka, 1954: 49–53).

much involved in tin mining in Larut, Perak. His income from the sale of tin in 1882 alone was valued at $180,000. He also owned bullock carts and ships (Burns, 1986: 66).

Another example of Malay aristocrats' involvement in business is the irrigation project in Krian, Perak. The Malay chiefs were said to have invested on a large scale in this irrigation work. The dam was 780 feet long, costing $40,000 (Gullick, 1985: 65). It was projected to provide irrigation water to 2000 acres of land. The Sultan ventured into this because he wanted his subjects to take up government land to cultivate paddy and, in return, pay him a small sum for the use of the water.

Business Activities Since the Federation Was Formed

The formation of the Federation in 1896 saw the four Malay states of Perak, Selangor, Negeri Sembilan, and Pahang brought under a union known as the Federated Malay States, which accelerated the arrival of investors with the state having a big role to play in attracting investors.[5] The Malay rulers adjusted well to the new situation, while the British did not deter them from engaging in mining and agricultural enterprises. Their participation in business activities was inevitable, as the Federation's establishment had their allowance reduced. Allowing them to engage in business enterprises was one solution to that problem. Furthermore, during this time, the state was required to contribute revenue to the federal coffers and it was difficult for the state to pay salaries to the aristocrats. Many cases in the state of Perak, Selangor, and Pahang bear testimony to this. Following the formation of the Federation, the British encouraged the Chettiars to lend money to the Malay aristocrats whose salaries and pensions were neither sufficient to finance their economic activities nor to sustain their extravagant lifestyle.

There were a number of cases where the Malay aristocrats borrowed money from the Chettiars. These include a loan of $11,350 that the Raja Muda of Perak took from Raman Chetty, a $7500 loan that the Yam Tuan of Negri Sembilan took from Muthiah Chetty, a loan of $1600 that Sultan Abdullah obtained from Vengadasalam Chetty, and a $251 loan

[5] See Raja (2018) for a detailed account of British involvement in agriculture and mining activities in the FMS.

that the Tunku Laksamana of Perak took from R. M. P. Suprama Niar Chetty (Suppiah & Raja, 2016: 59–60). The British allowed this as they were not in a position to help them sustain such a lifestyle that had to be maintained as one of the ways to retain their social status. They were therefore naturally inclined to borrow money from Chettiars, who practiced a liberal form of money lending. The liberal form of money lending refers to a simple procedure in granting a loan. The client was known as *maral* and the introducer was known as *maralder*. The word moral literally means "through or on contract basis." Through this method, the Chettiars did not require a guarantor or witness. The lending process was rather simple and fast. Malay aristocrats who borrowed money from Chettiars included government officials, members of the royalty, chiefs, village headmen and subordinate officers, and those who served in the British administration. Three cases are discussed to demonstrate the role of Malay aristocrats in business activities that engaged the Chettiars during the British Administration.

Pahang

Under colonial rule, the state of Pahang was mainly known for agriculture and mining, with coffee, coconut, tapioca, paddy, and rubber as the main crops. Several trade syndicates were involved in these cultivation and mining activities, the main being Liang Syndicate (coffee) in 1897; Messrs. Price, Boustead and Company (coconut) in 1900; Duff Coconut Plantation (coconut) in 1901; and Bibby and Ruxton (rubber) in 1905. The total acreage for all crops expanded each year, adding to state revenues mainly through land tax. Tin and gold were also mined extensively in Pahang. Prior to British intervention, Pahang was known for its rich mineral resources, such as gold and tin. The mines were first worked by the Malays, and subsequently by the Chinese and Europeans. Tin deposits were vigorously mined in the Ulu Tembeling district, and gold was mined in the Raub region. Pahang shipped 830,666 pounds of sterling gold in the early twentieth century (Fermor, 1940: 43).

Concession

The state of Pahang witnessed the involvement of the Sultan and aristocrats in business ventures. This was noticeable even before the British rule, and persisted until intervention in 1888. Prior to British intervention Sultan Ahmad (1881–1909) granted 39 concessions for the mining, planting, and logging ranging from two to several thousand square miles (Thio, 1969: 128). The Sultan was awarded a 10% mining royalty. The granting of concessions to foreigners helped to reinforce the financial position of the Sultan, *Bendahara*, and the other chiefs. The *Bendahara* benefited from the issue of *surat kuasa* and *titah* to concessionaires and minor chieftains (Gopinath, 1991: 58).

The chiefs saw the concessions as a means of enriching themselves. In one particular instance, the Kuantan Company had to pay $20,000 to the Bendahara for the extension of its lease and Hae Sing paid $10,000 to To' Gajah to start business in Pahang (Gopinath, 1991: 58). Sultan Ahmad was also involved in Pahang Corporation, which offered him 10% of its revenue annually (Gopinath, 1991: 77). For the Sultan, foreign investment helped him offset the loss of income that he had incurred, and thus, demanded a monthly allowance of $1000 from each of the firms. In 1887, the concessions granted by the Sultan were as follows:

Concessionaires	*Location*
Penjum Company	100 sq. miles in Lipis
Penjum Company	100 sq. miles in Semantan
Knaggs, Gowen, and Cameron	From the Penjum boundary to Kuala Telam
Mr. Davidson	Telam
Syed Muhammed Alsagof	Tanum, Chika, Kichau, and Raub
Syed Junid	A further concession in Jelai
Hae Sing	Bera and Trusang in Lipis
Mr. Watson	4 miles × 4 miles Semantan
Seah Song Seah	2 rivers in Semantan
Tuan Ho	2 rivers in Semantan
Tungku Usman	100 sq. miles to be selected

Source Gopinath (1991: 79)

Under British rule, the concessions were recognized but would be canceled if no work were done within the five-year period that had been allotted to prove their ability to work. It should also be mentioned that Pahang was a less well-off state and the Straits Settlements had to borrow money to support Pahang, which amounted to $610,000 in 1891 as the annual revenue of the state in that year was a mere $77,586 (Thio, 1969: 128–129). The new state of affairs after British rule began made the ruler's position problematic. With the Residential System, his allowance was capped at $18,000 per year, which was close to that of the Sultan of Perak and Selangor in addition to concession payments that were continued. The Sultan had demanded that the British raise his allowance from $1500 to $2000, and it was honored. It should be noted that the Sultan's net income before British intervention was $29,520 (Gopinath, 1991: 105). The examples above are strong evidence of Malay aristocrats' involvement in business before and after colonial rule. After the Federation was formed, the British encouraged them to undertake business to supplement their allowances.

The Pahang Corporation

The case of Pahang Corporation versus the Sultans is a testament to the kind of problem that the Malay rulers encountered as a result of their involvement in business affairs. The Pahang Corporation, in its letter dated February 28, 1896, highlighted the problem of the acquisition of concessions in the Kuantan and Rompin districts. The concessionaires, H. H. Cozens-Hardy and T. T. Paine, claimed that they were unable to enjoy the tenancy granted to them in Kuantan for the duration of 80 years, as promised in the concession. The difficulty they were faced was that the Sultan began imposing rules as he pleased. They wanted the concession issue to be directly connected to the mining regulations promulgated subsequently. This, according to them, would prevent the Malay rulers from behaving unreasonably. The Sultan insisted on his constitutional privileges in all aspects of internal affairs. Both Cozens-Hardy and Paine were of the view that the solution to the problem was then with the Colonial Office.[6]

The Pahang Corporation case represented the problem faced by the Western enterprise in their relationship with local rulers, who were likely to enforce rules and regulations as they preferred. The Resident, the Resident-General, or the High Commissioner in Singapore could not solve the issue. Subsequently, they had to bring the matter to the Colonial Office in London. The Colonial Office in London eventually decided that the land had to be granted to the Sultan based on his terms because the colonial authorities were unable to increase his allowances. This is a clear case that the wishes of the Malay sovereigns had to be met because the British were unable to pay their allowances. This was not the case in Pahang alone but even in the other Malay states where the colonial

[6] "Concession of the Corporation in the Kuantan and Rompin Districts," High Commissioner's Office (HCO), 2456/1896.

authorities could not afford to increase the allowance paid to the Malay rulers.

Sultan of Pahang's Application of Mining Land

There were also issues with Sultan's right to purchase land as he desired. This was the case with the Pahang Sultan's application for mining land in the state on November 10, 1900. The Sultan's request was not approved, following which he complained the payment he had requested had not been granted.[7] The Sultan questioned why the Resident had allowed him to acquire only 640 acres of unalienated land, and not all of Sungai Semantan from Kuala Lumpur to the Ulu, and even the tributaries to the right and left of Sungai Chika. The Sultan stressed the following point:

> I am pleased that the British Government should come into Pahang, my country, and put it properly in order and bring justice into it, but not that they should refuse my reasonable request. On account of that my large country is ready to receive companies, and the Government is collecting rent from those I promoted formerly. In my opinion there is nothing to hinder my being personally given the two small rivers I ask for I submit this matter to my friend with my hopes that he will quickly comply with my request, should he be unable to grant what I ask in this letter, I must write fully and appeal to the Justice of the English Government. (High Commissioner's Office (HCO) 1081/1901)

According to a common understanding between the Resident-General and the Resident, if the Sultan were to be allocated 640 acres of land as promised, he would no longer be entitled to receive his regular allowance of $12,000 per year. Since the Sultan was awarded an increment in allowance amounting to $36,000 per year, he should not have applied for the grant of land as well. It is interesting to note that the British administrators doubted that the Sultan was interested in the land because he had intended to sell it to capitalists in Singapore.[8] The Acting Resident-General stated that the Sultan's payment was drawn from the public funds of Pahang. He stressed that the funds were not even adequate to support the extensive development of the state's resources and had to be supplemented by loans from the neighboring state of Selangor; Pahang had

[7] "Sultan of Pahang's Request for Mining Land," HCO, 1081/1901.

[8] Letter from Acting Resident-General to High Comissioner, November 30, 1900.

already been indebted for almost $3 million. The whole reason why the British wanted to grant private land or mining land to the Sultan was to enable him to collect personal revenues like the Sultan of Perak.

The Pahang case shows the altercations between a Malay ruler whose state expenses were increasingly falling short of the revenue collected, as well as his efforts to raise his own allowances that drove the ruler into business activities. The Malay rulers were audacious enough to demand their rights from the British officials. It shows that the Malay rulers were not merely the figureheads or puppet rulers under the British, as claimed by some scholars (Shamsul, 2004: 19).[9] In his letter of December 29, 1900, the High Commissioner strongly felt that the British officials in the state were unfair to the Sultan and that he had been deceived.[10]

Mining Interest in Selangor

On March 21, 1905, the Sultan of Pahang made an application to the District Officer (DO) for 35 acres of mining land in Ulu Selangor.[11] The Sultan made two applications for mining land and hoped that they should be considered as special cases considering that the mining application books had been closed and that the District Office would not accept any further applications. The DO was hesitant to accept this as a special case and did not see why the Sultan's application should be handled differently. When the matter was brought to the attention of the Resident, he objected to the decision of the DO and requested that the application be approved as a special case and that the books be opened for him.[12] The mining land was approved by the DO on March 30, 1905. This case demonstrates that the British authorities made provisions to help the Malay rulers to engage in business as a means to appease them, while such privileges were not provided to Chinese and Indian capitalists.

[9] Shamsul, in his work (2004), claims that when the British took control of the administration in the Malay states, the Sultans and chiefs became figureheads.

[10] J. A. Swettenham, High Commissioner of FMS to the Acting Resident-General, W. H. Treacher dated 29 December 1900 in "The Highness The Sultan of Pahang's Application for Mining Land," File Pahang 1771/1900, Arkib Negara Malaysia (ANM) 1957/0582546.

[11] Application from His Highness the Sultan of Pahang for mining Land in Ulu Selangor, March 21, 1905, file 1684/1905, Selangor Secretariat, ANM 1957/0121734.

[12] Letter from Secretary to the Resident to District Officer (DO), Ulu Selangor dated March 29, 1905.

Selangor

After intervention in 1874, the British Government encouraged agriculture in Selangor and the initial crops included Liberian coffee, coconut, pepper, and *gambier*. European planters were the pioneers who focused extensively on Liberian coffee. The increase in agricultural produce in Selangor was also due to incentives provided by the government, such as the granting of favorable terms to land, the provision of financial assistance, and the introduction of legislations, such as the Selangor Land Code 1891, which required all land-related transactions to be registered in the local land office. The registration allowed landed properties to be purchased legally, thus providing the legal means by which the cultivation of rice could be expanded through irrigation works. The founding of the Selangor Planters' Association in 1892, aimed at protecting the rights of planters, was a significant step in the development of agriculture. The establishment of the Department of Agriculture in the Federated Malay States (FMS), in 1905 was an important indicator of the government's commitment to agriculture (Grist, 1950: 27–28). Mining, particularly tin mining, was extensively carried out in the districts of Ulu Bernam, Ulu Selangor, Klang, and Ulu Langat.

The other districts that were also known for mining were situated in the Klang Valley. The most productive mines were found at Sungai Puteh, Ulu Arang, Ulu Klang, and Petaling (Wong, 1965: 101–102). A number of mining companies were involved in tin mining, including The Malay Peninsula (East India) Malay States Mining Company (1873), Rawang Tin Company Limited (1884), and the Malay States Tin Mining Company. The British Government boosted productivity through free movement of capital and labor; the development of private businesses and enhanced communications infrastructure. In the early twentieth century, tin mining produced $3,357,033 in revenue, and the total area of land alienated for mining amounted to 68,000 acres (Wong, 1965: 104–105). Alongside these developments, in many instances, the commercial interests of the Malay aristocrats in Selangor could be observed. Two years after the Federation was established, the Resident wrote to the Sultan to interview him on state business.[13] Below are a number of cases that show Sultan's involvement in business affairs.

[13] Interview with Sultan on State Business—Asks to Fix Place, Selangor Secretariat File 1886/1896 dated April 25, 1898, ANM 1957/0076860.

Application for Mining Land in Rawang

On January 21, 1919, Sultan Suleiman Shah of Selangor, applied for 100 acres of mining land in the Forest Reserve of Rawang. The land came under the district of Rawang and Sungai Chin Chin. The Resident had little opposition and so approved the application. The decision was taken on January 23, 1919 and then submitted to the State Secretariat. The Resident indicated to the Secretariat that the Sultan already had a mining permit of over 100 acres on either side of the town of the Chin-Chin River.[14]

Sultan's Application for Prospecting Rights

There was another case in which on November 15, 1911 the Sultan applied for prospecting rights over 300 acres of land in the Mukim of Peretak in Kuala Kubu.[15] The District Officer did not grant the right to mine here because he felt that it would cause harm to the *dusun* (orchard) inhabited by the Sakai. The evidence presented shows that the Sultan was actively seeking to control mining and agricultural enterprises in the state.

Royal Families' Application for Business Loans

On May 5, 1918, Raja Haji Osman b. Raja Yahya from Klang made an application, on behalf of Tengku Maheran, for a loan of $1000 from the Resident of Selangor to clear his rubber estate at Bukit Tempurung in Mukim Klang.[16] The land amounted to 22 acres but only 14 acres were planted with rubber while the rest were vacant.[17] The Tengku Maheran was willing to settle the loan at a rate of $20 a month. The application was not approved on the ground that the Sultan had no grant title to the land as he was merely granted permission to occupy the land. Although the grant was not given, this incident suggests that the Sultan was very much involved in rubber planting business in the state.

[14] Application for 100 Acres of Mining Land in Forest Reserve in the Mukim of Rawang by His Higness the Sultan of Selangor, Selangor Secretariat File, 434/1919—ANM 1957/0203298.

[15] Letter from Sultan to District Officer, Ulu Selangor, Selangor Secretariat File S24/1911—ANM 1957/0160316.

[16] Application on behalf of Tengku Maheran Bin Suleiman for a loan of $1000, Selangor Secretariat File, 1869/1919—ANM 1957/0199714.

[17] Letter from Tengku Maheran to Resident signed on behalf of Raja Haji Osman b. Raja Yahya in Selangor Secretarit File 1869/1918—ANM 1957/0199714.

Perak

The state of Perak also saw the Sultan's involvement in business. It is not surprising, as Perak was one of the states that drew large numbers of investors after the Federation was formed in 1896. In that year, Perak was added to the FMS, and then onwards, the state witnessed considerable changes in the introduction of Western administrative practices and an expansion of infrastructure, which in turn attracted investors both from within and outside the state. Agricultural crops were grown on a wide scale: sugar cane, *gambier*, tapioca, coffee, pepper, paddy, and rubber were the main crops cultivated. In 1884, special rules for planting *gambier* and pepper were introduced in Perak. In the 1890s, tapioca was cultivated in a small scale in the Matang district; however, this was rather short-lived. By the end of 1896, 35,000 acres of land in the state had been in the possession of European coffee growers (Jackson, 1968: 191). Paddy cultivation too attracted the interest of planters, and in 1895, 8000 new land leases were issued for paddy planting which in turn resulted in a settled population and stable revenue for the state of Perak.

Mining, especially of tin and to a less extent, gold, was also carried out in Perak. The Bukit Mas Mining Company was involved in gold mining in the Batang Padang District in 1897 and was the only quartz gold mine in Perak. Its output in 1897 was 1100 ounces, in 1989, 22,200 ounces and in 1909 14,888 ounces (Fermor, 1940: 43). The first European tin mining company in the state was the Societe des Mines d' Etains de Perak (1883), which was soon followed by among others, by the Melbourne Tin-Mining Company (1888), Sandhurst Mining Company, Larut Tin-Mining Company, Gopeng Consolidated Mines, Tekka Mines, Kinta Tin Mines, Tambun Company, Gopeng Hydraulic, Kampar Company and Tronoh Limited (Yip, 1969: 97). The amount of tin exported from Perak in 1890 was 237,000 *pikuls* (1 *pikul* is the equivalent of 60.5 kg). In 1899 it increased to 319,000 *pikuls* (Yip, 1969: 61). The increase in the production of tin and gold was induced by the signing of the Pangkor Treaty of 1874 and the subsequent establishment of British administration in Perak; the introduction of dredging; the granting of special concessions to Western capitalists; as well as legislation including the Mining Code of 1895 and the Mining Law of 1899.

Sultan's Application for Agricultural Land

On August 3, 1910, Raja Alang Iskandar bin Sultan Idris of Perak applied for 27.5 acres of agricultural land in the Ampang Mukim.[18] Raja Alang applied to the Collector of Land Revenue, Kuala Lumpur for this land to cultivate rubber. The Collector was not willing to authorize his application because the value of the land had gone up and he felt the said land might be needed as a residential site.[19] While the Sultan failed to obtain the approval for the land, the fact remains that he had applied for a business venture and this is an indication that members of the Perak aristocrats were actively seeking to participate in business.

The Chettiars and the Malay Aristocracy[20]

> The Malay aristocrats were also involved in taking loans from the Chettiars. The loans were taken for various purposes. The main purpose was to supplement their allowances and pensions, which could not meet their daily expenses. It was also done to finance their economic activities, such as rubber and mining. Women in the Kedah royal family used the land as capital for rice cultivation. Besides, it was also meant for building houses, to purchase jewellery, silk, cars, and wedding expenses. It was also to maintain their feudal practice, such as cockfighting, keeping concubines, receiving and entertaining guests, bribery, spending sprees, and banquets. A large number of aristocrats who were village chiefs borrowed money to cover various expenses for their role in society, such as entertainment of invited guests and villagers who constantly came to their home with various complaints and requests for help. It was also meant to meet food expenses of officials visiting districts for feasts at the end of Ramadan, death expenses of persons without family and for giving large donations as a means of keeping up their status as role models. (Suppiah & Raja, 2016: 62–63)

There were also a number of Malay aristocrats who borrowed money from the Chettiar for agricultural purposes in Perak. In 1903, Raman Chetty

[18] Application from Raja Alang Iskandar bin Sultan Idris of Perak for 27 and half acres of agricultural land in Ampang Mukim on August 3, 1910, Selangor Secretariat File 3446/1910—ANM 1957/0152840.

[19] Collector to Secretary to Resident, Selangor, August 3, 1910.

[20] For a detailed study on Chettiars economic activities in Malaya, refer Suppiah and Raja (2016, 2020).

granted a loan of $11,350 to the Raja Muda of Perak with agricultural and mining land as security (Selangor Secretariat File (SSF) 3624: 1903). The Raja Muda also borrowed $25,000 from Selangor, pledging 27 acres of his rubber land to the Chettiars. The royalty also invested heavily in landed properties, such as houses.

Kedah

The Malay aristocrat's involvement in business could also be seen in the state of Kedah during the reign of Sultan Abdul Hamid Shah (1864–1943). Wan Mohd Saman the Chief Minister of Kedah, also a successful capitalist, constructed the Terusan Wan Mat Saman, a 22-mile long, 24-feet wide, and 5-feet deep canal, in the mid-1880s, to provide water for irrigation purposes (Sharom, 1970: 5). By doing so, he was able to transform barren swampland into a huge fields of rice cultivation that attracted large numbers of Malay settlers. He was said to have obtained royal concession on land adjacent to both sides of the canal and sold it to settlers (Gullick, 1985: 65). He was permitted to sell the land to the prospective settlers at a fixed rate of $3 per *relong* and could charge an annual rent of 50 cents per *relong*. Wan Mat Saman's success encouraged other Malay aristocrats applying concessions from the Sultan to construct canals, including Wan Yunus, the Magistrate District of Kota Star, Tuanku Minah (a member of the Royal Family) and Syed Osman (the territorial chief of the Yen district) (Sharom, 1970: 5).

Besides him, there were a number of others who borrowed money from the Chettiars for business purposes, including some female members of the Malay aristocracy. Even notable political figures, such as Tunku Abdul Rahman, who later became Prime Minister of the Federation of Malaya, borrowed money from the Chettiars. It was said that he borrowed some $4,636.58 with land as security, when he was serving as the District Officer of Kulim in 1935.[21] The Tunku also frequently received financial support from his mother, Che Manjalara, who borrowed money from Karuppiah Chettiar (Mahani, 2005: 119). It is evident that members of Kedah's Malay aristocracy encountered financial problems due to inadequate salaries and pensions that could not cover the cost of their lavish lifestyle.

[21] Letter from the Office of the State Secretariat to the Sultan of Kedah, 6 December 1933, File 4159/1353.

A significant number of the aristocrats borrowed money from the Chettiar for the purchase of jewels, silk, cars, land, house construction and to meet other family obligations (Mahani, 2004: 18). Che Manjalalara had offered land valued at $50,000 as a surety bond (Mahani, 2005: 119).[22] She was heavily indebted to Muthukarpen Chettiar, for shopping of textiles, fuel, metal appliances, and jewellery and, more importantly, for the purchase of landed property. As a matter of fact, Che Manjalara was one of the richest women among the royal family owing to her business of renting premises and paddy fields to Chinese capitalists.

A large number of Malay village chiefs too borrowed money from the Chettiar to cover the expenses to meet their social obligations, which were incurred mainly due to handouts of food and materials to their followers and village folk (Kratoska, 1984: 44–45). Due to this social obligation and increased regular spending, in addition to the fact that their demands for higher allowances were never met by the British, they had no choice but to borrow money from the Chettiar.

The Malay aristocrats also borrowed money from the Chettiar to finance their economic activities. A number of them borrowed by pledging land for rice cultivation, rubber plantation, and mining. They had easy access to land acquisition and ownership because, according to traditional practices, all land belonged to the Malay sultans. The State Councils regularly accepted their applications for land ownership. In Kedah, for example, the 1917 *Land Revenue Exemption Act* easily enabled the approval of 500 acres of land with a tax exemption (Mahani, 2004: 70). Therefore, the aristocrats used land as surety to obtain loans from Chettiar because the market value of the land owned by the Malay aristocrats was much higher than land owned by Malay farmers as these lands were mainly used for cultivation of crops and never left idle. Due to this reason, the Chettiar would usually loan money to the royal family.

Women in the royal family of Kedah used the land as capital for agriculture, particularly in rice cultivation, in addition to maintaining their lavish and extravagant lifestyles. Besides, land ownership was also used as a

[22] Che Manjalara was said to have incurred debts totaling $64,915 with seven Chettiar from 1930 to 1931. Her last loan was obtained by mortgaging two lots of land owned by her daughter, Tunku Habsah. Besides Muthukarpen Chettiar, Che Manjalara also often obtained loans from another Chettiar named S. N. A. R. S. Sukalingam Chettiar from Alor Setar. Of this total debt, there were two loans from Muthukarpen of $10,000 and the biggest loan totaling $28.860 with $4,329 outstanding at the time of her death. Of all of these loans, the first was for her son, Tunku Abdul Rahman (Mahani, 2004).

basis for facilitating applications for loans from the Chettiar. Besides Che Manjalara, her own daughters, Tunku Kalsom and Tunku Rokiah, also borrowed a lot of money from the Chettiar. On June 4, 1933, Tunku Kalsom's land in Kota Setar was auctioned off to settle debts owed to Kailasam Chettiar (Mahani, 2005: 131). Similarly, Tunku Rokiah incurred debts amounting to $8000 with S. L. N. Palaniappa Chettiar, which she had used for paddy cultivation (Mahani, 2005: 131).

It is evident from the examples above that Malay aristocrats in Kedah were actively involved in business affairs with capital obtained from the Chettiars. In the early stages, the British did not stop this practice because their rules made things difficult for the aristocrats. To alleviate their position, the British authorities facilitated the Chettiar to help the Malay aristocrats maintain their lavish lifestyle. The British allowed the Chettiar to loan money to the aristocrats and in turn deducted their allowances and pensions as a means to settle the debts. Thus, the Chettiar had the authority to undertake allowances and pension cuts. The absence of regulation on the part of the British led the Malay aristocrats to continue obtaining loans from the Chettiar. The Chettiar, therefore continued exercising the Power of Attorney exercised by the agents to collect debt in installments from their pensions and allowances. However, from 1905 onwards, the British no longer allowed this as a result of widespread abuse of the Power of Attorney, especially in cases where the pensions or allowances of Malay aristocrats who had passed away were still deducted for debt repayment by the Chettiars.[23] To ensure that this did not recur, the British authorized that before receiving the allowances, the village head treasurer must be present to act as witness and this was to be done in the presence of a clerk.

Nevertheless, the role of the Chettiar remained the same due to the requests from the aristocrats. To overcome this, the British enforced *The Powers of Attorney Enactment 1912*, which strictly prohibited the Chettiar from exploiting the Power of Attorney to obtain allowances from the royal family,[24] which required the holders of the Power of Attorney to obtain approval from the Resident or District Officer prior to the payment of allowances and pensions to the Chettiar. Consequently, the holders

[23] Circular, the Residents Office 1905: 68.

[24] Federated Malay States Government Order (FMS G.O.) 1921: 81.

could not act on their own discretion. Despite the legislation, the relationship between the Malay aristocrats and Chettiar remained unchanged with the Malay rulers and aristocracy frequently resorting to taking loans from the Chettiar to overcome their financial problems.

Conclusion

It is apparent from the above case studies that the Malay aristocrats were not only interested, but were also directly involved in business activities both prior to and after British intervention. Under British colonization their participation in business increased owing to both a fall in their sources of revenue collection, as well as the rising opportunities business presented by an expansion in capitalist activities. Their business-related activities stretched into mining and agriculture during British rule in both the Federated and Unfederated Malay States.

Their active involvement in business transactions was partly caused by the drastic reduction of their allowances by the British, which led the British to approve applications by the Malay aristocrats for mining and agricultural licenses without much encumbrance. In fact, special provisions were made to help with their applications. The British also facilitated the Chettiar to help the aristocrats to retain their lavish lifestyle, especially by approving deductions from their allowances and pensions. In doing so, this chapter has provided sufficient evidence to show that capitalist penetration helped transform the way the Malay ruling elites adapted themselves to the evolving colonial economy.

References

Amoroso, D. J. (2014). *Traditionalism and ascendancy of the Malay ruling class in colonial Malaya*. Petaling Jaya: Strategic Information and Research Development Centre.

Arasaratnam, S. (1979). Dutch commercial policy and interests in the Malay Peninsula. In B. B. Kling & M. N. Pearson (Eds.), *The age of partnership, Europeans in Asia before dominion* (pp. 1750–1795). Honolulu: The University of Hawaii.

Azmi, K. (1996). Ekonomi Malaysi Kurun ke-19: Sara Diri atau Komersil? In Badriyah Hj. Salleh & Tan Liok Eee (Eds.), *Alam Pensejarahan dari Pelbagai Perspektif*. Dewan Bahasa dan Pustaka: Kuala Lumpur.

Bach, R. L. (1976). Historical patterns of capitalist penetration in Malaysia. *Journal of Contemporary Asia, 6*, 458–476.

Bassett, D. K. (1965). Anglo-Malay relations 1865-1795. *JMBRAS, 38*(2), 183–212.

Burns, P. L. (1986). Kapitalisme dan Negeri-Negeri Melayu. *Kajian Malaysia, 4*(2), 55–74.

Cant, R. G. (1973). *An historical geography of Pahang* (JMBRAS Monograph).

Cheah, B. K. (1994). Feudalism in pre-colonial Malaya: The past as a colonial discourse. *Journal of Southeast Asian Studies, 25*(2), 243–269.

Drabble, J. H. (1972/1973). Land alienation and the first rubber boom in Malaya, 1903-1910. *Jernal Sejarah, 2*, 23–28.

Fermor, L. L. (1940). *Report upon the mining industry of Malaya*. Kuala Lumpur: Federated Malay States Government Press.

Gopinath, A. (1991). *Pahang, 1880-1933: A political history* (JMBRAS, Monograph, 18).

Grist, D. H. (1950). *An outline of Malayan agriculture*. Kuala Lumpur: Department of Agriculture, Federation of Malaya.

Gullick, J. M. (1953). A careless, heathen philosopher? *JMBRAS, 26*(1), 87–103.

Gullick, J. M. (1985). The entrepreneur in late 19th century Malay Peasant Society. *JMBRAS, 58*(1), 59–70.

Gullick, J. M. (1987). *Malay society in the late nineteenth century: The beginnings of change*. Singapore: Oxford University Press.

Gullick, J. M. (1991). The role of the Malay ruler between 1850 and 1950's. *Kajian Malaysia, 9*(2), 1–23.

Hale, A. (1885). On miners and mines in Kinta, Perak. *JSBRAS, 16*, 303–320.

Hashim, W. (1988). *Peasants under peripheral capitalism*. Bangi: Penerbit Universiti Kebangsaan Malaysia.

Jackson, J. C. (1968). *Planters and speculators*. Kuala Lumpur: University of Malaya Press.

Kathirithamby-Wells, J. (1980). The Dutch in the Straits of Malacca. In Z. A. A. Wahid (Ed.), *Glimpses of Malaysian history*. Dewan Bahasa dan Pustaka: Kuala Lumpur.

Kaur, A. (1989). The Malay Peninsula in the nineteenth century: An economic survey. *Sarjana, 4*, 69–86.

Khoo, K. K. (1972). *The Western Malay states 1850-1873: The effects of commercial development on Malay politics*. Kuala Lumpur: Oxford University Press.

Kratoska, P. H. (1984). Penghulus in Perak and Selangor: The rationalization and decline of a traditional Malay office. *JMBRAS, 57*(2), 31–59.

Lim, T. G. (1977). *Peasants and their agricultural economy in colonial Malaya*. Kuala Lumpur: Oxford University Press.

Loh, W. L. (2002). The colonial state and business: The policy environment in Malaya in the inter-war years. *Journal of Southeast Asian Studies, 33*(2), 243–256.

Mahani, M. (2004). Malay women's involvement in land ownership and the accumulation of wealth and indebtness in Kedah. *JMBRAS, 77*(1), 1–22.
Mahani, M. (2005). *Sejarah dan Sosioekenomi Wanita Melayu Kedah, 1881-1940*. Bangi: Penerbit Universiti Kebangsaan Malaysia.
Nonini, D. M. (1992). *British colonial rule and the resistance of the Malay peasantry, 1900-1957*. New Haven: Yale University Southeast Asia Studies.
Raja, S. S. (2018). *The economy of colonial Malaya*. London: Routledge.
Sadka, E. (1954). The journal of Sir Hugh Low, Perak, 1877. *JMBRAS, 27*(4), 5–108.
Sadka, E. (1968). *The protected Malay states 1874-1895*. Kuala Lumpur: University of Malaya.
Shaharil, T. (1981). Nineteenth century Kelantan: A Malay tributary state. *Jurnal Antropologi dan Sosiologi, Universiti Kebangsaan Malaysia, 9*, 43–59.
Shaharil, T. (1984). *After its own image: The Trengganu experience 1881-1941*. Kuala Lumpur: Oxford University Press.
Shaharil, T. (1985). Jentera Undang-Undang Kolonial: Suatu Alat Penembusan Kapitalisme di Desa Melayu. *Purba, 4*, 68–80.
Shamsul, A. B. (2004). *From British to Bumiputra rule: Local politics and rural development in peninsular Malaysia*. Singapore: Institute of Southeast Asian Studies.
Sharom, A. (1970). The structure of the economy of Kedah, 1879-1905. *JMBRAS, 43*(1), 1–24.
Smith, S. (1994). The rise, decline and survival of the Malay rulers during the colonial period. *Journal of Imperial and Commonwealth History, 22*(1), 84–108.
Suppiah, U., & Raja, S. S. (2016). *The Chettiar role in Malaysia's economic history*. Kuala Lumpur: University of Malaya Press.
Suppiah, U., & Raja, S. S. (2020). Peranan Golongan Aristokrat Dalam Menangani Masalah Keberhutangan Petani Melayu. In H. Hasan, N. Ashikin, & A. Halim (Eds.), *Raja dan Rakyat Berpisah Tiada*. Dewan Bahasa dan Pustaka: Kuala Lumpur.
Thio, E. (1969). *British policy in the Malay Peninsula 1880-1910*. Singapore: University of Malaya Press.
Winstedt, R. O. (1981). *The Malays—A cultural history*. Singapore: Graham Brash. Revised and updated by Tham Seong Chee in 1981.
Wong, L. K. (1965). *The Malayan tin industry to 1914*. Tucson: University of Arizona Press.
Yip, Y. H. (1969). *The development of the tin mining industry of Malaya*. Kuala Lumpur: University of Malaya Press.

CHAPTER 8

Malaysia's South Indian 'Coolies': Legacies of Imperialism, Colonial Capitalism and Racism

Viswanathan Selvaratnam

It was not by gold or silver, but by labour, that all wealth of the world was originally purchased –*Adam Smith*
The story I have to tell deals with human beings whom colonialism and its supporters treated, mistakenly, as puppets and factors of production –never as individuals –*Charles Gamba*

Introduction

The Malaysian Indian diaspora in 2020 is nearly two million or 7% of the estimated population of the country's 32.6 million people and about 80% of them are of South Indian origin. Malaysian Indians, after the Chinese, form the second largest minority community in the country. The majority of them are Tamils and a smaller number are Telugus and Malayalees. The bulk of them are third, fourth and even fifth generation descendants

V. Selvaratnam (✉)
Fellow, Malayan Institute of Economic Research (MIER), Kuala Lumpur, Malaysia

R. Rasiah et al. (eds.), *Contesting Malaysia's Integration into the World Economy*, https://doi.org/10.1007/978-981-16-0650-2_8

of 'coolie' sojourners brought under 'a new system of slavery' (Tinker, 1974) to British Malaya. These 'coolies' were recruited at the behest of Imperial Britain, then the world's leading colonial power, from the British colony of Madras Presidency (now the linguistically demarcated states of Tamil Nadu, Andhra Pradesh, Telagana, Karnatarka and Kerala) on subsistence waged indentured contracts and shipped across the Bay of Bengal to labour in servitude and surveillance in the empire's fast emerging Peninsular Malaya's colonial economy.

In Malaysia today, an estimated 800,000 descendants of the Empire's 'coolies' are categorized as one of the country's most marginalized, dispossessed communities. The predicament of the Malaysian Indian 'coolies' is not a matter of their personal choice but a legacy of British imperialism, colonialism, colonial capitalism and racism. For colonial capitalism, colonialism and post-colonialism, the South Indian 'coolie' was an expendable resource that was only essential in its primary quest for economic gains.

The legacy of the immense and crucial contribution of the South Indian 'coolies' to the political economy of the Malayan/Malaysian nation as well as for the accumulation of capital, both at the metropolitan centre and to the nation, and their present dire economic, political and social predicament with exceptions, has escaped the country's national as well as Western-centric historical narratives. In the dominant Malayan/Malaysian historiography most of the major historical and political studies are primarily concerned with the chronology and sequential narratives about the ruling classes and their leadership both in the colonial and post-colonial settings. In other words, as the noted Marxist historian Eric Hobsbawm points out that working-class history has been treated in terms of the nation's isolated historical narrative rather than of the broader history of the development of capitalism in a world-historical context (Hobsbawm, 1969, 1981, 2015). This has resulted in the differing interpretation and the fragmentation of the country's historiography. In addition, the artificial construct of unequal and separate 'ethnic blocs' by the colonial state in order to 'divide and rule' by keeping the country's different ethnic groups artificially apart was to maximize returns to metropolitan capital (Selvaratnam, 1976; Stenson, 1980).

This fuzzier and looser colonial construct has given great credence to the narrow 'plural society' model (Furnivall, 1948) rather than to the broader interconnected and intertwined political economy and its impact. As Stenson (1980: 2) succinctly points out that 'at no stage in Malayan history could it ever be said that the Chinese have been constituted as an effective "ethnic bloc" as well as one can say that of the Indians'. More importantly, the colonial states fictionally manufactured and artificially constructed insidious divisions of society have moulded and reinforced the country's present political, economic, social and religious structures.

The absence of 'history from below' as expounded by Sharil (1982) in his studies, it is relevant to understand the complex social relations of subordination and oppression of the country's peasants, proletariat and other dispossessed groups and their political ideologies, cultural values and struggles. Through such methodology studies, one could have an understanding of the major underpinnings of the country's colonial economy and its overall historiography. Hobsbawm in his introduction to John and Barbara Hammond's 'The Village Labourer' states that their work has 'brought out the discovery that poor men are just as much people as the rich and influential, though the history of the world has been written by or in terms of the latter, and the vast bulk of the documentation on which historians worked left the lives and struggles of the poor in darkness" (Quoted in Kaye, 1984: 137–138).

Thus, the lack of studies on 'history from below' has hindered a clear appreciation and understanding of the other balanced historical viewpoints among academics, students and the public at large. Unraveling this complexity requires economic and social historians as well as social scientists to move away primarily from the long-entrenched Eurocentric and Malay/Malaysian-centric narrow 'ethnic bloc' parameters of national historiography.

Sharil (2004) succinctly emphasized in his inaugural lecture that '... the methods for writing history that has evolved in Malaysia are simply inadequate...it is hemmed in from all sides by a kind of circumscribed parochialism... thus built high walls and glass ceilings that have deliberately cut them off from the healthy interaction with other Asian scholars as well as scholars in analogous fields of enquiry... this has resulted in a sterile scholasticism that knows little of and cares still less for the spirit of interdisciplinary dialogue ... as such, it can teach us little about who we are or who we may become... in this current state, historical studies have reached an impasse... thus the intellectual task that we should be setting for ourselves ...in order to understand and explain the intricate changes of the contemporary world and Malaysia's place in that order... we need to revisit and recapture the spirit of the order'.

Sharil Talib thus, aptly urged Malaysia's historians in their historical narratives, whatever their ideological predisposition may be, to re-orientate and reconstruct both their thinking and approach towards the study of Malayan/Malaysian historiography. Thus, it may be legitimate for historical studies previously researched and resolved to be reconsidered and reinterpreted in the light of new material and interpretations but with a broader perspective.

In the study of the historiography of the Malayan/Malaysian plantation economy and labour, there appears to be an obscured or fragile connection between the intellectual and philosophical roots of the European liberalism, British imperialism and the penetration and rise of colonial capitalism. One of the pertinent questions to ask and recapture in the study of the historiography of the Malayan/Malaysian political economy is what has been the interconnected and intertwined historical constellations between European economic liberalism, the East India Company, the laissez-faire mercantile trade with China and East and Southeast Asian countries and expansion and penetration of colonial capitalism, the transformation and integration of British Malaya into the world capitalist system.

In a seminal study entitled 'The Intimacies of Four Continents' Lowe (2015: 137) takes issues with prevailing historiographical studies for their lack of interest in unraveling the robust linkages that existed between Europe, Africa, Asia and the Americas in the eighteen and nineteenth centuries. The failure to do so, she reiterates, has obscured the strong interconnection between European thinking on colonialism, imperial trade, slavery and indentured labour and the continents of Africa, Asia and the Americas and the emerging world capitalism. Applying extensive archival and unique interdisciplinary research across the continents, she connects the intellectual and the polemical philosophical discourse in Europe to the happenings in the four continents of Africa, America, Asia and Europe and their intimate connections with the emerging world capitalist system. Her study reveals how global capitalism and its precedent, Empire, operated to discipline and organize peoples, places, and the presentation of historical knowledge and limit 'what can be thought and imagined' to a concept of liberal humanism premised on progress and redemption yet contingent on the continued subjugation of its subjects.

In a similar vein, Ince in his study of *Colonial Capitalism and the Dilemmas of Liberalism* (2018: 159) highlights that '... liberalism and empire has produced a detailed inventory of such cross-pollinations that have resulted from attempts to reconcile liberal universals with colonial particularisms. These include, among others, a stadial theory of human development that yet infantilized the colonized, a brand of cosmopolitan pluralism that conditioned imperial arrogance and refused to judge non-Europeans, and the fatalistic view of the colonized as being incapable of progress and hence subject to the protective rather than the civilizing mission of the empire.

The asymmetrical and discriminative liberal ideology among eighteenth- and nineteenth-century European thinkers, especially those like Montesquieu and John Stuart Mill, according to the erudite 2018 study by Pitts entitled *Boundaries of the International: Law and Empire,* legally concretized and imposed on their colonies Eurocentric structured and skewed international laws. The enabling factors for the imposition of unequal laws were the world-wide nineteenth-century political triumphalism of European powers, imperial expansion and colonization. This was followed by the implementation of these one-sided Eurocentric laws by European colonial administrators who came to govern the emerging political and economic relationship with their non-European subjects in the continents of Africa, Americas and Asia, including British Malaya.

Interestingly, in a similar vein Sharil (1982: 453) pointed out in his article entitled 'A Revolt in Malaysian Historiography ...that the colonial government officials who accompanied the process of bureaucratic expansion were not creatures from the countryside; they were town dwellers and were unsympathetic to the peasantry. They executed their duties with little understanding and moderation'.

The prism of colonial capitalism and the imposition of Eurocentric laws highlight the uneven material dynamics that connect the different ideological expressions between the ruling colonial class and their subjects demonstrating the extent to which colonial primitive accumulation assimilated (destroyed and reconstructed) or articulated (subordinated and managed) existing relations of production in the colonies (Ince, 2018: 159). Sharil (1982) teases out and highlights the political and administrative might of the colonial state that evolved a system of subordination, destruction and reconstruction of the economic and social life of the Terengganu peasantry and drove them into poverty. In the same vein, this chapter will demonstrate that the race-class ideology of colonialism and colonial capitalism and its subordination, repression and exploitation of the South Indian 'coolie' too drove them into a similar fate of poverty.

In line with Sharil's (2004) call to reorient and reconstruct both the thinking and approach towards the study of Malayan/Malaysian historiography and in light of the scholarship of Lowe (2015), Ince (2018), Pitts (2018), Beckert (2014), Beckert and Rockman (2016), Williams (1944) and other studies, this chapter attempts to provide a greater focus on the interconnected relationship between British imperialism, colonial capitalism, the colonial state and the complex intertwined entanglement with the many layers of the despotic indirect British rule. In short, colonialisms' political, economic and cultural penetration into the Malay Peninsula was closely interconnected and intertwined with the policies of imperialism, colonialism, racism and world capitalism.

Marx throughout his writings emphasized the historical interconnectedness between the expansion of European colonial trade, territorial conquest (trade followed by the flag, hegemony, exploitation and repression), the emergence of the capitalist mode of production and the expropriation of labours' surplus-value for capital accumulation. Thus, Marx's framework underpins the centrality of political economy in the capitalist mode and relations of production, the expropriation of labour's surplus value and the proletrianization and exploitation of labour into a permanent and low-waged working class.

The evolution and functioning of Marx's unequal and exploitative class structure serves as an aperture to view the progression of Malaya/Malaysia's capitalist development and accumulation of capital in a peripheral economy not merely in a limited sense but in the broader global sense. Frank (1967), Hobsbawm (1969), and Wallerstein (1983) after Marx, have set the agenda in their studies by highlighting the dynamics of the historical interlink of imperial conquest, political hegemony and dominant power. This gave rise to European capitals' drive for commodification of labour and profits through coercion, surveillance, exploitation and repression of both the indigenous peasantry and migrant labour on a world-wide scale. It has contributed to the continuous schisms and schematic changes in the economic and social formation in many colonial societies, including British Malaya.

Imperial Expansion, Colonial Capitalism and Quest for Labour

In the aftermath of the landmark Pangkor Treaty of 1874, direct British colonial expansion, political domination and administration set the stage for the emergence of a new and unequal social formation and political order. It caused a shift 'from the informal imperialism of free trade to the more formal imperialism of protectionist economic expansion' (Stenson, 1980: 14). What mattered most of all was the major tilt in political, economic and administrative power from the indigenous Malay feudal ruling classes to the direct control of the British that was underpinned by an era of consent and compliance to colonial state's rule. This chasm enabled the Eurocentric and asymmetrical administrative and legal system of the colonial state to penetrate the whole country. With inviolate territorial sovereignty, and the assertion of administrative control of the day-to-day political order, the British officials were able to chart out the prime economic benefit imperial Britain and European capital could actualize from their new colonies with greater velocity.

It became apparent to Imperial Britain's officials that the newly annexed and directly politically-cum-administratively consolidated colony of the Malay Peninsular was, apart from an exclusive market for its finished goods, a storehouse of natural wealth. It was endowed with huge tracks of 'extremely fertile' soil and a 'climate conducive for the cultivation on plantation scale of highly profitable and exportable tropical crops for both the imperial and global market'. F. A. Toynbee, an early pioneer planter in the State of Selangor, pointed out to prospective European entrepreneurs that the state had thousands and thousands of acres of good land 'admirably suited' for planting coffee, with the prospect of good returns for their investment (Selvaratnam, 1960: 33). In particular, the consolidation of British sovereignty and administrative control with resident colonial officials in the main districts of the colony created a venal commercial environment for the expansion and exploitation for European plantation agriculture, mining and trade. In the Marxian sense, the colony was ideally suited to be exploited and transformed into capital by its metropolitan bourgeoisie. Thus, the implantation of an acquisitive imperial superstructure therefore ushered a new era of metropolitan capitalist expansion and economic exploitation in the colony.

Large-scale Western agricultural enterprises, on a commercial scale into colonial West Malaya, were incentivized when the colonial state targeted European entrepreneurs, some of them who had failed in their plantation ventures in colonial Ceylon and the Caribbean, with vast tracts of virgin forest land suitable for commercial agriculture in perpetuity for a pittance to cultivate coffee as the premier cash crop. A further inducement for these European entrepreneurs was the high and rising price for coffee in the world commodity market and the coffee boom in the 1890s (Selvaratnam, 1960). Apart from coffee, European planters were encouraged to cultivate tea, cocoa, cinchona, pepper, nutmegs and coconuts as minor commodities to cushion failures, if any, in their primary coffee venture. European planters originally operated as individual small producers or as joint proprietors, and in a few cases, as syndicates with minimal capital outlay or limited capital backing with the anticipation to extract huge profits and accumulate despite the volatility of the world commodity market.

From the onset, these European fortune seekers and venture capitalists realized that apart from their limited fixed and circulating capital at their disposal, to successfully exploit and profit from their risky undertakings and accumulate capital from the vast 'hidden riches of an almost unknown and jungle-covered' colony and provide raw material to fuel Britain's industrialization, an insatiable supply of cheap and docile labour was crucial. In the words of the pro-European capitalist entrepreneur's *Annual Report of the Straits Settlement of 1887* 'A large handy supply with a pittance of a wage (in servitude) is considered an essential prerequisite for an erratic plantation economy'. This was to be so too for the development of the colony's infrastructure such as roads, railways and public utilities mainly to support the growth and exploitation of its political economy. The nascent capital-strapped European entrepreneurs, apart from cheap and servile labour, in order to expand rapidly its productive processes to appropriate labours' surplus value and accumulate capital required, the colonial state to buttress it with both legal and extra-legal law and order mechanisms as well as provide capital with subsidized interest rates, trade protection and regulated markets. In other words, as Yuen (2013: 42) points out 'The system of law introduced into British Malaya laid the legal foundation of capitalism in a colonial context'.

European entrepreneurs and imperial officials in the newly found colony realized that it was near impossible to lure the indigenous Malay peasantry in sufficient numbers to labour in the plantation and tin economy as well in the supportive infrastructural developments. The Malay peasant was by tradition deeply embedded and intertwined into a feudal system dominated by the Malay ruling classes that legitimized and protected their political, economic and cultural space (Gullick, 1958: 126). Basically, the Malay ruling classes, to protect and hold on to their traditionally vested feudal identity and political power-base, were not prepared to deplete the numbers of their population (Milner, 2016).

Their power base was basically dependent on the revenue they appropriated from the surplus-value generated by their subject classes through the feudal mode of production. Therefore, the traditional Malay ruling classes wanted to retain and subjugate their subjects on land for padi (rice) cultivation, which was the vital stable diet (Abraham, 1997: 82) as well as to extract revenue and services. A combination of these traditional feudal relationships reinforced and cemented their socio-economic status and political power-base.

Further, colonial racism portrayed the myth of the lazy native's work ethic, his feeble intellect and inability to understand a labour contract as well as his aversion to live and work continuously in servitude on foreign-owned and managed plantations that were rigidly structured, highly regimented and punitively administered (Alatas, 1977). On the contrary, in particular, the inhibiting and debilitating factors led the Malays to shun the European capitalist ideology of a regimented and rigorous low-waged employment. Wisely, they escaped the enslavement by the European capitalist in his own soil (Aiyer, 1938: 5).

The then available labour, categorized as industrious and productive was the indentured Chinese migrant 'coolies' and they had been used by British planters to labour in the pepper, beetle-nut, nutmeg and other spice plantations in the Prince of Wales' Island (Allen, 2012: 231). They were informally controlled by tightly linked kinship networks, clan organizations and secret societies and these groups went 'to the extent of protecting them from unjust and arbitrary local and colonial governments' (Gungwu, 1986: x). The 'sinister' and 'secretive' Chinese 'coolies', taking advantage of their informal community-based protection and the labour scarcity in the colony, demanded higher wages. They were also more inclined to work for higher wages in the well-established Chinese-owned plantation, mining and related industries that long predated the establishment of European enterprises.

For the embryonic European plantation and mining entrepreneurs who were seeking large profits with minimal capital outlay and an early retirement back to Europe from the tropical hellhole. Thus, in an increasingly marketized and competitive world economy, an expendable, low-waged, reliable and stable supply of unfree and coerced labour was a prerequisite. Both, primary commodity cultivation and extractive tin mining industry in their infancy were highly work as well as labour intensive. This demanded a large and insatiable supply of workers for its opening, day-to-day operation and expansion.

Further, to be cost-effective and competitive in the highly volatile world commodity market that was intrinsically tied to price vagrancy, European enterprise to be profitable, had to be a competitive producer. Shortage of labour tended to raise wages, squeeze profits and stunt capital accumulation. Thus, it was crucial that the nascent European enterprises had an insatiable supply of cheap, unfree, malleable and readily expendable labour. The only available option for Imperial Britain to meet its new colony's critical shortage of cheap labour was from among the unemployed or underemployed and poverty-stricken peasants from the densely populated Madras Presidency of British India (Kondapi, 1951: 2–5). The argument of Frederick Weld, the British Resident in Selangor was, that unlike the Chinese 'coolie', the South Indian was 'peaceful and easily governed'. South Indian 'coolie' was also considered to be a countervailing force to both the risky and impractical Chinese labour as they were relatively well-organized, high-waged and 'troublesome' to manage.

Not surprisingly Imperial Britain's interconnected and intertwined exploitative and repressive colonial policies created the enabling environment for the recruitment of South Indian 'coolies' on a mass-scale. The imperial policy of 'de-industrialization' of British India contributed to '… massive disruption of the livelihood with the demise of traditional industries, dislocated local economies, new demand of cash payments for upward spiraling rents, a high incidence of eviction, and widespread of employment' (Mahmud, 2013). The dispossessed and poverty-stricken peasants, mainly from the Adi-Dravida or untouchable caste groups, were enticed by locally commissioned recruits to go and work overseas with the promise of a better life and return after three to five years with a 'small fortune' (Kumar, 1975).

Concomitantly, Imperial Britain by the early 1800s had informally replaced slave labour with the trade in 'coolies' (Meagher, 2008) from across various parts of India and in 1837 the British Parliament legalized it as an iron-cast and sustainable provider of cheap and able-bodied 'coolie' labour on a massive scale for the empire's far-flung colonies (Kumar, 2017: 2). The additional debilitating factor was the Southern India Famine of 1876–1878. It caused untold distress to large sections of the population and induced large numbers of agricultural labourers and handloom weavers to emigrate to work as indentured 'coolies' in the colonial plantations (Roy, 2006: 361–362).

Apart from the economic underpinnings, the justification for the recruitment and the deployment of the 'coolie' in servitude was ideologically governed by the British pseudo-scientific eugenics' theory. Francis Galton, the Anglo-Saxon high-priest of the theory of eugenics, who globally propagated the credence of a highly controversial genetically endowed natural superiority between the European white races and others. Thus, he advocated white-supremacy, imperialism and slavery. The race ideology in its varying forms penetrated into the fabric of the colonial state to shape and solidify white supremacy as well as the subject society. Within the framework of the racial ideology, the South Indian 'coolie' was made to know that he is an inferior being and therefore destined and stamped to be always subordinate 'coolies' to the white man. To know his place, the 'coolie' was marginalized and slotted at the bottom of the country's race and class social hierarchy. This 'separate and unequal' bigotry doomed the 'coolies' to a dismal life and prevented the bulk of them from any form of social mobility. Under this systematic coercive and debilitating class and racist system, the bulk of the 'coolies' were not permitted to either acquire recognized positions as leaders, negotiators or be represented by a trade union and this was to remain so until the Second World War. The 'coolies' only recognized role was that of petitioners: and that too as humble petitioners (Tinker, 1974: 227).

Thus, in Colonial Malaya as well as in Britain's other colonies, the centuries old legacy of white political and economic hegemony coupled with the ideological barrier of class and race were the natural order of things and the 'coolie' was naturally suited for labour in servitude. Therefore, the ideology of class and race permeated throughout the colony and was used both as a central formal and informal weapon of exploitation and repression to shape the daily live experience of the South Indian 'coolie'. The ideology of race was the '...engine of colonial power...and closely interwoven...' (Hale, 2013: 74) from the inception in the administration and economic exploitation of the colony and its population.

Empire's Rubber Country

The initial crop Europeans ventured into on a plantation scale was coffee. Coffee, as mentioned earlier, was in the boom crop in the late 1880s and early 1890s. However, a worldwide production glut and export of huge quantities of Brazilian coffee resulted in a huge depression in its price in the world commodity market in 1896. On the heels of the world price set-back for coffee, the colony's coffee plantations were beleaguered with a devastating blight. The future of the economic viability of coffee as a profitable cash crop in the world commodity market combined with the devastating blight was spearheading a bleak future for the European Planters' Raj, the South Indian migrant 'coolie' population and the colony's economy.

If the fortune hunting European planter's economic future was to be ruined by the glut and slum in the price of Brazilian coffee in the world market, it was the extensive transplantation of the 'boom crop', the Brazilian *hevea brasilliensis* or natural rubber (NR) into the colony that saved the fledging fortunes' of the European planters and the nascent political economy of British Malaya. The demand for rubber began just before the turn of the twentieth century as pointed out by Tully (2011: 51) 'rubber had come to stay: mass industrial society could not function without it'. The pioneer plantation scale rubber cultivation in Malaya was in 1895 on a 43 acres estate in Bukit Lintang, the Straits Settlement of Malacca by the Chinese capitalist Tan Chay Yan and in a small 5 acres plot in the State of Selangor by a European planter T. H. Hill (Drabble, 1973: 19).

The phenomenal growth in the demand for natural rubber by the burgeoning motor industry during the first two decades of the twentieth century created a 'tremendous rubber rush beyond imagination'. With the 'rubber rush' European capital investment in rubber cultivation took a sharp upward trend. New plantations that were both distinctly isolated politically and socially as well as segregated residential enclaves, stretched from the north to the south in the western half as well as in Pahang and Kelantan in the eastern half of the Malay Peninsula. As the rubber boom escalated, many more European companies ventured in the development of rubber plantations and their acreage grew at a phenomenal rate with heavy planting all over the country. In less than two decades from the start of the rubber boom, British Malaya in 1915 had 1,198 rubber plantations with a planted acreage of 703,535. Out of this, 347,750 acres were under production. By 1920, 779,123 acres were under rubber cultivation and further the escalation for world demand in rubber saw the exponential growth both in the number of plantations and acreage. Under the shield and legal protection of imperial policy and the colonial state, British Malaya gained the distinction of being the empire's and the 'white man's' rubber country and by far the world's largest producer and exporter of the crop.

More importantly, this was achieved with the conversion of European individual or joint plantation holdings were mainly London-based limited liability joint-stock companies. These huge profit-generating European companies were floated in London by agency houses at highly enhanced value which raised considerable capital for new plantation cultivation as well as boosted the wealth of many of the original proprietors and gave prosperity 'beyond imagination' for the new shareholders, largely in the metropolitan centre, with no benefits to the South Indian 'coolie'.

The most prominent and influential metropolitan-based companies to take advantage of the 'rubber rush' and were to become household names for the next seven decades were Socfin, Guthrie, Sime Darby, Harrisons & Crosfield, Dunlop, Boustead, United Plantations and Duff Development. To protect and further their economic interest, the metropolitan-owned plantation companies established both in London and in Malaya powerful associations.

Their continuous process of capital accumulation was strategized, implemented and sustained through a complex and effective web of socio-political networks of 'official policy making, informally through an exclusive web of metropolitan and colonial clubs, more formally through regular consultations in London between the Rubber Growers' Association, mining interest groups and the colonial office, and by representatives in Malaya on all relevant official councils and boards' (Stenson, 1980: 29). Their overwhelming strategy was to work together to pressure the Crown and the colonial regimes in India and Malaya to inextricably link their development of the colonial economy, mainly the plantations, with a persistent flow of an indispensable supply of cheap and servile South Indian 'coolies' to man the relentlessly expanding and profitable European ventures. Under such a strategy, the encapsulated and isolated South Indian 'coolie' was not able to pull out his or her labour power nor was he or her able to renegotiate the terms of bondage for better wages and living conditions.

At the local level, the European-dominated Planters' Association of Malaya (PAM) was reorganized in 1934 to became the United Planting Association of Malaya (UPAM), and like its predecessor, continued to be the plantation industry's most influential pressure group. The UPAM steered the Colonial State's policy formulation as well as its implementation, particularly in matters pertaining to the condition of workers' employment, their wages and working as well as living conditions in the industry's favour. The overreaching dominant policy of the UPAM was to pressure the Colonial State to keep the wages of the South Indian 'coolie' at the subsistence level so as to maintain minimal labour cost.

The rubber boom combined with the tin industry merged and integrated the country's colonial political economy to the global commodity market that was subjected to the vagaries of the world price of these two primary commodities. More importantly, British Malaya was systematically integrated and intertwined into the fast-developing capitalist economic chain of world trade which stretched from the plantations and tin mines to the entrepôt of Penang, Port Klang and Singapore to western industrial ports and cities, the vagaries of the capitalist world's volatile commodity markets and global capitalism. This development was further invigorated through the rise of a Chinese comprador class that served the colonial economy as intermediaries (Yuen, 2013).

South Indian 'Coolie' Labour: The Indentured and *Kangany* System

The first large-scale importation of South Indian indentured 'coolies' across the Bay of Bengal to the twin Crown Colony of Penang and Province Wellesley took root in the 1840s when European planters recruited and deployed them to toil in servitude for five years in their labour-intensive sugar plantations (Sandhu, 1969: 78; Chanderbali, 2008: 58). The subsequent upsurge in large-scale South Indian 'coolie' migration commenced from the late 1870s onwards when more European planters ventured eastwards into the British colony after their plantation undertakings in the Caribbean and Sri Lanka had failed.

The pro-colonial capitalisms' indentured 'coolie' recruitment and their emigration to British Malaya was orchestrated and governed by the British Indian Immigrants Protection Ordinance of 1876 and the Indian Act No. 5 of 1877. Under the ordinance, a Protector of Immigrants was appointed in 1880 by the British Empire's Madras Presidency with recruiting inspectors stationed in various places within the Presidency. The Protector of Immigrants through recruiting inspectors, appointed and licensed a chained network of recruiting agents at the village level. The recruits were led to one of the immigration depots that replicated 'a prison camp in appearance' at the port cities of Madras (Chennai) and Nagapattinam.

The processing and shipment of the recruits was primarily done by the appointed agents mainly in the port cities of Madras and Nagapattinam (Marjoribanks & Marakkayar, 1917: 30). With the finalization of the medical and contractual documentation the indentured 'coolies' were then shipped across the Bay of Bengal with little supervision on a 'treacherous and excruciating sea journey' to British Malaya, mainly by the British India Steam Navigation Company. During the sea voyage, many 'coolies' perished due to disease, thirst, insufficient and improper food and the dead were simply thrown overboard.

Despite the many deaths during the perilous sea voyage, the number of 'coolies' arriving annually jumped from about 5,000 in 1880s to more than 28,000 by 1900. The majority of them were deployed and concentrated in the plantation and public sector enclaves in Peninsular Malaya's western states of Kedah, Pulau Pinang, Perak, Selangor and Negri Sembilan and the southern and eastern states of Johor and Pahang respectively. The growing world demand for rubber from the mid-1900s followed by the exponential growth in large-scale cultivation of plantations, increased the demand for more and more labour by the turn of the nineteenth century. Plantation agriculture was highly labour-intensive. An abundance of workers was required for clearing and burning densely forested virgin jungles into well-drained land, terraces, roads, nursery beds, planting, fertilizing, weeding, tapping, latex collecting, coagulating, processing them into sheets and grading them for exports increased. In other words, a large, cheap, docile and expendable South Indian 'coolie' labour force was vital for the transformation of virgin forest into fertile and profitable plantations for colonial capitalism.

Concomitantly, South Indian 'coolies' were required in large numbers by the colonial state to construct and expand the colony's vital infrastructural facilities. The 'coolies' were used to build roads, bridges, railways, public buildings, drainage and irrigation canals, municipal sewerage systems and other ancillary public services as well as maintain them. Their primary function was to construct, expand and sustain the basic but crucial facilities for the advancement and profitability of colonial capitalism.

Thus, the Planters' Raj clamoured for an increase in the recruitment of South Indian'coolies'. The colonial state responded by establishing a government-subsidized Indian Immigration Fund in 1908 to boost 'coolie' immigration and its continuous replenishment to meet the increasing labour demands of the exponentially expanding European plantations. By 1910, the annual indentured 'coolie' arrivals reached the 10,000 mark (Sandhu, 1969: 157).

The complete lack of concern for the continuous indignities and ill treatment suffered by the 'coolies' 'generally (described as) simple, ignorant, illiterate, resourceless people belonging to the poorest classes of this country' in the colonies was taken note by the Imperial crown (Kumar, 2017: 212). In particular, the arbitrary and abusive use of the criminal penal code, suicides and murders on plantations, mortality on ships and the system and its brutal abuses, degraded the self-respect of Indians (ibid.). This led to the appointment of the Sanderson Commission in 1909 that eventually put an end to the brutal indentured system. Even before the abolishment of the exploitative and repressive indentured 'coolie' recruitment system by the Sanderson Commission Report in 1910, the Planters' Raj had devised and implemented the cheaper and equally coercive and exploitative *kangani* system of labour recruitment and to a lesser extent encouraged free 'coolie' immigration. This was to replace the bureaucratically cumbersome as well as the high-cost indentured system. Native intermediaries were used as recruiters at the local level in South India as well as the local planters at the level of their respective plantations used selected *kanganies* (headman) to recruit 'coolies'. *Kanganies* who were invariably from the upper caste and wielded considerable power over their Adi-Dravida recruits, were financially incentivized to recruit 'coolies' from their native villages and their precincts. Not surprisingly, the *kanganies* too victimized the 'coolie' recruits by entangling them into a debt-bondage. The 'coolies' subsistence wage was far from sufficient for their daily survival or even to free themselves from their debt obligations. Though the *kangani* recruitment system drastically reduced the cost of procurement of the 'coolie' from $47.50 to $29.39 between 1903 and 1938, the Planters' Raj did not think it to be fit to warrant a wage rise for the South Indian labourer. By the eve of the Second World War, it was estimated that a near total of two million (1,910,820) South Indian 'coolies' had arrived in the colony either through the indentured or *kangani* system (Sandhu, 1969: 305).

Many 'coolies' perished in this brutal and coercive colonial capitalist economy due to diseases, largely malaria, poor diet and harsh working conditions for long hours. On some plantations, the mortality rates were huge 'as many as 60 rising to 90% of the labourer's died within a year of their arrival' (Sandhu, 1969: 171). These appalling and deplorable living conditions were prolonged for a long time (Sasidaran, 2012), and the education and medical facilities were far from adequate (Tinker, 1976: 153). Though the Federated Malay States Labour Code (enacted in 1912 and revised in 1923) required plantations to pay a minimum wage, provide adequate housing, education and medical facilities for their workers and that children under ten were not to be employed. The Committee that was empowered by the colonial state to supervise the recruitment, wages and the general working and living conditions of the 'coolie' was 'heavily weighted in favour of the employers' (Tinker, 1976: 153). The reasoning for the European plantations to maintain a low-wage ideology was justified by the erroneous notion that the Indian 'coolie' 'needed little for his daily subsistence'. However, the primary objective of colonial capitalism was to ensure the ready availability of a cheap '...stream of able-bodied men to go through the grinding mill' (Aiyer, 1938: 22).

The marooned 'coolies', apart from their psychological adjustment to the new harsh environment, were subjected to disproportionate judicial and extra-judicial laws. The laws were promulgated to tame and discipline the 'coolies' as well as to acquiesce them into the monotonous and punitive time-work-discipline routine. In addition, the 'coolies' had to complete their indentured bondage that they had pledged to or had tied themselves into. Many of the 'coolies' recruited under the by *kangani* system invariably became indebted to the recruiting *kangani*. If the 'coolie' was insubordinate or failed to fulfill either his indentured contract or settle his debt, he was subjected to physical abuse, 'habitually flogged', fined or jailed (Amrith, 2010: 240).

At the level of the plantation, to facilitate the appropriation of surplus value and capital accumulation, a despotic race and class-based hierarchical system of hegemony and coercive system of labour organization 'on a military/industrial lines' was instituted. This rendered the 'coolie' helpless against the brutal exploitation of colonial capitalism and the colonial state. Thus, for the majority of South Indian 'coolies' it was a daily struggle to find meaning in their life in servitude as it was near impossible to buy their freedom out of the system. Subsequently, they were gradually evolved into a permanent proletarianized working-class labour force to be recycled from one generation to another into the colonial capitalism huge wealth generating mono-crop rubber to be followed by palm-oil plantations.

Neither did the system's scale of inequality, control, surveillance and repression allow the 'coolie' to organize themselves into unions till the 1940s, just before the start of the Second World War. However, an upsurge of sporadic industrial unrest among South Indian 'coolies' did emerge in the 1920s and 1930s. This was due to the drastic reduction of wages followed by retrenchment and repatriation of workers back to India following both the depression of 1920–1921 and the Great Depression of 1929. Even the conservative and pro-capital British economist P. T. Bauer pointed out that the Indian workers' 'wages in 1932 were near starvation rates and were totally inadequate for the maintenance of dependents' (Bauer, 1948: 51).

In the terms of Engels (Engels, 1973), like their working-class counterparts of industrial Britain, these 'coolies' were made to be 'toiling machines' under inhuman hours and harsh working conditions all year round on meagre subsistence wages. The wages were just sufficient for their mere physical subsistence and reproduction and therefore had no relationship to work-load and productivity. In servitude, under the hierarchically structured, closely managed, controlled and isolated plantation and public sector compounds, the South Indian 'coolie' was absolutely dependent on his white employer for his daily bread. Even as late as 1936, the Colonial Government of India due to the constant agitation from Indian nationalist movements, sent the pro-British V. S. Srinivasa Sastri to conduct an official inquiry into the working and living conditions of Indian labour in Malaya (Srinivasa Sastri, 1937). In a letter dated 20th December, A. Thamboo of the Kinta Indian Association and the joint secretary of the Central Indian Association of Malaya (CIAM) to V. S. Srinivasa Sastri called for the general betterment of working and living conditions among Indian estate workers. Thamboo raised twenty-six issues faced by the South Indian 'coolies' in Malaya. The key critical issues arose from the 'coolie' being deprived of the officially stipulated standard wage rate. They were subjected to long working hours; poor housing and sanitary facilities. Vernacular education provision for children was poorly organized (and the ones in operation had poorly qualified teachers). The overwhelming skew in sex-ratios towards males led to murders, assaults and suicide. There was also a serious Imbalance in wages between Chinese and Indians doing the same job. There was also little enforcement to stop the issuance of fresh licences to toddy shops. Women were also not given jobs in the same place as their husbands. Labour settlements were not allocated free land to house labourers in the country.

The South Indian 'coolies', from one generation to another, were isolated, segregated and tied to plantation and public sector housing and were locked into a subsistence wage ideology for their daily survival. Their children were subjected to a system of rudimentary vernacular education which made them devoid of alternative work options. This forced them into a culture of dependence and condescension and remained within their colonial and capitalist organized work system as a separately identified, marginalized and proletarianized labour force from generation to generation. Despite the exploitative policies of European capital in terms of low wage accompanied by poor living and working conditions, there appeared to be very little overt resistance by the 'coolies' till the late 1930s. In Marxian terms, the 'coolie' had evolved into a settled proletarian without access to land, alternative skills and savings to physically survive in a harsh and inhibiting colonial and capitalist collaborating economic environment. This enabled the 'coolies' brutal exploitation, misery and social degradation, an endemic cancer in the colony's capitalist labour system to continue to operate in British Malaya till 1938 and beyond.

The appalling persistence of poverty and continuing exploitation and repression of the South Indian 'coolie' by colonial capitalism, with the complicity of European plantation capital gave rise in the 1930s to concerns on basic issues by the various middle class led Indian associations across the Malay states. In particular, the 'coolies' miserable economic conditions and their social plight was widely vented and articulated at the annual conferences of the various Indian associations across the country. The Indian associations, mostly led by prominent English-educated professionals and businessmen both from the upper class and caste communities, initiated in 1936 the formation of the CIAM. Apart from voicing and protecting the community's overall class and cultural interests in the rapidly expanding political economy of the colonial state, the CIAM, more for altruistic reasons, raised the debilitating economic and social issues faced by the country's South Indian 'coolie'. Foremost among them were their wages and working conditions, land settlements, repatriation and *toddy* (an alcoholic drink tapped out of the coconut palm). As Sandhu (1969: 110) points out, the CIAM '...waged an incessant war of memoranda, petitions, resolutions, meetings and speeches championing the cause of the Indian labourer in Malaya. Whilst constantly urging the Indian National Congress and legislature to ban emigration of labour...'.

Although there was a boom in rubber prices between 1933 and 1936, which rose by 250%, the UPAM strongly resisted efforts to restore the wages of the 'coolie' even to the pre-Depression level. Instead, the UPAM in 1938 recommended a wage reduction in anticipation of a threatened recession. The CIAM's critical voice on behalf the lamentable low-wages, working and living conditions of the 'coolie' class had little traction on colonial policy, until the visit of Jawaharlal Nehru in 1937 to Malaya. Nehru's visit acted as a catalyst to raise the overall political consciousness of Malayan Indians, in particular of the working class. It gave rise to the formation of new type of reformist associations led by the lower strata of Tamil-speaking estate level *kanganies* and school teachers with membership from the working class. The primary objective of these associations was to uplift the economic condition and social status of the Indian working class in British Malaya.

In 1938, the Government of India, taking cognizance of the fact that their natives were being 'discriminated on every side' as well as a Malaya-born Indian 'is treated as an alien in the land of his birth!' banned the emigration of all unskilled Indians to Malaya. The influential Indian-owned newspaper, *The Hindu*, in a scathing editorial pointed out, 'To permit the emigration of Indians to a country where they are treated with such little consideration seems consistent neither with the self-respect of India, nor with the best interests of prospective emigrants' (quoted in Parmer, 1960: 64). On the contrary, the planters, colonial officials and pro-British agents by and large painted a rosy picture of the situation.

Rise of Labour Militancy

The colonial state's continuing repressive labour laws and policies, combined with colonial capitalisms low wage ideology, harsh working and living conditions and humiliating treatment, did culminate in a major strike just before the Second World War. In February 1941, a militant and well-organized Klang Strike was carried out by over 900 workers from several estates in the vicinity and led by the Klang District Indian Union. The factors that triggered the rise and spread of worker militancy were the persistence practice in the arbitrary reduction in wages to near starvation levels; retrenchment and repatriation during economic downturns; poor living conditions; and the lack of proper medical facilities and schools for their children. In particular, when 'coolies' had passed their productive cycle and literally squeezed out as 'sucked oranges', they were either repatriated or those who lost their roots in India became vagrants in towns. A Penang lawyer in 1933 pointed out that 'That repatriation to India of over 180,000 unemployed Indian labourers, many of them mere "bag of bones", showed that Indian labour in Malaya was simply an object for exploitation' (quoted in Stenson, 1980: 44). A feature for the unrest among the 'coolies' was also the perennial problem of overt and covert humiliating treatment that was being meted out to them by the plantation's European and subordinate Asian managements. The strike was brutally crushed by the Colonial State and among the strikers who displayed defiance, six were gunned down by Gurkha soldiers from the locally stationed British Army Brigade (Gamba, 1962: 252; Stenson, 1980: 63–64; Wilson, 1981). There were also similar strikes among plantation workers in Negri Sembilan from December 1940 to January 1941. The local police were used it to break the strikes (Selvaratnam, 1976: 239).

The initial catalyst that infused and manifested the rapid rise and spread of class awareness, anti-imperialism and political radicalization among Indian labour was the myth of invincibility of British military might and its defeat in December 1941 by the Japanese with relative ease. This impetus was further ignited by the Japanese occupation and immediate dislocation of the plantation industry and public sector provisions, that had serious repercussions on the livelihood of Indian labour throughout the country. The establishment of the Indian National Army (INA), which also included a women's wing, under the charismatic nationalist and anti-imperialist, Subhas Chandra Bose, drew into its fold a large number of now radicalized South Indian working-class men and women from the plantations and public sector enclaves to join the freedom struggle (Selvaratnam, 1976: 242; Toye, 1991; Hildebrand, 2016). The Japanese occupation of Malaya until September 1945 and its immediate aftermath had a devastating impact on the living conditions of the population at large and for the Indian working class in particular. A near 75,000 of them were literally forcefully taken by the Japanese between 1942 and 1945, to build the Burma-Siam Death Railway. It is estimated that only about 22,000 of them returned by mid-1946 and the rest were uncounted for or in all likelihood perished (Sasidaran, 2019: 29). On the heels of the shattered life of the Indian 'coolies', the reoccupying British planters, in collusion with colonial state, sought to revitalize their distraught plantations at minimum cost and imposed a drastic reduction on the wages of the poverty-stricken South Indian 'coolies'. This led to the eruption of an intense class struggle between the impoverished and radicalized Indian workers trapped in the plantations and the reoccupying planters backed by the might of the colonial state (Stenson, 1970: 3).

The workers were mobilized by their respective left-oriented estate unions at the local level and backed by both the General Labour Union

(GLU) and Pan-Malayan Federation of Trade Unions (PMFTU), which were in turn allied to the Malayan Communist Party (MCP) (Khong, 1984: 85–7). Earlier to this, was the spread among Indian workers of the doctrines of the Self-Respect or Dravidian Movement from Tamil Nadu as espoused by E. V. Ramasamy Naicker or Periyar. The parochial and class-oriented militant Tamil youth movement, the Thondar Padai or Youth Corp, that took roots in Northern States of Colonial Malaya, was rooted on Periyar's teachings (Stenson, 1980: 136).

The reoccupying European plantation companies in collusion with the colonial state deployed the same Indian workers who had been subjected to unemployment, appalling poverty, other indignities and malnourishment. Though the plantation industry manned by the poverty-stricken Indian 'coolies' was nursed back to record levels of production and profits, the lion's share of the profits gained by the surplus output produced by them was siphoned away by the European-owned and managed plantation companies back to London, and closed the widening gap of the British balance of payments. Even a tiny portion of the huge profits accrued by the plantation companies was not apportioned to alleviate the poverty and miserable subsistence conditions of the Indian 'coolies' (ibid.: 113).

The distressed and discontented Indian workers triggered an upsurge of militant unionism led by the Central Committee of the Selangor Estate Workers Union. By the end of 1946, organized labour unrest became a common feature among plantation labour (Gamba, 1962: 271). In March 1947, the union's demands, apart from a pay rise equal to that of their Chinese counterparts, were war bonuses, sick pay, confinement leave, abolition of eviction from labour lines within twenty-four hours, provision of proper living quarters with suitable sanitary conditions, good drinking water, separate kitchens, bathrooms and latrines and the removal of trespass restrictions by plantations (ibid.). The union's demands were supported by the MCP with whom the militant Indian-led unions led by G. A. Ganapathy, P. Veerasenan and others forged alliances between 1945 and 1948. This coalition between the Chinese and Indian working class was further bolstered by ties with the left-wing, anti-British and anti-feudal Malay groups, in particular the Malay National Party (MNP), which demanded freedom for 'all the oppressed people of Malaya' (Sani, 2008: 21). The growth and ramifications of a multiracial and nationalist mass working-class alliance with social and political protest, in coalition with a united front between the MCP, the Malayan Democratic Union

(MDU) and MNP were seen as a hostile, subversive and potent opposition to both the vital economic interests of Imperial Britain and the feudal political ideology of the Malay aristocracy. UMNO's Malay elite leadership that commanded a substantial body of mass Malay support saw this left-wing alliance and activism as highly subversive and a clear threat to their traditional position of Malay supremacy. British colonial capitalism saw the challenge as a potential death knell to the significant strategic and economic importance of Malaya, both to their imperialism and to the 'Free World' (Selvaratnam, 1976: 257). In fact, the Malayan dollar earnings were vital to Britain's post-war recovery and in bridging the huge balance of payment gap with the United States (Stenson, 1980: 113).

Collapse of Labour Militancy

An approach to coherently enhance the colonial state's capability to recognize, understand and scuttle the increasing alliance among the country's Chinese, Indian and Malay working classes and the MCP was implemented. The primary aim was to crush the rise of any form of left-oriented multiracial nationalist and revolutionary movements and trade unions that opposed the colonial order. To contain the growth of militant unions, the colonial state amended the 1940 Trade Union Enactment to stringently regulate the registration unions. John Brazier, a former union official with the British Railways, was appointed as Trade Union Adviser, with the express task of fostering moderate, servile unionism in line with the colonial economic order. The amended Trade Union Enactment drastically reduced the number of trade unions, from 305 in 1947 to 41 in 1949 and also led to the plummeting of union membership, from 195,113 in 1947 to 41,305 by 1949 (Gamba, 1962: 355). Through a combination of oppressive labour laws and with Brazier's connivance as well as with the even-handed role of the Registrar of Trade Unions, the colonial state successfully weeded out all of the trade unions that were purported to be radical and significantly weakened the MCP and GLU's hold over the country's unions. The rising militant workers' struggle was thus crushed by the might of both the British Empire and metropolitan capital. Imperial Britain's governing Labour Party that professed to be anti-empire with a decisive policy to 'liquidate its Empire' (Haqqi, 1960: ix) when in power instead developed and unleashed a highly potent repressive policy strategy to enforce labour discipline, subjugate the people and take the country back to the pre-war colonial-regime days.

Hereafter, only pliable, 'apolitical', 'tame' and 'responsible' unions were allowed to operate. One such union that fitted the colonial state's needs was the Negri Sembilan Estate Union with majority Indian membership. Its leader was P. P. Narayanan, an anti-communist and a unionist, espoused both pro-government and pro-employer sentiments. Narayanan's union was allowed to enter plantations to mobilize workers to be members in order to 'accommodate workers' welfare issues rather than negotiate for workers-rights'. With the blessings of the colonial state, the planters and Brazier, in 1954 Narayanan formed the National Union of Plantation Workers (NUPW), the sole union of the country's plantation workers.

The historical trajectory of Malaya/Malaysia would have taken a different turn had the Chinese and Indian working-class struck a multiracial national alliance with the majority of the Malay proletariat and peasantry, led by the PMFTU and GLU. However, a veil of progressive nationalism did not emerge among the majority of the rural Malays under the influence of the Malay aristocracy and UMNO. The fear of the Malay rulers' and the aristocracy was their submergence and 'racial extinction' by the Chinese and a multiracial nationalist alliance was not therefore in their deep-rooted aristocratic and feudal interest (Ahmad Fauzi Abdul Hamid, 2007: 385).

To counter the demand, the British colonial state in June 1948 declared a State of Emergency with wide ranging powers to arrest, shoot to kill and occupy or destroy property without fear of legal challenge. Further, a plethora of arbitrarily instituted oppressive laws including the draconian Sedition Act was used to curb free speech and radical trade unions. The British flooded the country with security forces and Commonwealth troops. The counter-insurgency strategy of the British succeeded to split the working class and root out and isolate the MCP's challenge. Radical South Indian trade union activists, such as S. A. Ganapathy, P. Veerasenan, R. G. Balan and C. S. V. K. Moorthy, who all held positions in the MCP and who were leaders in the PMFTU and GLU, were dubbed as subversive communists planning to overthrow the government in order to establish a Communist State allied to Russia and China. The 'Red Bogey' was lashed up as a serious threat to both the colonial state (Cheah, 1983) and the huge 'imperial assets' in the country.

Some of these leaders were deported to India, while the extreme excesses of British imperialism were demonstrated when others were incarcerated locally or executed on trumped-up charges. Ganapathy was convicted for arms possession and executed by the British, while Veerasenan was killed by the security forces (Selvaratnam, 1976: 242; Saminathan, 2020).

The Emergence of the United Malays National Organisation

The landmark development in the country's history was the emergence, in March 1946, of an exclusively race and mass-based political party, the United Malay National Organization (UMNO), representing the country's majority-Malay community and led by a largely English-educated aristocratic leadership (Roff, 1967). The UMNO's elites, with the support of the Malay masses, the Malay rulers, British capital and its organ the *Straits Times,* were vehemently opposed to Britain's imposition of the multiracial and united Malayan Union constitution in April 1946. Their opposition to the Malayan Union lay in the belief that if enacted a significant majority of the Chinese and Indians resident in Malaya would become citizens. Their hostility was further aggravated by subsequent events (Cheah, 2007: 7).

The rising strength of a nation-wide working-class movement allied to the MCP and GLU and their call for a National Association elected democratically through universal suffrage of the peoples of Malaya and Singapore in May 1946. This initiative underpinned by a 'People's Constitution' was embraced by a round table assembly in December 1946 convened by the All-Malayan Council of Joint Action (AMCJA) and with representatives from the MIC, MDU, MNP, PMFTU, the Malayan People's Anti-Japanese Army (MPAJA) ex-Comrades Association, the Women's Federation and the New Democratic Youth League (ibid.). The British rejected the AMCJA-PUTERA (the Malay-based Pusat Tenaga Rakyat) proposals. Instead, the UMNO's leaders and Malay rulers, with the support of British vested economic interests, unilaterally succeeded in arraying these radical forces and in secret negotiations succeeded in concluding a Malay-centric Federation of Malaya Agreement. The establishment of Federation of Malaya in 1948 laid the foundation for the traditional Malay aristocracy and the growing influential bureaucratic elite in the colonial administration to gradually dominate the politics and administration of the new federation as well as the independent Malayan state in 1957.

UMNO Dominated Post-colonial State

Britain granted independence to Malaya in 1957 under a new secular constitution that ushered in a parliamentary democracy modeled on the Westminster system. In theory, political power was supposed to be transferred by the departing British rulers to the tripartite 'rightist' ideological-based leadership of the Alliance Party, a coalition of three pro-British and pro-capital communal parties led by UMNO. UMNO's overarching slogan was and is 'Malaya for the Malays'. The Alliance (and since 1974, Barisan Nasional or BN) was purported to be a political partnership between the right-wing leadership of UMNO, and the Malayan Chinese Association (MCA) as well as the Malayan Indian Congress (MIC), representing the country's two other minority 'ethnic blocs', the Chinese and Indians, and from 1974 other regional minority parties. The leadership of each of the component parties basically shared an overriding identical class interest between themselves rather than with the mass membership of their respective political base. Neither did the Alliance/BN leadership dismantle or reform colonial capitalism and the free market economy. Thus, the transfer of power that was expected to bring about benefit to the country's population at large accomplished little for the people, including the South Indian 'coolie' now an integral part of independent nation. The entrenched colonial legacy of racial discrimination, segregation, subjugation and exploitation, the predatory to the growth of metropolitan and world capitalism, still continues to be used by the country's new ruling bourgeoisie to protect its dominant power base and advance its vested interests. Thus, the Malaysian Indian working class though rooted in the country's history with shared traditions for well over a century have been treated decisively at variance to the independent constitution as a distinctly separate and unequal minority community that has contributed to their continuous social and economic insecurity and deprivation.

Conclusion

The chapter is a brief attempt to narrate the storyline of the gross exploitation and oppression of the Indian labour force in British Malaya that immensely contributed to capital accumulation in both the metropolitan centre and Malayan nation. The largely Indian-origin creators of this wealth have remained dispossessed and impoverished. The chapter attempted to distinguish, highlight and interpret the constellation of different interconnected and intertwined colonial policies that have left a durable devastating impact on the Malaysian South Indian 'coolie' diaspora as it has had on the Malay peasantry as discerned and narrated by Shaharil (1982). For over a century, a class-cum-race based ideology of exploitation and repression was used by British imperialism and colonial capitalism to accumulate capital at the metropolitan centre at an enormous human cost. The human cost of a massive unimaginable scale was borne by a majority of Malaysia's South Indian 'coolies' and their descendants who had been brought in by the thousands through the indentured and *kangany* systems. Both these systems were a mere replication of the old slave trade in a new grab for the continuing accumulation of capital both for imperial Britain and the world capitalist system. The exploitative and repressive system, bondaged and locked the 'coolies on military/industrial lines' based labour organization with meagre wages. The isolated and closed work structures buttressed by the coercive mechanisms of the colonial state's and colonial capitalism's legal and extra-legal systems respectively have contributed to their major economic, social and cultural deprivation and alienation and widened the gulf between the majority of the South Indian 'coolies' and rest of Malaysian population. Further, the isolated and oppressed South Indian 'coolies' were proletarianized into a permanent workforce and were in turn marginalized and precluded from the mainstream of the nation's economic and political activities.

In a similar manner Shaharil's (1982) important study on Malay peasantry at the grass-roots level captures and highlights the disruptive impact of British colonial political hegemony and direct administrative rule had on the intricate and weak traditional economic and social relations of Malay rural society. In the new order of things, the colonial state's administrative machinery and imposition of documentary prove of land ownership and land tax drastically impinged upon and impacted on the accepted and customary age-old tradition of land ownership and rights in the agrarian peasant society. This led to the obstruction of the traditional economic and social relations as well as to their struggle for existence especially those who were poor and 'possess little above the margin of subsistence'. A constellation of factors, mainly brought into play by the expansion and centralization of rule, mainly economic, the payment in cash of land rents, land mortgages and tenancy, reduced a substantial number of traditionally land-owning peasants into poverty.

The studies on the Indian working class and the Malay peasantry in British Malay is a pathetic and poignant story of colonial economic exploitation, social strangulation and poverty. This chapter illustrates the underside of British colonialism and the constellation of the hegemonic mechanisms to accumulate capital at the metropolitan centre was employed and maintained to systematically exploit, repress and impoverish both the South Indian 'coolies' and the Malay peasantry.

References

Abdul Fauzi Abdul Hamid. (2007). Malay anti-colonialism in British Malaya: A Re-appraisal of independence fighters of Peninsular Malaysia. *Journal of Asian and African Studies, 42*(5), 371–398.

Abraham, C. R. E. (1997). *The roots of race relations in Malaysia: Divide and rule*. Kuala Lumpur: INSAN.

Aiyer, N. K. A. (1938). *Indian problems in Malaya*. Kuala Lumpur, F.M.S.: The Indian Office.

Allen, R. B. (2012). Re-conceptualising The 'new System of Slavery". *Man in India, 92*(2), 225–245.

Anwarul Haque Haqqi, A. (1960). *The colonial policy of the labour government (1945–51)*. Aligarh, India: Aligarh Muslim University.

Armith, S. S. (2010). Indians overseas? Governing Tamil migration to Malaya 1870–1941. *Past and Present, 208*(August), 207–261.

Alatas, S. H. (1977). *The myth of the lazy native*. London: Frank Cass.

Bauer, P. T. (1948). *The rubber industry: The study in competition and monopoly*. London: Longmans.

Beckert, S. (2014). *Empire of cotton: A global story*. New York: Random House.

Beckert, S., & Rockman, S. (2016). *Slavery's capitalism: A new history of American economic development*. Philadelphia: University of Pennsylvania Press.

Cheah, B. K. (1983). *Red Star over Malaysia: Resistance and social conflict during and after the Japanese Occupation, 1941–1946*. Singapore: Singapore University Press.

Chanderbali, D. (2008). *Indian Indenture in the Straits Settlements, 1872–1910*. Leeds: Peepal Press.

Cheah, B. K. (2007, July 13). Malayan Union and its impact. *The Sun*.

Drabble, J. (1973). *Rubber in Malaya, 1876–1922: The Genesis of the industry*. Kuala Lumpur: Oxford University Press.

Engels, F. (1973). *The conditions of the working class in England*. Moscow: Progress Publishers.

Frank, A. G. (1967). *Capitalism and underdevelopment in Latin America: Historical studies of Brazil and Chile*. New York: Monthly Review.

Furnivall, J. S. (1948). *Colonial policy and practice: A comparative study of Burma and Netherlands India*. Cambridge: University of Cambridge Press.

Gamba, C. (1962). *The origins of trade unionism in Malaya: A study in in colonial labour unrest*. Singapore: Eastern University Press.

Gullick, J. M. (1958). *Indigenous political systems of Western Malaya*. London: Athlone Press.

Gungwu, W. (1986). Foreword. In C.-H. Yen. *A social history of the Chinese in Singapore and Malaya 1800–1911*. Singapore: Oxford University Press.

Hale, C. (2013). *Massacre in Malaya: Exposing Britain's My Lai*. Stroud: The History Press.

Hildebrand, V. (2016). *Women at war: Subhas Chandra Bose and the Rani of Jhansi regiment*. New Delhi: Harper Collins.

Hobsbawm, E. (1969). *Industry and empire*. Harmondsworth: Penguin.

Hobsbawm, E. (1981, 19 March). *In search of people's history in London review of books* (Vol. 3, No. 5).

Hobsbawm, E. (2015). *Labouring men: Studies in the history of labour* . London: Weidenfield & Nicolson.

Ince, O. U. (2018). *Colonial capitalism and the dilemmas on liberalism*. New York: Oxford University Press.

Kaye, H. J. (1984). *The British Marxist historians*. Oxford: Polity Press.

Khong, K. H. (1984). *Merdeka: British Rule and The Struggle for Independence in Malaya, 1945–1957*. Petaling Jaya: Strategic Information Research Development (SIRD).

Kondapi, C. (1951). *Indians Overseas, 1838–1949*. New Delhi: Indian Council of World Affairs.

Kumar, A. (2017). *Coolies of the empire: Indentured Indians in the sugar colonies, 1830–1920*. Cambridge: Cambridge University Press.

Kumar, D. (1975, January). Landownership and inequality in the Madras Presidency, 1853–54 to 1946–47. *The Indian Economic & Social History Review*, 229–246.

Lowe, L. (2015). *The intimacies of four continents*. Duke University Press.

Mahmud, T. (2013). Cheaper than a slave: Indenture labour, colonialism and capitalism. *Whitter Law Review, 34*, 215–243.

Marjoribanks, N. E., & Marakkayar, A. K. G. T. (1917). *Report on Indian Labour Emigration to Ceylon and Malaya*. Madras: Government Press.

Meagher, A. J. (2008). *The coolie trade: The traffic in Chinese labourers to Latin America 1847–1874*. Bloomington: Xlibris Publishing Co.

Milner, A. (2016). *Kerajaan: Malay political culture on the eve of colonial rule*. Petaling Jaya: SIRD.

O'Brien, P. (1982). European economic development: The contribution of the periphery. *The Economic History Review (New Series), 35*(1), 1–18.

Parmer, N. (1960). *Colonial labour policy and administration: A history of labour in the rubber plantation industry in Malaya, 1910–1941*. New York: J. J. Augustin Inc.

Pitts, J. (2018). *Boundaries of the international: law and empire*. Cambridge: Harvard University Press.

Roff, W. R. (1967). *The origins of Malay nationalism*. New Haven: Yale University Press.

Roy, T. (2006). *The economic history of India, 1857–1947* (2nd ed.). New Delhi: Oxford University Press.

Saminathan, M. (2020). *Remembering the legacy of Malayan Trade Unionist S.A. Ganapathy* (unpublished paper).

Sandhu, K. S. (1969). *Indians in Malaya: Some aspects of their immigration and settlement (1786–1957)*. Cambridge: Cambridge University Press.

Sani, R. A. (2008). *Social roots of the Malay Left*. Petaling Jaya: Strategic Information and Research Institute (SIRD).

Sasidaran, S. (2012, October). A reflection of the plantation industry—Its origin, quest and challenges: Part 1. *The Planter, 88*(1039), 733–737.

Sasidaran, S. (2019). *Revisiting the death railway: The survivors' accounts*. Kuala Lumpur: University of Malaya Press.

Selvaratnam, V. (1960). *A history of Western enterprise in the state of Selangor from 1874 to 1895*. Department of History: University of Malaya (Singapore).

Selvaratnam, V. (1976). *Metropolitan control and South Indian Proletariat on the Malaysian Frontier: The persistence of powerlessness and poverty*. Ph.D. thesis, University of Manchester.

Sharil, T. (1982, Januari–Julai). A revolt in Malaysian historiography. *Akademia, 20 & 21*, 447–465.

Sharil, T. (2004). *Inaugural Lecture: Interrogating the state and craft of History: The Malaysian historiographical journey*. Kuala Lumpur: University of Malaya.

Srinivasa Sastri, V. S. (1937). *Report on the Conditions of Indian Labour in Malaya*. Kuala Lumpur: Government Press.

Stenson, M. R. (1970). *Industrial conflict in Malaya: Prelude to the communist revolt of 1948*. London: Oxford University Press.

Stenson, M. (1980). *Class, race and colonialism in Peninsular Malaysia*. Brisbane: Queensland University Press.

Tayyab, M. (2013). Cheaper than a slave: Indentured labour, colonialism and capitalism. *Whittier Law Review, 34,* 215–243.

Tharoor, S. (2016). *An era of darkness: The British Empire in India*. New Delhi: Aleph Book Co.

Tinker, H. (1974). *A new system of slavery: Export of Indian labour overseas, 1830–1920*. Oxford: Oxford University Press.

Tinker, H. (1976). *Separate and unequal: India and Indians in the British Commonwealth, 1920–1950*. London: C. Hurst & Co.

Toye, H. (1991). *Subhas Chandra Bose: The Springing Tiger*. Mumbai: Jaico Publishing House.

Tully, J. (2011). *The devil's milk: A social history of rubber*. New York: Monthly Review Press.

Yuen, W. T. (2013). *Chinese capitalism in Colonial Malaya 1900–1941*. Bangi, Malaysia: National University of Malaysia Press.

Wallerstein, I. (1983). *Historical capitalism*. London: Verso.

Williams, E. (1944). *Capitalism and slavery*. Chapel Hill: University of North Carolina Press.

Wilson, H. E. (1981). *The Klang Strikes of 1941: Labour and capital in colonial Malaya*. Research Notes and Discussion Paper No. 25. Singapore: Institute of Southeast Asian Studies.

CHAPTER 9

Sustaining the Hakka Chinese Identity in Sabah: The Role of the Basel Church

Danny Tze Ken Wong

Introduction

During his tenure at the University of Malaya, Professor Shaharil Talib was instrumental in introducing Fernand Braudel's *longue durée* to many young scholars. He was hoping to challenge the manner in which Malaysian history was being written at the time—encouraging many to explore issues in Malaysian history by taking a long panoramic view, in chronological terms as well as digging into distant past to draw inferences. Using his influence as both scholar and leader, he was able to encourage many to explore new topics in Malaysian and Southeast Asian history by emphasising on Braudel's vast, panoramic view, and downplaying the importance of specific events. The topic of this chapter is something that has to be discussed by focusing on the question of objectivity when writing about one's own community. More importantly, Shaharil also

D. T. K. Wong (✉)
Faculty of Arts and Social Sciences, University of Malaya,
Kuala Lumpur, Malaysia
e-mail: dannyw@um.edu.my

R. Rasiah et al. (eds.), *Contesting Malaysia's Integration into the World Economy*, https://doi.org/10.1007/978-981-16-0650-2_9

talked about looking at the evolving identity of a people from a broad perspective.

Chinese presence in Sabah had begun long before the establishment of the British North Borneo (Chartered) Company rule in the state in 1881.[1] The earlier Chinese were mainly petty traders who came from the Straits Settlements and the southern Philippines, and were engaged in trade with the indigenous population. The opening of Labuan in 1846 by the British Government also resulted in some Chinese presence on the island as well as on the west coast of the mainland.[2] These early connections, as well as the group of Chinese who came for the aborted attempt by the Americans to develop their settlement at Kimanis in 1865, resulted in very few Chinese settling in Sabah before the establishment of the Chartered Company rule.[3] It was only after the setting up of the Chartered Company administration that the Chinese began to come to Sabah in large numbers. By the beginning of the twentieth century, the Chinese community had become a permanent feature in the state.

The Chinese community in Sabah is made up of at least five major dialect groups namely: Hakka, Cantonese, Hokkien, Teochiu, and Hailam. Among these, the Hakka community is the largest, making up about 58% of the Chinese community in 2000 (Population and Housing Census of Malaysia, 2000). Mainly due to their numbers, the Hakka dialect has become the *lingua franca* of the Chinese community in the state. Such features are distinctive rather than common, and have few parallels in other parts of Malaysia or Southeast Asia. The numerical dominance of the Hakka is indeed a deciding factor in the dialect being the main Chinese dialect in Sabah.[4]

This paper will explore the role of a Christian church, namely, the Basel Church in forging Hakka identity in Sabah by tracing the historical ties between the church, through the Basel Missionary Society of Switzerland, and the North Borneo Company which was the first modern administrative entity that governed the state between 1881 and 1946. This is followed by a critical analysis of the various means through which the

[1] To date, there are several works on the Chinese of Sabah; among them are Purcell (1980); Han (1976); Wong (1998) & Wong (2000a).

[2] For a study on the Chinese in Labuan, see Tarling (1970).

[3] For a discussion on the Kimanis venture, see Tregonning (1965); see also his 1954; see also Keith (1980).

[4] For a study on this, see my work, Wong (2003a).

Basel Church had contributed to the process of shaping Hakka identity in Sabah. Finally, this paper will discuss the challenges faced by the Basel Church in sustaining its Hakka origin (identity) in the face of changes that were taking place within the Hakka community and the Chinese community at large.

There have been some attempts to investigate the Hakkas by academicians and laymen alike, but the results have been wanting. David Fortier, an American anthropologist, was perhaps the first to have conducted a study on the Hakka community in Sabah, by investigating the evolution of the Hakka settlers in the interior plantation region of Sapong, near Tenom.[5] However, due to his anthropological approach, Fortier did not disclose exact information on the individuals he had interviewed, and provided little clue to the larger picture of the community in the state. In a survey conducted in the same area, it was clear that the Hakka community in Sapong were established mainly in the 1950s, and that ever since their establishment, the three settlements at Mile 8, Mile 10, and Mile 14 maintained strong ties with the Basel Church, and that the church had established congregations at all these settlements.

K. G. Tregonning's survey volume on the history of modern Sabah also provided some information on the Hakka community in the state.[6] Having consulted most of the official records available to him, Tregonning's study provided important historical background for further research on the community. However, as his study is a survey on the history of Sabah, the Hakkas were only mentioned in brief. Niew Shong Tong's study provided some glimpses on the immigration process of the Hakkas into the state.[7] According to Niew, the Hakkas first arrived in Sabah immediately after the collapse of the Taiping Rebellion in 1864.[8] While this has not been ascertained, it is clear that many families had some links to the Taiping Rebellion. Another work on the Hakkas in Sabah is a small booklet jointly produced by the Department of Sabah Museum and State Archives and the United Sabah Hakka Association in 1990,

[5] Fortier (1964).

[6] Tregonning (1965).

[7] Niew (1993).

[8] The Taiping Rebellion (1850–1865) that started in Guangxi in 1850, was initially joined mainly by the Hakka. Its leader, Hong Xiuquan, was influenced by Christian missionaries from the Basel mission and maintained ties with them for a time. See Spence (1996).

in conjunction with the 10th World Hakka Convention, held in Kota Kinabalu, Sabah.[9] The booklet, which is an accompanying programme book for an exhibition on the Hakka community in Sabah, contains a brief account of the arrival of the Hakkas in Sabah, followed by a survey of prominent Hakkas in the various towns of Sabah (Sandakan Hakka Association, 1986: 348–353).

More recent studies on the Hakkas in Sabah include the work by Zhang Delai, (Chong Tet Loi) whose *Hakka in Sabah* is the most comprehensive survey published on the subject.[10] Other works published include several by the present writer offering a closer look into the history of the Hakka community in Sabah.[11]

This study takes the long view historical approach, by looking at the development of the Hakka identity in Sabah since 1882 and the manner it was sustained throughout the decades; its ties to the Basel Church, as well as the way this church provided the impetus to reinforce this identity. The study utilises both official and non-official records and writings. The former includes correspondences and documents of the British North Borneo (Chartered) Company.. The non-official sources are mainly publications by various organisations relating to the Hakka community in Sabah. This comprises of materials published or kept by the Basel Christian Church and publications by the various Hakka associations in the state.

Historical Ties Between the Basel Church and the Hakkas

The Basel Church in Sabah traces its origins from the community of Hakkas in the Guangdong province. They were the Hakkas whom the Basel Missionary Society of Switzerland was carrying out its missions' work. The Basel Missionary Society was a Christian evangelical mission established in 1815 in the city of Basel in northern Switzerland. Its objective was to bring the Christian faith to different parts of the world. Throughout its 200 years of existence, its main missions were in Cameroon, Ghana, Nigeria, Sudan, India, Latin America, Borneo, and

[9] Sabah Museum (1990).

[10] Zhang (2002).

[11] See Wong (2000b), see also Wong (2003b, 2005).

China. In China, the society started work in 1847, initially among the Hokklos community in Chaozhou, but failed. It was then that the mission moved to work among the Hakkas. The circle of Hakkas concentrated in the Hakka heartland of Guangdong's northeast region, including Meixian (Moi Yen), Zijin (Tze Kim), Wuhua (Ng Fah), Longchuan, Huiyang (Fuiyong), Baoan (Bao On), Heyuan (Ho Yen), and Qinyuan (Ching Yen). Some of these areas were in fact the poorest in the province.

The Basel Missionary Society came to the Hakkas at a time when southern China had just experienced the Taiping Rebellion (1850–1864). Most of those who were involved in the rebellion were Hakka peasants from Guangdong and the neighboring province of Guangxi. Hong Xiuquan, the leader of the rebellion was himself a Hakka with ties to some of the Basel Missionaries. The aftermath of the rebellion saw the Qing Government carrying out a series of punitive actions aimed at exacting retributions from those who were involved in the rebellion. Many families were implicated in the rebellion either by active involvement or by mere association of familial ties. Due to such pressure, many of the Hakkas decided that they should go abroad to avoid incrimination and the difficult life in their homeland.[12]

The Basel Missionary Society's work among the Hakkas was carried out using a two-pronged strategy. First, the mission went all out to convert the Hakkas to Christianity and at the same time, built churches and mission stations. A theological seminary was established by the mission at Lilang with the aim of providing training to local Christians in the hope that they too may become pastors (church leaders) and missionaries among their own people. Second, the Basel Missionary Society also established a series of schools which provided education to these Hakkas. These activities bore fruits as by the 1870s, the Lilang seminary had produced a small number of Hakka Christian leaders. They were appointed catechists by the mission and sent to work among their own communities (Lutz & Lutz, 2008: 4).

More importantly, the Basel mission had also taken on the task of providing a way out for the Hakkas, particularly those who were already Christians, from being constantly harassed or persecuted by the Qing

[12] Many Hakka families who arrived in Sabah professed to having links with the Taiping Rebellion. In fact, one family even claimed that their forefather was the youngest son of Hong Xiuquan, the leader of the Taiping. Interview with Doreen Hurst nee Funk (Hong), Canberra, August 2004.

Government for their involvement in the Taiping Rebellion. It was under such circumstances that the mission began to look beyond the shores of China and started to help to settle some of these Hakka Christians abroad, including North Borneo or Sabah.

The following sections will look into three areas where the Basel Church had been pivotal in helping to forge the Hakka identity in Sabah,

1. The migration process and creation of Hakka settlements
2. The establishment of churches and schools
3. Church members' involvement in Hakka associations

Basel Mission and Immigration of Hakkas to Sabah

The Basel Missionary Society started to establish links with the North Borneo Company in 1881 when Reverend Rudolph Leschler (Basel Christian Church of Malaysia, 1983: 4) [13] was approached by the company's agent who was in search of immigrants who would settle in Sabah. The idea was part of the company's first ever immigration scheme introduced and operated by Sir Walter Medhurst.[14] It was aimed at bringing the right type of Chinese immigrants to North Borneo. The North Borneo Chartered Company was hoping to emulate the successes of Singapore and the Malay States in utilising Chinese labour and capital in achieving economic progress. Medhurst was a former British Consul in Shanghai and appointed by the North Borneo Company as its first Immigration Commissioner. His task was to bring Chinese immigrants and capital into North Borneo aimed at developing the state.

Medhurst's initial venture resulted in the arrival of a large number of Chinese who were predominantly traders and businessmen. For a while, the presence of these Chinese brought a sense of prosperity in the major

[13] Rudolph Leschler (1824–1908), was born into a family of pastors in Wittenburg, Germany. After graduating from the Basel Theological College, he was sent to China in 1847 as a missionary of the Basel Mission. He initially assigned to the Hoklos of Swatow until 1852, when he started to work among the Hakka in Guangdong province until he left China in 1899. A pioneer in Christian ministry among the Hakka, he also published a *Romanised Hakka Colloquial Gospel of Matthew*. He was chiefly responsible in engineering the emigration of the Hakka from China to Sabah.

[14] Several studies are available on the immigration of Chinese into Sabah, among them Oades (1961); Niew (1993); and Wong (1999).

towns of North Borneo as shops were being set up by these new arrivals. However, the company soon realised that the merchant class was not the type of Chinese required for the development of the state. After that, the emphasis was to bring immigrants who were more suitable for opening up land. However, out of this original venture came the first batch of Hakka immigrants who were part of the Basel Missionary Society flock who responded to Medhurst's call. They were considered by the Chartered Company as the right type of immigrants needed for Sabah's future development. Hence, efforts were made to further accelerate the immigration process between the North Borneo Company and the Basel Missionary Society to bring new batches of Hakka immigrants into Sabah.

Upon learning of Medhurst's offer, Rev. Leschler decided to send two delegates to Sabah in November 1882 (Tregonning, 1965: 132). After inspecting the land offered to them, and having held discussions with Governor William H. Treacher, their reports resulted in the immediate emigration of two groups of Hakka Christians to Sabah. On 14 January 1883, thirteen Hakka Christian immigrants landed in Kudat after making the journey on the *S. S. Fokkien*. They included 'a delegate for a large number of intending immigrants from the same districts and who mediate making North Borneo (Sabah) their home' (*British North Borneo Herald*, 1 March 1883). There were also among them, women and children. This feature distinguishes them from other early Chinese immigrant communities in Southeast Asia who that mainly comprised of males.

Favourable terms were offered with the Hakka immigrants provided land and financial advance. Apart from that, they were also given temporary lodging, as well as tools and seeds to start planting. It was under similar terms that further Hakka migration to Sabah was promoted between 1882 and 1889. In 1885, Medhurst left the company's service and though the immigration process continued for a while, by 1889, the first wave of Hakka immigration to Sabah through the Basel Missionary Society had come to an end.

New immigration schemes were started to bring in more Chinese, and the initial initiatives that started between the Basel Missionary Society and the North Borneo Company came to a temporary halt. It was not until 1913 that new arrangements were made between the two parties for more Hakka immigrants to come to Sabah. Between 1889 and 1913, however, many Hakkas entered the state either as free immigrants or to join their family members who had arrived earlier.

In 1913, the North Borneo Company, once again, entered into an agreement with the Basel Missionary Society to bring in new Hakka immigrants to Sabah. Much of the initiatives came from Sir West Ridgeway, the company's Chairman, who was very keen to bring in more immigrants to become settlers instead of labourers. As a result, in 1913 Ridgeway managed to bring in a group of northerners who settled on the outskirts of Jesselton (Kota Kinabalu).[15] At the same time, the company had also arranged to have another large group of Hakkas to be brought into Sabah. This effort resulted in the creation of three new Hakka settlements on the west coast of Sabah, namely in Inanam, Menggatal, and Telipok. These new immigrants were brought in under some of the most favourable terms ever provided by the company—five to ten acres of land with easy terms, financial advancements, and promises from the government to provide land for churches and schools. The creation of these three settlements also helped to ensure the Hakka Christians' domination on the west coast of Sabah.

The Basel Missionary Society remained a reliable recruiter for the Chartered Company. Arrangements were made to encourage more Hakka Christians, who were considered to be the 'right class' of immigrants,[16] and who were regarded as the mainstay of the agricultural and industrial population of the state.

The new Hakka settlements along the Tuaran road connecting Inanam, Menggatal, Telipok, Temparuli, and Tuaran resulted in the further development of a group of Christian Chinese smallholders, similar to those who had arrived earlier in Kudat. Due to their access to favourable land concessions and government subsidies, the Hakka Christians had by the 1920s, become important rubber smallholders in Sabah. The landholding of most Hakka settlers was small, normally ranging from five to 15 acres. Thus in 1919, the predominantly Hakka smallholders had cultivated 7578 acres of rubber against a total of 47,739 acres planted state-wide,[17] which was more than one-sixth of the state's total. While their holdings could not match the European-owned rubber estates, they remained important contributors to the development of the Sabah economy.

[15] See Tan (1997).

[16] "Governor Gueritz to Court of Director", 7 December 1905, *CO874/746*.

[17] British North Borneo Company, *Annual Report on Agriculture* (1919).

Further immigration processes on the part of the Chartered Company helped ensure that more Hakkas were being brought into Sabah. Of all the programmes, none was more effective than the Free Passage Scheme. Introduced in 1921, the scheme was a means by the Chartered Company to bring settlers into the country. The scheme involved inducement from the Chartered Company for those settlers already in Sabah to apply to bring in their relatives, with expenses covered by the government. Upon arrival, these new immigrants would either join their relatives or apply for land on their own. The implementation of this scheme had benefited many, but more so were those associated with the Basel Missionary Society, as many of the existing settlers were made up of this group of Hakkas. Between 1921 and 1941, the Free Passage Scheme had brought in close to 10,000 Chinese immigrants, and almost all of them were Hakkas.[18]

However, it must be pointed out that participation in the scheme did not directly involve the Basel Missionary Society. Its implementation had relied on the initiatives of the Hakka settlers themselves to recruit their relations. The scheme helped enhance Hakka identity through sheer numerical reinforcement—also as a result of having women as part of its composition—ensuring that the Hakka remained the largest dialect group and its language the *lingua franca* among the Chinese in Sabah. Most of these new immigrants were settled on the government-subsidised settlements in Inanam, Menggatal, Telipok, Tuaran, Pinangsoo, Tamalang Bamboo, Buk Buk, and Penampang. The spread of this dialect owes a great deal to the Basel Church in enforcing its usage and its spread to other parts of the state.

If the identity of a people is also associated with the material culture of the community and its way of life, then the emergence of these Basel Church-related Hakka settlements in Sabah, particularly on its west coast, has helped introduce many special characteristics of the Hakka people to the general lifestyle of the Chinese in Sabah. Hakka food such as spring-rolls (*Chun-Kyuen*), meatballs (beef) (*Nyuk Yen*), stuffed tofu (*Nyong Teufu*), and the famous sliced meat with yam (*Kieu Nyuk*) have become very much a part of the Chinese classical cuisine of Sabah.

[18] *North Borneo Annual and Administrative Reports* (1921–1940).

Hakka-Speaking Churches and Schools

Despite taking an active role in assisting the Hakka Christians in migrating to Sabah, for many years, the Basel Missionary Society did not send its clergymen to the state. Hence, for their spiritual life, the early Hakka immigrants depended very much on their lay leaders. Many of these leaders had received training in theology, and hence were able to provide some form of leadership to the new settlers. However, for religious purposes, many initially joined the Anglican Church which had a Hakka section. The Anglican Church had even despatched one of its clergymen, Reverend Richard Richards, to study the Hakka dialect in Hong Kong and Guangzhou. It is interesting to note that the baptismal register of the Anglican St. James' Church contained the names of those who were from the Basel denomination—who would later leave the Anglican Church once their own clergyman had arrived from China.

The first Hakka clergyman despatched by the Basel Missionary Society was Reverend Wong Tien Nyuk, who was initially working among a group of Chinese coal miners in Labuan before being sent to Kudat (Basel Christian Church of Malaysia, 1983: 20). There, he provided the necessary leadership thus far shouldered by lay leaders such as Wong Shuk Ming, Lee Siong Kong (Basel Christian Church of Malaysia, 1983: 18–19), and later Lo Tian Cheok (Wong, 1997: 118).[19] It was from such beginnings that the church began to grow. Later, other clergymen from the Basel Missionary Society were also sent to Sabah, among them was Yap Hien Mu. All these pastors, along with their European missionary counterparts, conducted their worship services and other religious ceremonies in the Hakka dialect.

The two decades between 1900 and 1920 were a significant period in the development of the Basel Church in Sabah. Alongside the development of the railway lines on the west coast from Jesselton to Tenom and Melalap, a number of Hakka-speaking churches were established by the Basel mission. The first one being in Papar in 1903, and one in Jesselton a year later. This was followed later by churches in Beaufort (1910) and Tenom (1912).[20]

[19] Lo Tian Cheok later became a member of the State Legislative Council.

[20] See Basel Christian Church in Malaysia, 1983 (Basel Christian Church of Malaysia, 1983: 18–19) for the brief history of the various parishes.

Between 1882 and the beginning of World War I, the Basel mission grew quite steadily. Apart from the Hakka clergy, the Church also had its fair number of European missionaries who were there to oversee the functioning of the church and schools. When war broke out in 1914, the Church had to face some unpleasant experiences. As many of the European missionaries were either German or Austrians, they were detained and later deported as enemy subjects since North Borneo was a British protectorate. As a result, the Church suffered from the want of leaders and teachers. Financially, as the Church had depended on the Basel Missionary Society, the freezing of enemy properties created some very undesirable experiences for it.

The difficult experience of war prompted the Church to rethink its position. A synod was held in 1925 to discuss the future direction of the church. It was decided that in order to avoid future repetition of their war experience, the church had to be independent of the Basel Missionary Society in Switzerland. As a result of the synod, a North Borneo Self-Established Basel Church was proclaimed. The establishment of this new church meant that the running of the church was entirely in the hands of the Hakka immigrants and their Hakka pastors. This development was crucial for the future development of the church, including the use of the Hakka dialect as the main language spoken in the church and schools.

In the field of education, the Hakkas made good progress through the role played by the Christian churches, particularly the Society for the Propagation of the Gospel in Foreign Parts (SPG) and the Basel Church, which were very much Hakka-based churches. In 1886, the Hakka Christians (of Basel) in Kudat started classes for their children at the premises of one of its members. The class later grew to be a proper school in 1901, called Lok Yuk, meaning 'willing to educate'. Since then, Lok Yuk schools could be found in almost every major town on the west coast of Sabah wherever a Basel Church was established, including Lauson (1903), Jesselton (1905), Menggatal (1930), and Inanam (1924). In Sandakan, the Basel Church started an English school in 1912, called the Sung Siew School: its first master was Reverend Fritz, a Basel missionary of Austrian origin, who was assisted by a Chinese master, Reverend Yap Hien Mu (Basel Christian Church of Malaysia, 1983: 20). The school was the first Chinese-based school which conducted lessons in English. The Basel Church also started another school in Papar which offered instruction in English. The school, named Anglo-Chinese School, was started sometime after 1922 under the leadership of Chin Chung Tat.

Leadership in the Hakka Dialect Association

One of the direct roles played by the Hakka leaders, both lay and clergy from the Basel Church, was their involvement in the Hakka dialect associations in Sabah. The involvement began almost as soon as the Hakka Christians arrived in Sabah. The first Hakka association was established in Sandakan in 1886 through the setting up of the San Sheng Kung Temple by a group of business leaders originating from Guangdong province. It also had a school offering lessons in the Cantonese dialect.

Some Hakka leaders, including a few from the Basel Church, were also heavily involved in the establishment of the Tan Gong Zhu Miao Temple, near the Chinese settlement at the suburb of Sandakan. The temple was dedicated to the deity of Tan Gong, usually venerated by Hakka from the Huizhou prefecture. Most of the Hakka on the east coast, including Sandakan, were from Huizhou. Several Hakka Christian leaders from the Basel Church also served as trustees to the temple. Among them was Lam Man Ching, a Hakka from Bao An who was later made the Capitan China for Sandakan. Another Hakka leader was Liau Nyuk Kui who was a businessman involved in agriculture and livestock. Other than the Tan Gong Zhu Miao Temple, the Hakkas in Sandakan also established two other temples, namely, Pan Gu Tian Wang Temple and Lie Shen Gong Temple (Sandakan Hakka Association, 1986: 43).

Most importantly, both Lam and Liau were also founding members of the Ngo Chen Hui Kon—which later became the Yan Who Hui Kon, the forerunner of the Hakka Association in Sandakan. It was through this association that the Hakka identity was sustained and preserved.

Over in the west coast, there was no effort to organise the Hakkas into association, at least not until 1940. There is no clear explanation for this situation, apart from the possibility that there was no immediate need for the Hakkas to get themselves organised as was the case in the west coast. The most likely explanation lies with the fact that the majority of the Hakkas on the west coast were closely linked to the Basel Church. The migration processes that took place there were strongly tied to the many schemes jointly organised by the Basel Missionary Society and the North Borneo Company. Therefore, much of the community life of the early Hakkas on the west coast had probably evolved around the churches that were set up by the Basel Church. This was different from the situation in Sandakan where many Hakkas were not linked to churches. The cases of the Hakka-linked temples are clear evidence. As most of their needs and problems were usually presented to the government through their church leaders, the need to organise was not undertaken until much later.

The Hakkas in the west coast only started to organise in 1940 when a Hakka association was established in Jesselton. Interestingly, almost all the leaders of the association were leaders and members of the Basel Church. In fact, the chief organiser was Reverend Lee Wok Sin, the main pastor of the Basel Church on the west coast, who duly became the first chairman of the association. The decision to form a Hakka association on the west coast was in fact a response to the calls by a regional Nanyang Hakka Association in Singapore (Zhang, 2002: 102). It is also likely that by 1940, there were already a large number of Hakkas who had arrived and settled on the west coast but were not members of the Basel Church. Many either came as part of the Free Passage Scheme or as free immigrants.

In a way, this new development is a reflection of the changing nature of the post-war Hakka population in Sabah whereby a large percentage were not Christians nor associated with the Basel Church. Many actually came down as free immigrants and had nothing to do with the church. Nevertheless, the links between individuals from the Basel Church and the leadership of the Hakka associations in Sabah have continued well into the present day.

Challenges of Post-independence

When Sabah joined the Federation of Malaysia in 1963, Hakkas consisted of roughly 60% of the total Chinese population in the state. This figure would remain constant throughout the entire period from 1963 until the present day. The Basel Church, now renamed Basel Christian Church of Malaysia (BCCM), had also grown to become one of the largest non-Catholic churches. This growth, both in the number of churches and membership, however, did not necessarily mean the strengthening of the Hakka identity that had been forged during the pre-independence days. In fact, starting from the mid-1950s, even the special position of the Basel Church as the bastion of Hakka identity had begun to suffer from some degree of erosion. Despite the continued usage of the Hakka dialect in almost all of its transactions, new changes were starting to reshape the identity of the Basel Church.

The first major change was the introduction of the English language in many of the church's activities. This is a reflection of the receptiveness of the Hakka Christians within the Basel Church towards English education. Many have looked to English education as a mode of change towards modernisation. Thus, many of the younger generations were sent to study in English medium schools with significant numbers gaining tertiary education abroad. When these new graduates returned, many felt that they were more comfortable with the English language and demanded the introduction of English worship services to be added to the original Hakka worship services. By 1953, the churches in Jesselton and Sandakan had already started worship services in English (Basel Self-Established Church of Borneo, 1955: 23). Today, there are five churches with English services and one church in the Kota Kinabalu area that conducts its transactions entirely in English language.

Apart from the challenges posed by English language, the Basel Church's Hakka identity was also undermined by the establishment of Mandarin-speaking worship services in the churches. This again, is a phenomenon of the 1980s onward when more children from the Basel Church started attending Chinese independent secondary schools. Many were attracted by the promise of having the opportunity of gaining proficiency in Chinese, English, and the Malay, as opposed to just Malay and English education offered at the national secondary schools as well as the national-type schools, which all of the Basel Church-sponsored schools have become. Many of these independent school leavers however were more fluent in Mandarin than in any other language. Hence the demand for Mandarin-medium church worship services in addition to the traditional ones in Hakka.

Another contributing factor was the changing nature of the membership of the Basel Church. From the time when the church was started in the late nineteenth century, up to the 1950s, almost 100% of the members of the Basel Church were Hakkas. As the church expanded through its mission work and schools, and became successful, its membership grew and thus transcending dialect barriers and divisions. And as more non-Hakkas joined the church, the church's Hakka identity somehow became diluted. According to Zhang Delai, intermarriages between Hakka members and non-Hakkas also contributed to the change in the Hakka identity of the Church,

"The constituents of the Church also underwent changes. Throughout its existence, there had been intermarriages between members and people of other dialects or races. These non-Hakkas as well as non-Chinese were readily assimilated if they were comfortable with the predominantly Hakka atmosphere. Occasionally, the assimilation of non-Hakka dialect members made it necessary to start Mandarin worship services. Moreover, the non-Hakka multitude paved the way for a heterogenous dialect-speaking church leadership. Active non-Hakka members were enlisted as stewards, and were subsequently elected into congregation committees and thus eligible for parish and central council posts" (Zhang, 2002: 65).

Conclusion

The Basel Christian Church of Malaysia's position as a Hakka church stemmed from its historical origins in Guangdong. When the church was started in Sabah, it was among the Hakka Christian immigrants, hence ensuring that the church remained a Hakka-based entity. As the church was expanding, it was helped by the government's efforts in bringing more Hakka settlers, which benefited the church greatly.

Throughout its more than a hundred years in Sabah, the church has played a vital role in helping to enhance and sustain the Hakka identity in Sabah that centred around the Hakka dialect as well as the Hakka way of life. These were done through the various activities carried out by the church, especially through its church services and schools. There were also efforts by individual church leaders who were involved in the establishment of Hakka associations and provided leadership to these organisations. However, despite all these, it must be pointed out that the church had never declared itself as the champion of Hakka identity, and neither did it at any time—overtly or otherwise—introduce a programme that was geared towards promoting or enhancing Hakka identity. Whatever role that was visible, was merely a reflection of the church's original nature as a Hakka-based church and a perpetuation of such nature.

With the passage of time, it is obvious that the traditional barriers of dialect differences have become less important. The church's position as the bastion of Hakka identity was challenged by several external changes such as the preference for other dialects and new languages. Ironically, the church's position as a Hakka church was also eroded by its successful expansion which resulted in the incorporation of many non-Hakkas into its ranks.

The chapter argues that the Basel Church, through its institutionalisation of Hakka-ness, both in terms of language and activities (e.g. churches and schools), have been instrumental in enhancing the Hakka identity among the Chinese in Sabah. The immigration process facilitated by the Basel Missionary Society resulted in the Hakkas having numerical superiority over other dialect groups, thus ensuring its pre-eminent position as the largest community in Sabah. However, the paper also shows that despite such initial advantages, this Hakka identity became threatened by changes that were taking place, so much so that even the church's own Hakka identity is now at stake.

References

Basel Christian Church of Malaysia. (1983). *BCCM centenary magazine 1882–1982.* Kota Kinabalu: Basel Christian Church of Malaysia.

Basel Self-Established Church of Borneo. (1955). *Annual report.* Jesselton: Basel Self-Established Church of Borneo.

British North Borneo Company. (1919). *Annual report on agriculture.* Sandakan: North Borneo Company.

British North Borneo Herald (hereafter *BNBH*), 1 March 1883.

Fortier, D. H. (1964). *Culture change among Chinese agricultural settlers in British North Borneo.* Ph.D. Thesis, Columbia University.

Han, S. F. (1976). *The Chinese in Sabah.* East Malaysia, Taipei: The Oriental Cultural Service.

Keith, H. G. (1980). *The United States consul and the Yankee Raja.* Brunei Museum Monograph, 4.

Lutz, J. G., & Lutz, R. R. (2008). *Hakka Chinese confront protestant Christianity, 1850–1900, with the autobiographies of eight Hakka Christians and commentary.* London: M. E. Sharpe.

Niew, S. T. (1993, June). A brief history of the Hakka immigrants in East Malaysia. *Asian Culture, 17*, 187–195.

North Borneo Annual and Administrative Reports (1921–1940).

Oades, R. (1961). *Chinese emigration through Hong Kong to North Borneo since 1880.* M. A. Dissertation, Hong Kong University.

Population and Housing Census of Malaysia. (2000). *Sabah.* Kuala Lumpur: Department of Statistics Malaysia.

Purcell, V. (1980). *The Chinese in southeast Asia.* London: Oxford University Press (Reprint).

Sabah Museum. 1990. *The Hakka in Sabah.* Kota Kinabalu: The Department of Sabah Museum and State Archives & The United Sabah Hakka Association, in conjunction with the 10th World Hakka Convention, 1990, Kota Kinabalu.

Sandakan Hakka Association. (1986). *Sandakan Hakka association centenary anniversary, 1986–1986* (pp. 348–353). Sandakan: Sandakan Hakka Association.

Spence, J. (1996). *God's Chinese son.* New York, NY: Norton.

Tan, C. B. (1997). The northern Chinese of Sabah, Malaysia: Origins and some sociocultural aspects. *Asian Culture, 21,* 19–37.

Tarling, N. (1970). The entrepot at Labuan and the Chinese. *Sabah Society Journal, 2,* 101–116.

Tregonning, K. G. (1965). *A history of modern Sabah.* Singapore: University of Malaya Press.

Tregonning, K. G. (1954, November). American activity in North Borneo, 1865–1881. *The Pacific History Review, 23*(4), 357–372.

Wong, T. K. D. (1997). "Lo Tian Cheok" n Lee Kam Hing and Chow Mun Seong (comp.). *Biographical dictionary of the Chinese in Malaysia.* Petaling Jaya: Pelanduk Publications.

Wong, T. K. D. (1998). *The transformation of an immigrant society: A study of the Chinese of Sabah.* London: ASEAN Academic Press.

Wong, T. K. D. (1999). Chinese migration to sabah before the second world war. *Archipel, 58*(3), 131–158.

Wong T. K. D. (2000a). The Chinese in Sabah: An overview. In L. K. Hing & T. C. Beng (Eds.), *The Chinese in Malaysia* (pp. 382–406). Kuala Lumpur: Oxford University Press.

Wong T. K. D. (2000b). The Hakka in Sabah, 1882–1946. *Sabah Society Journal,* 1–36.

Wong T. K. D. (2003a, December 13–14). *Early Hakka businessmen and entrepreneurs of Sabah, 1882–1941.* In International Conference on Hakka in Asia Pacific, organised by the Hakka Research Institute, Taiwan Central University and Miao Li County Government.

Wong T. K. D. (2003b). The search for modernity: The Chinese in Sabah and English Education. In M. W. Charney, T. C. Kiong, & B. Yeoh (Eds.), *Chinese migrants abroad: Cultural, educational, and social dimensions of the Chinese diaspora* (pp. 145–160). Singapore: Singapore University Press & World Scientific.

Wong, T. K. D. (2005, December). The Hakka of Sabah and English education. *Oceanic Culture Journal,* (Taiwan) (1), 67–85. [in Chinese].

Zhang, D. (Chong Tet Loi). (2002). *The Hakkas of Sabah: A survey of their impact on the modernization of the Borneon Malaysian state.* Kota Kinabalu: Sabah Theological Seminary.

CHAPTER 10

Hegemonic Instability in the Evolving Geopolitics of Southeast Asia

Johan Saravanamuttu

Introduction

Since the Vietnam War (1955–1975), Western dominance in Southeast Asian geopolitics has seen a steady decline. However, colonial legacies may be said to still have had influences during the post-Vietnam War and post-Cold War periods of Southeast Asian geopolitics. While European (French, Dutch and British) geopolitical presence has dissipated in current day Southeast Asia, there continued to be a system of Western-inspired but watered-down American-led arrangements aimed at maintaining regional stability among Southeast Asian states particularly during the Cold War and to some extent even till the present time. Importantly, regional geopolitics have increasingly been tempered by the emergence of Association of Southeast Asia Nations (ASEAN) regionalism in the late 1960s and the progressive fashioning of ASEAN constructs for regional stability. This chapter advances the idea that regional geopolitical constructs and norms have progressively led to the discarding of colonial

J. Saravanamuttu (✉)
Asia-Europe Institute, University of Malaya, Kuala Lumpur, Malaysia

R. Rasiah et al. (eds.), *Contesting Malaysia's Integration into the World Economy*, https://doi.org/10.1007/978-981-16-0650-2_10

legacies. Constructivist scholars posited that ASEAN over time evinced an agency in crafting its own regional institutions and norms to leverage on the notion of 'ASEAN centrality' in stabilising regional politics into the twenty-first century. Hitherto, the notion of "hegemonic stability" in international relations literature implied that a major hegemon, such as a European power like Britain or the United States, would undergird regional stability. With the apparent decline of an American-led world order even before the Trump Administration and the emergence of a more multipolar global system, balancing by other major powers may have already superseded American hegemonic stability in Southeast Asian regional politics. It may be too early to speak of a "post-hegemonic" world order (Cox, 1996; Acharya, 2018) but the evidence is strong that hegemonic stability, such as there was, as conceived by various proponents, neo-realist, liberal and Marxist, is being unravelled or reconfigured at the current conjuncture of global politics.[1]

This chapter posits that hedging and balancing have outpaced bandwagoning as new strategies in the foreign policy of Southeast Asia.[2] Such a change may have occurred even in the post-Cold War era when the United States failed to seize the so-called "unipolar moment". The changing character of global politics has allowed for a large measure of agency and flexibility in the foreign policy of small and medium states in the ASEAN formation. Moreover, hegemonic stability, such as may have existed, has been disrupted by China's putative rise in the twenty-first century. However, hegemonic stability of a more multipolar sort in the wider Asia-Pacific region has been buttressed by states such as Japan, Australia and South Korea, which so far have remained as US allies.[3] The

[1] Some analysts have been debating the validity of hegemonic stability. See, for example, Gowa (1989), who suggests that it is the anarchical world order which leads to a stable world economy devaluing the role of hegemons. On the other hand, an empirical analysis of the concept found it to be adequately robust (Kwon, 2012).

[2] Bandwagoning refers to categorical support or alliance with a hegemonic power while balancing, seen on a continuum, is at the other end of the spectrum. Hedging strategies, in the midpoint of the same continuum, implies keeping options open. For gradations of such hedging strategies vis-à-vis China, from the perspectives of Malaysia and Singapore, see Kuik (2008: 166 and *passim*). For a perspective on "double hedging" from an Indonesian perspective, see Mubah (2019). Others like Lee (2017) have also used notions such as "hard" versus "soft" hedging.

[3] Japan, South Korea and Australia have maintained alliances with the hegemonic United States and in my view contributes to a softer notion of hegemonic stability in a more

new balancing by regional states takes a leaf from the Obama Administration's policy of "Rebalancing" and follows *a fortiori* upon a new "America First" posture of the Trump Administration, which appears to eschew direct military and even high levels of political involvement outside of the United States.

The Notion of Hegemonic Stability

We begin with a brief interrogation of hegemonic stability theory (HST), which has been the subject of considerable scrutiny by international relations scholars. The use of the term is attributable to Robert Keohane (1984) in his discussion of institutionalisation of international regimes which was considered necessary to manage economic disruptions, transactions costs across borders and the efficient regulation of the world economy. The main proponent of this liberal view is Kindleberger (1973) who studied the Great Depression of 1929–1939. Among the strongest proponents that a single hegemon is necessary for this task is Robert Gilpin (2000, 2001), who exemplifies a neo-realist perspective. Gilpin has mounted a strong defence of HST in the face of various conceptual and empirical critiques, viz.

Lack of a counterfactual makes it impossible either to validate or refute the theory of hegemonic stability... For these reasons, even though the hegemonic stability theory (HST) does not provide a foolproof account of the eras of British and American leadership of the world economy, it does hold up quite well by the standards of the social sciences, including economics (Gilpin, 2001: 97).

There are three major conceptualisations of hegemonic stability: Marxist/World-System (Arrighi, Wallerstein); Liberal (Kindleberger) and Realist (Gilpin, Krasner).[4] What the liberal and realist perspectives tend to underplay or even ignore is the orchestration of the cycles of capitalist accumulation of direct benefit to global hegemons. Arrighi (1994) suggests that this occurs in three phases of systemic expansion, hegemonic

multipolar world. In Southeast Asia, the Philippines remains the only formal ally of the United States although Singapore is close to the United States, while seemingly going along with the hedging strategies of other ASEAN states.

[4] I have left the names mentioned here without full citations, which can be found in Mendes (2018). His excellent survey of literature provides a clear characterisation of these perspectives (Mendes, 2018: 443 and *passim*).

crisis and then breakdown. Based on this theory, hegemony stability according to Arrighi has seen four cycles:

> [I]n the last 500 years, four world powers stood out for the building of production and accumulation chains: Genoa, United Provinces, Great Britain and the US. These political units became more powerful one after another, and except in the case of the last one, were replaced according to predictable historical pattern. This pattern consisted of a phase of productive economic expansion, followed by a phase of financial accumulation, and then decline. (Mendes, 2018: 440)

The prospect of US hegemonic decline or even breakdown appears to be a distinct possibility in the second half of the twenty-first century. We shall return to this subject later. Most importantly we are interested to show how the dominance and hegemony of the United States and, by implication, hitherto colonial hegemony, in the Southeast Asian region may have floundered in the period after the founding of the ASEAN. These two phases of US hegemony in Southeast Asia, a period of intense conflict of Communist versus non-Communist states and the US intervention in Vietnam in the 1950s leading to the Vietnam War. In the post-Vietnam War environment, major powers continued to exercise considerable influence in the region politically and economically. An ascendant China and the continued Russian engagement no doubt contributed to the disruption of the hegemonic stability of the United States as it started to disengage militarily from Southeast Asia under the Guam Doctrine. However, it could be argued that given continued American global economic pre-eminence, hegemonic stability prevailed in the Southeast Asian region in the post-Vietnam War and post-Cold War environment of the late twentieth century.

This, the more so, because hitherto Communist states began to embrace market capitalism and neoliberalism after the collapse of Communism in Eastern Europe and the end of the Cold War. There is thus considerable discussion in the literature of the lost "unipolar moment" even as the United States emerged as the main superpower underpinning the global neoliberal economic order. The idea of a post-hegemonic world order premised on critical theory (Cox, 1996) and constructivism (Acharya, 2018) suggests that US hegemony may have become progressively diluted over time.[5] Cognizant of the critical theory of Cox, this chapter leans on constructivism as a lens to visualise the Southeast Asian regional order and the current reconfiguration of "hegemonic instability" or hegemonic contestation and balancing by various powers in the region. It argues that such an historic moment occurring in the first half of the twenty-first century allows for the further valorising of middle power statecraft by Southeast Asian states.

A constructivist perspective to the understanding of emerging Southeast Asian geopolitics suggests that just as there was a case made for hegemonic stability underpinning a particular politico-economic structural neoliberal order, so too could such an order be disrupted growing multipolarity and "hegemonic instability" now articulating within the Southeast Asian regional formation. The emergence of such a historic moment, one could argue, sees the embedding of autochtonous Southeast Asian norms and the progressive debunking of colonial or Western vestiges in the region's geopolitics. This is also a moment when political and economic agency via middle power statecraft could be said to complement ASEAN socialising and the enhancement of regional norms of coexistence and peace building. Indonesian and Malaysian foreign policy practice provides some prime examples of such middle power statecraft (Ping, 2005).[6]

Emergence of a Consolidated ASEAN Construct

The Vietnam War (1955–1975), which saw the United States supplanting French presence in Indochina, was the defining event of post-colonial geopolitics of the Southeast Asian states in the Cold War period and even post-Cold war period. The Sino-US rapprochement of 1971 occurred when the war was still ongoing and even hurtled the region into the Sino-Vietnamese War of February 1979. The United States and Vietnam only normalised relations in 1995, two decades after the end of the Vietnam War. Throughout the 1980s, the region continued to be bifurcated into Communist and non-Communist components. The post-Vietnam War Cambodian conflict loomed large as the major bone of contention among

[5] See further discussion of this in the section on "Hegemonic Instability".

[6] For an examination of how such statecraft is practised by Malaysia in context of Southeast Asian changing geopolitics, see Saravanamuttu (2013).

the two sides. In Philippines, a natural ally of United States, the American military installations of the Clarke Airfield and Subic Naval base were abandoned only in 1991 after the end of the Cold War.

In 1981, the Western-aligned non-Communist ASEAN states had just won overwhelming support for an UN-sponsored International Conference on Kampuchea (ICK) which adopted a "Declaration on Kampuchea" reiterating the various ASEAN demands for a comprehensive political settlement of the Cambodian conflict through negotiations. Malaysia was instrumental through the then Foreign Minister, Tan Sri Ghazali Shafie, in setting up the Coalition Government of Democratic Kampuchea (CGDK), which held on to Cambodia's UN seat for the most part of 1982–1990 period. Other ASEAN states took the lead on the Cambodian question in the ensuing period of diplomatic impasse between Indochina and ASEAN which endured until 1987. In 1988, political developments in Thailand gave a fillip to breaking the impasse when the government of Chatichai Choonhavan started to pursue a new flexible Indochina policy which came to be known by its dictum of "turning battlefields of Indochina into markets". This led to an immediate improvement of relations with Cambodia and Vietnam. Thailand's sponsorship of the several dialogues and eventually saw the convening of the meeting of the newly formed Supreme National Council of Cambodia in June 1991 in Pattaya. Indonesia, which also acted concurrently as co-chair of the Paris peace talks, had played a highly significant role in bringing together all parties to the Cambodian conflict in several rounds of the "Jakarta Informal Meetings" (JIM). The idea of such meetings was agreed upon in July 1987 by Vietnam and Indonesia, with the blessings of Indochina and ASEAN, respectively.

Besides the internal parties to the Cambodian conflict, JIM saw the participation of all the Indochina and ASEAN states, thereby allowing for the first face-to-face meetings of all the regional parties in the conflict. Even though the first JIM failed to resolve outstanding issues, it nevertheless propelled a new dynamic in the peace process which led to other meetings between the various parties to the conflict, including the meeting between Norodom Sihanouk, Son Sann and Hun Sen in Paris of November 1988; between Thailand and Vietnam in January 1989 and between Vietnam and China also in January 1989.

By the time of the ASEAN Summit of January 1992, Malaysia had already openly declared support for Vietnam's and Laos' intention to join the regional body. In the event, the Singapore Declaration reiterated support for the UN role in the Cambodian peace process and ASEAN's willingness to partake in international programmes for the reconstruction of Vietnam, Laos and Cambodia, and in an obvious overture to Indochina, it welcomed all Southeast Asian countries to accede to the ASEAN Treaty of Amity and Cooperation (TAC). As part of political and security cooperation ASEAN commitment to ZOPFAN (Zone of Peace, Freedom and Neutrality) and the Southeast Asian Nuclear Weapon Free Zone (SEANWFZ) was re-emphasised. By the annual ASEAN Foreign Minister's meeting in Manila in July that year, both Laos and Vietnam acceded to the TAC. The ASEAN Summit of July 1994 in Bangkok inaugurated the ASEAN Regional Forum (ARF) and the subsequent Ministerial Meeting in Brunei, the next year, saw Vietnam participating as a full-fledged ASEAN member and the setting up of an Asia–Europe Meeting (ASEM), alongside the ARF. The SEANWFZ came to fruition in December 1995, when the ASEAN Heads of Government signed the draft treaty in Bangkok.

The Bali Summit and signing of the TAC 1976 was arguably the historic moment of the rapprochement of the non-Communist and Communist sectors of Southeast Asia. The hegemonic stability provided by the United States and Western powers remained embedded in Southeast Asia as the Indochina states began to embrace capitalist practices and neoliberalism. ASEAN trade preference agreements and other economic postures are validation of this. Vietnam could even be said to an exemplar of such practices. The US–China rapprochement opened the possibility of China ties with all ASEAN states, thereby diluting in some ways the rigidity of Western hegemony without debunking neoliberal hegemonic stability which became even well-entrenched in Southeast Asia with two sets of states, Communist and non-Communist on board.

This period of geopolitical development did nonetheless allow for ASEAN agency in foreign relations as it attained a peak in its web of "constructivist" structures. ASEAN initiatives included increasing its Western and non-Western Dialogue Partners, the setting up of the ARF in 1994, the Asia–Europe Meeting (ASEM) in 1996, ASEAN Plus Three (APT) in 1997 and the East Asia Summit (EAS) in 2005. As noted by Mahbubani and Sng (2017: 48ff.), political divisions engendered by the Cold War were resolved when the fear of communism was overcome by the absorption of the Communist states into the regional body in the second half of the 1990s. Such a move, they suggest, demonstrated the wisdom of its founding leaders to "hang together or hang separately" in the words of Singapore's former foreign minister, S. Rajaratnam. Having trumped communism and embraced the market economy, ASEAN was on its way to develop a dense regional network for an "ecosystem of peace" (p. 48 ff.). These developments also allowed the socialising among members of the ASEAN consensus decision-making model known as the "ASEAN way". More importantly, it provided a process of confidence-building among Southeast Asian states which encouraged them to advance the notion of "ASEAN Centrality" in the socio-political relations of the Southeast Asian region.[7] Over time, foreign policies of hedging and balancing major powers in the region outweighed the older strategy of direct bandwagoning with superpowers such as the United States or Russia.[8]

Signs of Hegemonic Instability

As noted earlier, in the last 500 years or so, four world powers stood out for their building of production and accumulation chains (Mendes, 2018). Except for the United States up to the point of writing, three powers encountered the pattern of financial accumulation and expansion, followed by decline and breakdown. We will now examine in greater detail the US situation from a geopolitical standpoint at this current conjuncture of Southeast Asian history.

By the time the second term of the Obama Administration (2012–2016), the policy of making the United States the "pivot to Asia" in the rebalancing of power dynamics was a central theme of geopolitics in the Asia-Pacific region and Southeast Asia. There were clear indications that this policy was directed at the significance of the Southeast Asian states in

[7] Many books have been written about ASEAN. The constructive perspective is provided by Acharya (2001). A good review of "ASEAN at 40" is the December, Vol. 29, No. 3, of *Contemporary Southeast Asia*.

[8] Refer to footnote 2 for definitions of these strategies. For a discussion of the growing literature in Southeast Asia on the subject of hedging and hedge diplomacy, see Liow (2005), Kuik (2008), Lee (2017) and Mubah (2019).

the new geopolitics of Asia and the crucial role that they could be play. Most importantly, the American pivot to Asia was to counter the ambitions of a rising China. Analysts saw that "Southeast Asian states risked becoming pawns in a geopolitical clash between the two extra- regional superpowers" (Kitchen, 2012: 6) with the unprecedented economic rise of China, which was likely to become the world's largest economy by 2030 (Majid, 2012: 22). China appeared to have persuaded regional states of its benign goals especially in the economic sphere but its territorial disputes with regional states in the South China Sea presented the more aggressive face of Beijing, even as these states became more dependent economically on China. Importantly, the American pivot to the region to rebalance the strategic challenge posed by China's rise allowed regional states to hedge against China's less transparent intentions. But at that point of time it was not clear whether the Obama presidency was as yet aware of China's new major policy of "One Belt One Road" (OBOR) or Belt and Road Initiative (BRI) which was launched in 2013.

China's launch of the BRI had come in tandem with its growing economic presence in Southeast Asian states. Practically every ASEAN state has China as its major trading partner and ASEAN as a whole has overtaken the United States as China's major second largest trading partner in 2019, behind the EU.[9] In Malaysia, for example, China takes pole position as largest trading partner with total trade topping some USD78 billion in 2018 and as the largest direct foreign investor in Malaysia for a number of years, overtaking countries such as United States, Singapore and Japan.[10]

By the time of the Trump Presidency, the OBOR was clearly a target of US foreign policy. Even before President Trump had enunciated his American First foreign policy, China had pivoted to the greater Eurasia region with the new policy orientation. In 2013, President Xi Jinping launched China's OBOR initiative, later known as the Belt and Road Initiative (BRI). The Trump Administration's somewhat belated response to the BRI has come by way of the Indo-Pacific strategy to be further discussed below. It would seem that such a strategy was clearly aimed

[9] See: https://asia.nikkei.com/Economy/Trade-war/US-overtaken-by-Southeast-Asia-as-China-s-No.-2-trade-partner, accessed 19 August 2019.

[10] Investment figures available for 2019, show that China (US$3.7bilion) was slightly ahead of the US (US$3.5 billion). See: https://www.mida.gov.my/home/facts-and-figures/posts/, accessed 31 July 2020.

at containing China's ambitions. These were clear signals that American hegemony was under the veritable threat of China's ascendancy.

Thus, it is no surprise that Asian geopolitics also took a radical turn with the emergence of the Trump presidency, which saw the effective abandonment of Obama's Asian pivot and the adoption of the America First posture. That said, the main theme of US foreign policy seemed to be tailored to check and contain China's economic ascendancy, one way or another. For Southeast Asian states, this change of strategy seemingly undervalued their role or importance in American foreign policy or alternatively aimed to recast Southeast Asia in a different light with respect to US foreign policy. A major signal came with Trump's withdrawal from the Trans-Pacific Partnership (TPP), which although excluded China, had too much of an Obama imprint. In sharp contrast, the Trump Administration took the high road leading ultimately to an all-out trade war with China. In geopolitical terms, the Trump Administration advanced the Indo-Pacific Strategy, which was dovetailed with the newly fashioned National Security and National Defence strategies. The Indo-Pacific, which subsumes the Asia-Pacific, is a huge swathe of intercontinental territories that stretches from the West Coast shores of the United States to the Western shores of India and said to contribute two-thirds of the global GDP (Indo-Pacific Strategy Report, 2019).

The idea of a Free and Open Indo-Pacific (FOIP) was announced at the APEC Summit of 2017. America's competitors and rivals have given various labels under the FOIP. First, China is seen as a "revisionist power" said to not adhere fully to international norms and rules and is considered both to be coercive and expansionist. Second, Russia is said to be a "revitalised malign actor" based on its military, economic and other activities, while North Korea has been dubbed as a "rogue state". The Indo-Pacific strategy of the United States will be pursued through its military *preparedness*, its *partnerships* in a *networked region* through alliances and ongoing engagements with Japan, South Korea, Australia and the Southeast Asian states (ibid.). The document outlines the Indo-Pacific Strategy as a comprehensive plan and alludes to a multiple set of economic and military collaborations with the regional states through such specific goals as improving the interoperability of military hardware and software with allies and securing them as partners for peace operations and anti-terrorism.[11] Various ASEAN countries have been given a specific mention.[12]

The US document gives a neo-conservative spin to US foreign policy under Trump and continues to call on allies and partners on which the superpower has customarily relied but it fails to conceal the fact that a rising China severely challenges the hegemony of the United States in the region. Moreover, the cautious treatment in the document of China as "revisionist" but not objecting too much to its economic presence suggests the devaluing of the older Asia-Pacific idea to one where US hegemony and relationships could be better served by stronger relationships with Southeast Asian states and traditional allies like Japan and Australia.

ASEAN responded through the ASEAN Outlook on the Indo-Pacific announced on 23 June 2019 by an Indonesian-led initiative. While welcoming the idea, the document stated that the Asia-Pacific and the Indian Ocean were closely integrated, emphasising the importance of the evolving norms, principles and rules-based security and economic architectural structures that has already been put in place by ASEAN, viz.:

Consistent with decades of ASEAN's role in developing and shaping regional architectures in Southeast Asia and beyond, and with ASEAN's norms and principles as contained in the ASEAN Charter and other relevant ASEAN documents, ASEAN Outlook on the Indo-Pacific envisioned by ASEAN consists of the following key elements: A perspective

[11] With respect to Southeast Asia, the compendium National Security document states that: "...the Philippines and Thailand remain important allies and markets for Americans. Vietnam, Indonesia, Malaysia, and Singapore are growing security and economic partners of the United States. The Association of Southeast Asian Nations (ASEAN) and Asia-Pacific Economic Cooperation (APEC) remain centrepieces of the Indo-Pacific's regional architecture and platforms for promoting an order based on freedom" (https://assets.documentcloud.org/documents/4332186/12-2017-National-Security-Strategy.pdf, accessed 17 August 2019).

[12] With respect to Malaysia, it stresses the importance of the relationship, which includes military exercises, interoperability, a total of 100 defence engagements annually, including collaboration to defeat the ISIS in the region. It specifically notes the following: "Malaysia also participates in similar patrols in the Sulu and Celebes Seas with Indonesia and the Philippines aimed at countering violent extremists. The Malaysia Maritime Enforcement Agency formally committed to host the Southeast Asia Maritime Law Enforcement Initiative (SEAMLEI) Commanders' Forum in December 2019" (p. 39).

of viewing the Asia-Pacific and Indian Ocean regions, not as contiguous territorial spaces but as a closely integrated and interconnected region, with ASEAN playing a central and strategic role; An Indo-Pacific region of dialogue and cooperation instead of rivalry; An Indo-Pacific region of development and prosperity for all; The importance of the maritime domain and perspective in the evolving regional architecture.

The statement was a polite but firm statement that ASEAN centrality still played a crucial role in maintaining regional order and stability and that ASEAN possessed the necessary security and economic structures in maintaining geopolitical peace.[13] For ASEAN, the new geopolitical development of apparent US downplaying of Southeast Asia has favoured a renewal of new regional economic trade agreements such as the Regional Comprehensive Economic Partnership (RCEP). The RCEP will harmonise existing ASEAN free trade agreements and build new ones in an arrangement made up of some 2.3 billion people with a GDP of US$24.8 trillion.[14]

Hedging and Balancing China

South China Sea

The South China Sea (SCS) has been the thorn in the side of ASEAN–China relations. Despite differences and mutually overlapping territorial claims, ASEAN states have taken a consistent common position vis-à-vis China since 2002 through the Declaration of Conduct (DOC) and since 2018 via Code of Conduct (CoC) negotiations. Two sets of players are involved in the SCS dynamics: the claimants to its territories, islands and features; and the outside powers and states which have an interest in maintaining sea lines of communications and freedom of navigation.

Malaysia is a major claimant in the SCS, along with China, Vietnam, the Philippines, Brunei and Taiwan. ASEAN as a group in theory continues to engage China through the 2002 Declaration on the Conduct

[13] Cf. Saha (2019) and Parameswaran (2019).

[14] See https://theaseanpost.com/article/multiplicative-effects-rcep-asean-trade. The 16-member RCEP (ASEAN 10 plus Australia, China, India, Japan, Korea and New Zealand), touted as the world largest trade deal, would supplant the US-led TPP which has become of limited value after the US withdrawal. India's participation at the time of writing is still being negotiated.

of Parties in the South China Sea (DOC), which underscores universally recognised norms of international law based on the 1982 United National Convention on the Law of the Sea (UNCLOS). China's extravagant claims in the SCS are based on its controversial U-shaped map, with the nine-dash-line, drawn in 1947 extending to territories claimed by Malaysia and Brunei at its southern-most end. But what is particularly worrisome is the character of its claims, which remain rather vague, given that the nine-dash line of its map at the southern extremity has never been explained in the lexicon of international law.

The Philippines advanced its case against China on the basis of its proximity to the Spratly group of islands and its presence in ten or so islands and islets in that broad area. In 2016, the Permanent Court of Arbitration on UNCLOS ruled that China's claims to features, which are not islands, as well as its nine dotted line in SCS, have no standing in international law.[15] The decision, while not accepted by China, has put it on the defensive and a poor legal footing while giving the ASEAN states some measure of legitimacy to their claims. The overall ASEAN stance in the SCS is also indirectly helped by the US insistence, although not as a claimant, to freedom of navigation in the SCS. It has been estimated that US$5.3 trillion worth of goods transit through the SCS annually, with US$1.2 trillion of that total accounting for trade with the United States. Thus, the continued contestation of the two superpowers in the SCS is to be expected and ASEAN states can leverage on this as a foil in their CoC negotiations with China. The United States has recently ramped

[15] For the full text of the award, see Permanent Court of Arbitration (2016). On the nine-dash line, the text reads as follows: "DECLARES that, as between the Philippines and China, China's claims to historic rights, or other sovereign rights or jurisdiction, with respect to the maritime areas of the South China Sea encompassed by the relevant part of the 'nine-dash line' are contrary to the Convention and without lawful effect to the extent that they exceed the geographic and substantive limits of China's maritime entitlements under the Convention; and further DECLARES that the Convention superseded any historic rights, or other sovereign rights or jurisdiction, in excess of the limits imposed therein". As to features such as reefs and shoals, it concluded as follows: "that none of the high-tide features in the Spratly Islands, in their natural condition, are capable of sustaining human habitation or economic life of their own within the meaning of Article 121(3) of the Convention; that none of the high-tide features in the Spratly Islands generate entitlements to an exclusive economic zone or continental shelf; and that therefore there is no entitlement to an exclusive economic zone or continental shelf generated by any feature claimed by China that would overlap the entitlements of the Philippines in the area of Mischief Reef and Second Thomas Shoal".

up its FONOPs (Freedom of Navigation Operations) in the SCS with 2019 seeing a record number. In July 2020, two US aircraft carriers, *USS Ronald Reagan* and *USS Nimitz*, carried out elaborate military exercises with its strike groups.[16] The unmistakable message to Beijing was the US resolve to maintain freedom of navigation in the SCS.[17]

Among the littoral ASEAN states, Malaysia has been fairly effective in its stance and claims. It has occupied a number of reefs and atolls, and stakes its claims based on its 1979 map, which extends its continental shelf along the Sabah and Sarawak coast into the Spratly and Kalayaan area. Its submission on an extended continental shelf in 2019 drew the ire of Beijing. This was in addition to an earlier submission in 2009, together with Vietnam, on their joint continental shelves. As early as June 1983, Malaysia occupied the Swallow Reef (Terumbu Layang Layang), which was subsequently turned into a tourist resort for bird watching and diving, complete with an airstrip. The Malaysian posture has drawn protest not just from Beijing but also from the Manila and Hanoi. On occupying Swallow Reef, Malaysia deployed three F-5 fighters to Labuan to provide military backing to its claims. In 2004, Malaysia completed the Teluk Sepanggar naval base, which will house its two Scorpene-class submarines the first of which, *KD Tunku Abdul Rahman*, docked into port in September 2009, while the second, *KD Tun Razak*, arrived in July 2010 (Saravanamuttu, 2012).

[16]According to an expert who monitors such events: On 4 July, the *USS Nimitz* combined with the *USS Ronald Reagan* (CVN-76) CSG to form the Nimitz Carrier Strike Force. The *USS Nimitz* was accompanied by the guided missile cruisier *USS Princeton* (CG 59) and two guided-missile destroyers, the *USS Sterett* (DDG 104) and *USS Ralph Johnson* (DDG 114). The *USS Ronald Reagan* was escorted by the guided-missile cruiser *USS Antietam* (CG 54) and guided-missile destroyer *USS Mustin* (DDG 89). Each CSG was also accompanied by a nuclear attack submarine (Thayer 2020a).

[17]In July 2020, the United States made one of its strongest statement on the SCS. Although the United States is not party to the UNCLOS, State Secretary, Mike Pompeo, cited the award issued by an Arbitral Tribunal set up under the UNCLOS which stated that China's nine-dash line, among others, had no basis in international law. Secretary Pompeo underscored that "[t]oday we are aligning the U.S. position on the PRC's [People's Republic of China] maritime claims in the SCS [South China Sea] with the Tribunal's decision" (Thayer 2020b). Pompeo also seemingly acknowledged the claims of the ASEAN states, namely, the Philippines, Vietnam, Malaysia and Indonesia, which have overlapping jurisdictions with China.

By July 2020, China had agreed to resume negotiations on the second draft of the CoC document with the ASEAN states against the backdrop of the United States throwing its support behind the ASEAN states in various statements about China's aggression in the SCS. Malaysian authorities reported that between 2016 and 2019, the Chinese military encroached as many as 89 times into its waters in the SCS. China is also said to be intruding into the waters around the Indonesia's Natuna Islands. The Philippines in July 2019 complained that China had amassed some 113 vessels around the Pag-asa Island in the Spratly group which it administers. In March 2020, China sank a Vietnamese fishing vessel and apparently made claims which went beyond its nine-dash line. Most crucially, the actions by China included the establishment of the so-called administrative districts over the Spratly and Paracel island groups. China made the notification in April 2020 with the two administrative units created under the Sansha city in Hainan.[18] The "Nansha District" covers the Spratly Islands and the "Xisha District" covers the Paracel Islands, which are disputed areas, which is also claimed by Vietnam amidst denials by China that it is setting up an Air Defense Identification Zone (ADIF) over the SCS.[19]

The complex dynamics of the SCS disputes have allowed the ASEAN states to adopt hedging and balancing as strategies in dealing with China and collectively contain China's ambitions and assertiveness in the SCS. The implied strategy of balancing China involves the willing United States, an ally of the Philippines, as an important foil to check China's ambitions in the SCS. Such delicate balancing and hedge diplomacy includes the dimension of ASEAN agency in maintaining a consistent common stance anchored on "ASEAN centrality" as the basic premise of its engagement with Beijing.

The BRI Projects

Unlike its aggressive stances and actions in the SCS, China's BRI projects in Southeast Asia present the more amorphous "soft power" face of China. However, three sorts of issues surfaced especially during the

[18] See: https://www.globaltimes.cn/content/1186004.shtml, accessed 24 July 2020.

[19] There are numerous reports and analyses of the developments, issues, disputes and incidents in the SCS. *Thayer Consultancy Background Briefs* provides an excellent source of updates on latest developments. I have also drawn from sources such as *The Diplomat* magazine, *Malaysiakini*, *Aljazeera* and *The Times of India*.

first phase of the BRI, namely, project delays, ballooning deficits and sovereignty concerns (Yamada & Palma, 2018; Priyandita & Wijaya, 2018; Saravanamuttu, 2018).[20] A regular complaint was that BRI projects usually require Chinese workers and Chinese material inputs with reduced forward and backward linkages to the local economies. The other major complaint has been dubbed "the China debt trap" primarily illustrated by the Sri Lanka case where its Hambantota port has been leased to China for 99 years because of payment problems. Malaysia under Najib Razak and the Philippines under Rodrigo Duterte have been the main supporters of China's BRI thrust in Southeast Asia while Indonesia has adopted a more circumspect approach and until now has not designated any of China project as BRI-related (Negara & Suryadinata, 2018). The US$6 billion joint venture for Jakarta–Bandung High-Speed Rail launched in January 2016 is said to be outside of Indonesia's BRI definition. The ASEAN states have as yet no concerted or collective policy vis-à-vis the increasingly large number of projects tied to the BRI in the region. Three ASEAN states, it would seem, have gone some distance with the BRI projects, namely, Myanmar, Thailand and Laos.

In Myanmar, the oil and gas pipeline from Kyukphuk to Kunming—a 50.9–49.1 percent China–Myanmar joint venture—has been completed and was up and running since April 2017. The 771 km pipeline is designed to carry 22 million tonnes of crude a year with Myanmar using 2 million tonnes annually from it. It ends in Kunming, where PetroChina has built an oil refinery with the capacity to process 13 million tonnes of crude annually. China has also been involved in building the Myitsone Dam in Kachin State which has been halted because of issues of conservation, compensation and Kachin rights. Under the deal, 90 percent of electricity produced goes to China on which China claims to have expended US$800 million.

Two projected China-sponsored high-speed rail projects in Thailand have hit many snags since they were launched in 2010. However, in June 2017, a new deal was inked for the 252 km Bangkok–Nakhon Ratchasima portion, to be linked eventually to Kunming. Concerns have ranged from the passing of a new law by the Thai government to allow Chinese engineers to work on the project to issues of debt burden and the adverse impact of the project on forest reserves. In Laos, the BRI high-speed

[20] For an overview of the BRI projects, particularly their environmental impact on Southeast Asia, see *Trends in Southeast Asia*, 2019, No. 18.

railway to be built by China, and completed by 2021, with a cost of US$6.7 billion sourced mainly from China's Exim Bank, represents a quarter of the country's GDP and may turn into a debt trap (ibid.).

In Malaysia, China's economic presence via the BRI projects featured as electoral issues in the 2018 general election. The East Coast Rail Link (ECRL) project bankrolled with its ballooning costs came under severe criticism from the incoming premier in the run-up to the 9 May 2018 general election. China's Exim Bank was to finance the major expenditure with a RM38.5 billion while the remaining RM16.5 billion was to be financed from a *sukuk* issue. Mahathir, then leading a coalition of opposition parties, had indicated that the costs were unacceptable and that the project would be scuttled should they come to power. However, it was later decided that the project could still proceed at a later date given that RM20 billion had already been expended on it, with the new government renegotiating new terms[21] During the election campaign period, Mahathir asserted that the ECRL along with projects like property development bankrolled by a China company, the "Forest City" project in Johor, were indications that the Najib government was indirectly surrendering Malaysia's sovereignty to China. Within less than a year of assuming power, Mahathir, after an initial rebuke of Najib's embrace of the BRI, began to show a willingness to re-embrace the BRI and its related projects. The Mahathir turn-around also more or less coincided with what has been suggested by observers as Phase 2 of the BRI. At the second BRI Forum held at the end of April 2019, attended by over 5000 participants from 150 countries including leaders such as Russian President Vladimir Putin and President Abdel-Fattah al-Sisi (Egypt), Mahathir in his speech was all praise for the BRI: "Without a doubt, the utilisation of these passages will enrich all the littoral states along the way, as much as the great nations of the East and West. I am fully in support of the Belt

[21] See: https://www.themalaysianinsight.com/s/56285, accessed 26 June 2018. Malaysia would have stood to lose some RM22 billion should the project be cancelled, according to then Finance Minister, Lim Guan Eng. The project's loan from the Exim Bank of China, is kept abroad and paid to the state-owned construction company, China Communications Construction Co Ltd (CCCC) in China, which the new government considered "strange". In the end, Tun Daim Zainuddin, a member of Mahathir's Council of Eminent Persons, was able to renegotiate a deal which brought down the price of the ECRL to RM44 billion. See: https://www.thestar.com.my/business/business-news/2019/04/12/ecrl-to-go-ahead-as-costs-reduced-by-rm2pt5b-to-rm44b, accessed 16 August 2019.

and Road Initiative. I am sure my country, Malaysia, will benefit from the project".[22]

Unlike the situation of the SCS, the BRI projects in mainland and island Southeast Asia has allowed China to keep ASEAN states somewhat divided, which each country having to craft its own responses and strategy vis-à-vis China's dominant hand.

Hegemonic Instability

The foregoing section on the firm responses of the ASEAN states to China's presence in the SCS as well as some negative sentiments to its BRI projects provide evidence that despite China's inexorable rise in the Asian region and globally, at this point of time China is perhaps still in the mould of "the partial power" (Shambaugh, 2013). Such a narrative suggests that China's foreign policy is still too self-centred and that its capacity to project a positive global image still remains work-in-progress. Shambaugh's idea that China is still weak in influencing global events was before the initiation of the BRI. That said, in the era of the Coronavirus and with the minimal economic presence of the United States and the European states in the Asia-Pacific region today and a Trump-driven US foreign policy, would virtually ensure that China remains as the preeminent power in the region. Regional states have virtually Hobson's choice with respect to a full, if critical, engagement with China on all fronts. In Southeast Asia, the China behemoth partakes in virtually all major infrastructural developments, and occupies top pole position in trade for most countries. Political engagement is bound to follow if not already evident.

The foregoing discussion of geopolitical and other developments pertaining to Southeast Asia shows that hegemonic instability rather than hegemonic stability seems to the order of the day in the region. The economic ascendancy of China has not been matched by any corresponding US or Western response but by a defensive strategy of the containment of China's ambitions. The Trump Administration continuance of trade war and trade sanctions and stances on the SCS issues are the indication of more steps in the same direction.

[22] See: https://www.thestar.com.my/news/nation/2019/04/27/dr-m-endorses-the-bri, accessed 25 August 2019.

The international relations literature has over the recent past been replete with a narrative of America's global decline. Paradoxically, President Trump's slogan of "making America great again" seems to admit that such a decline had indeed occurred. Trump's postures and policies which have been discussed earlier also tend to confirm that if not an American decline per se, certainly the America crafted world order seems to be fraying (Acharya, 2014). There is understandable angst among American intellectuals about decline of the current American-led world order. Other non-American analysts have increasingly alluded to the changing dynamics of global politics and its more pluralistic and "multiplex" structure could well-being greater agency to non-Western parts of the world as Acharya has argued (Acharya, 2018). The power shift from the West to the East, Yuen (2019) argues, is also predicated on the decline of American soft power or "prestige" and the closing of such a gap by its putative rival China and this is especially evident in Asia. Singapore's Kishore Mahbubani, whether in his books or on well-watched presentations and debates on the internet, has routinely upbraided American analysts for not recognising China's significance or ascendancy.[23]

Farid Zakaria writes about the "self destruction of American power" (Zakaria, 2019) where not just the "unipolar moment" after the end of the Cold War was squandered but where the world order of norms and rules America created has been abandoned by the Trump Administration. One of the doyens of American academe, Joseph Nye, has similarly written about the decline of American hegemony (Nye, 2019). In his long essay Nye suggests that Wilsonian thought leadership and American "exceptionalism" provided the early underpinning that eventually led to the liberal world order. He suggests that "we are at the end of an economic period – that of Western led globalization – and a geopolitical one, the post-Cold War 'unipolar moment' of a US led global order" and it could well be that non-Western powers such as China and India play a much larger role in sustaining a new global order (Nye, 2019: 73).

If we accept the broad premise of an American decline, or even the end of the American-led world order as suggested by Acharya, greater agency in foreign policy could become vested in and cohere more definitely among non-Western powers and in non-Western regions. In such a "hybridised" global environment of hegemonic instability, the notion

[23] See Mahbubani (2020) which suggests, among other things, that US policymakers today have failed to understand the nature of China's rise.

of middle power statecraft advanced earlier could yield stronger beneficial outcomes for the ASEAN states. ASEAN's approach to US initiatives such as the Indo-Pacific strategy has rightfully been anchored on ASEAN centrality, so too in its dealing with China vis-à-vis issues in the SCS. ASEAN multilateralism, its security architecture, track two diplomacy and its "dense eco-system of peace" (Mahbubani & Sng, 2017: 44ff.) would no doubt remain as the basis of overall foreign policy with respect to dealing regional powers. More importantly ASEAN, despite its overall institutional weaknesses, seems able to act as a norm setter for regional stability through its much-celebrated "ASEAN way".

Conclusion

Hegemonic stability has been disrupted by China's rise but China has definitely not emerged as yet as a hegemonic power globally. Even if China were to become the world's largest economy in the next two decades, in terms of nuclear capability, the United States and Russia far exceed China's incapacity. However, could the current transitional phase of global politics, as least from a Southeast Asian lens, be a prelude to a "hegemonic crisis" given the obvious declining status of the United States as a superpower? As hypothesised by Arrighi and Silver (1999), such a crisis would include the following broad features: interstate-rivalries and inter-enterprise competition; social conflicts, emergence of new configurations of power. The problem with such generic features is that we often find them occurring over very long periods of time. Ever since the end of the Cold War, when the United States was unable to seize the unipolar moment as many have noted, new configurations of power have emerged in Europe, Latin America, Africa and Asia. Theorists of middle power statecraft such as Ping (2005) view such hybridised global political environments as particularly germane for greater agency and flexibility in the foreign policy of small and medium states. There is little doubt that up to the point of writing the United States remains as the superpower across most regions of the world even as its influence and prestige wanes (Yuen, 2019).

However, it may well be argued that the United States has maximised its expansionist phase within the current neoliberal economic order and that new hegemons such as China are overtaking the United States economically, although not militarily, especially in regions like Southeast Asia and possibly Africa. At the time of writing, a further disruption of

American hegemony may be caused by the episode of the Coronavirus pandemic but a full discussion of this subject is beyond the scope of this chapter.[24] It is worth repeating that the much-discussed decline of an American-led world order has certainly ushered the emergence of a more "multiplex" global system (Acharya, 2018) and a level of hegemonic instability if not crisis. It would be somewhat premature to speak of a "post-hegemonic" moment.

From the Southeast Asian perspective, this current post-colonial historic moment of hegemonic instability has allowed for considerable flexibility in foreign policy and economic direction. The ASEAN regional construct has served Southeast Asian states well in terms of deploying common political and economic instrumentalities and strategies in addressing superpower presence and dominance in the region. Much of such actions fall within the ambit of middle power statecraft. The dense web of common structures the group has constructed over some five decades through its socialisation of the regional norms of coexistence and socio-economic collaboration ensures that each ASEAN state would not be left alone to draw on its own means to hedge and balance the dominance of hegemonic powers.

References

Acharya, A. (2001). *Constructing a security community in Southeast Asia: ASEAN and the problem of regional order*. London and New York: Routledge.

Acharya, A. (2014). *The end of the American world order*. Cambridge: Polity Press.

Acharya, A. (2018). *Constructing global order: Agency and change in world politics*. Cambridge: Cambridge University Press.

Arrighi, G. (1994). *The long twentieth century: Money, power, and the origins of our times*. Brooklyn, NY: Verso.

ASEAN at 40; Progress, Prospects and Challenges (Special Focus). (2007, December). *Contemporary Southeast Asia, 29*(3).

ASEAN Outlook on the Indo-Pacific. https://asean.org/asean-outlook-indo-pacific. Accessed 25 Aug 2019.

Chua, A. (2020). Divided we fall: What is tearing America apart? *Foreign Affairs, 99*(4): 158–164.

[24] See Chua (2020) for a review essay on the polarisation of politics in the United States and suggesting that the United States is reaching "systemic breaking point" in the face of the Coronavirus pandemic.

Cox, R. W. (1996). Towards a post-hegemonic conception of world order: Reflections on the relevancy of Ibn Khaldun. In R. W. Cox with T. J. Sinclair (Eds.), *Approaches to world order*. Cambridge: Cambridge University Press.

Gilpin, R. (2000). *The challenge of global capitalism: The world economy in the 21st century*. Princeton and Oxford: Princeton University Press.

Gilpin, R. (2001). *Global political economy: Understanding the international economic order*. Princeton and Oxford: Princeton University Press.

Gowa, J. (1989, April). Rational hegemons, excludable goods, and small groups: An epitaph for hegemonic stability theory? *World Politics, 41*(3): 307–324.

Indo-Pacific Strategy Report: Preparedness, Partnerships, and Promoting a Networked Region. (2019, June 1). The Department of Defence, United States.

Keohane, R. O. (1984). *After hegemony: Cooperation and discord in the world political economy*. Princeton: Princeton University Press.

Kindleberger, C. P. (1973). *The world in depression, 1929–1939*. Berkeley: University of California Press.

Kitchen, N. (2012, November, 6–7). Executive summary. In *The new geopolitics of Southeast Asia*. LSE IDEAS Special Report SRO15.

Kuik, C. C. (2008). The essence of hedging: Malaysia and Singapore's response to a rising China. *Contemporary Southeast Asia, 30*(2), 159–185.

Kwon, R. (2012). Hegemonic stability, world cultural diffusion, and trade globalization. *Sociological Forum, 27*(2), 324–347.

Lee, J. Y. (2017). Hedging strategies of the middle powers in East Asian security: the cases of South Korea and Malaysia. *East Asia, 34*, 23–37.

Liow, J. C. (2005). Balancing, bandwagoning, or hedging? Strategic and security patterns in Malaysia's relations with China, 1981–2003. In K. L. Ho, & S. C. Y. Ku (Eds.), *China and Southeast Asia: Global changes and challenges*. Singapore: Institute of Southeast Asian Studies and Centre for Southeast Asian Studies.

Mahbubani, K. (2020). *Has China won? The Chinese challenge to American primacy*. New York: Public Affairs.

Mahbubani, K., & Sng, J. (2017). *The ASEAN miracle: A catalyst for peace*. Singapore: National University of Singapore (NU) Press.

Majid, M. (2012, November). Southeast Asia between China and the United States. In *The new geopolitics of Southeast Asia*. LSE IDEAS Special Report SRO15, pp. 21–35.

Mendes, M. V. I. (2018). Is it the end of North-American hegemony? A structuralist perspective on Arrighi's systemic cycles of accumulation and the theory of hegemonic stability. *Brazilian Journal of Political Economy, 38*(3), 434–449.

Mubah, A. S. (2019). Indonesia's double hedging strategy toward the United States-China competition: Shaping regional order in the Indo-Pacific? *Issues &*

Studies: a Social Science Quarterly on China, Taiwan, and East Asian Affairs., *55*(4), 1–17.

Negara, S. D., & Suryadinata, L. (2018). Indonesia and China's belt and road initiatives: Perspectives, issues and prospects. *Trends in Southeast Asia*. No. 11, ISEAS-Yusof Ishak Institute.

Nye, J. (2019). The rise and fall of American Hegemony: from Wilson to Trump. *International Affairs,* 95(1), 63–80.

Parameswaran, P. (2019, June 24). Assessing ASEAN's new Indo-Pacific Outlook. *The Diplomat*. https://thediplomat.com/2019/06/assessing-aseans-new-indo-pacific-outlook/. Accessed 18 Aug 2019.

Permanent Court of Arbitration, Award. PCA Case No 2013-19. (2016, July 12). In the matter of the South China Sea Arbitration before an Arbitral Tribunal Constituted under Annex VII to the 1982 United Nations Convention on The Law of the Sea between The Republic of the Philippines and The People's Republic of China.

Ping, J. (2005). *Middle power statecraft: Indonesia, Malaysia and the Asia-Pacific*. Oxford: Ashgate.

Priyandita, C., & Wijaya, T. (2018, May 4). Winning hearts on China's Belt and Road. *The Diplomat*. https://thediplomat.com/2018/05/winning-hearts-on-chinas-belt-and-road/. Accessed 23 June 2018.

Saha, P. (2019). *ASEAN's Indo-Pacific outlook: An analysis*. https://www.orfonline.org/expert-speak/aseans-indo-pacific-outlook-an-analysis-52542/. Accessed 19 Aug.

Saravanamuttu, J. (2012, November). Malaysian in the new geopolitics of Southeast Asia. In *The New Geopolitics of Southeast Asia*. LSE IDEAS Special Report SRO15, pp. 47–52.

Saravanamuttu, J. (2013). Malaysian in the new geopolitics: A critical-constructivist perspective. *The Journal of Diplomacy and Foreign Relations, 13*(1), 5–17.

Saravanamuttu, J. (2018, July 23). *Malaysia's Embrace of the belt and road initiative and its implications for bilateral and regional relationships*. Paper presented at the International Political Science Association (IPSA) Conference, Brisbane.

Shambaugh, D. (2013). *China goes global: The partial power*. New York: Oxford University Press.

Thayer, C. A. (2020a, July 8). Background brief: South China Sea: U.S. Aircraft carrier strike groups conduct exercises. Thayer Consultancy ABN # 65 648 097 123.

Thayer, C. A. (2020b, July 18). *Background brief: South China Sea: How to evaluate the new U.S. policy*. Thayer Consultancy ABN # 65 648 097 123.

Trends in Southeast Asia. (2019). No. 18. *The belt and road initiative: Environmental impacts in Southeast Asia* (A. M. Lechner, M. T. Chee, A. Tritto, A.

Horstmann, C. T. Hoong, J. R. Owen, & A. Campos-Arceiz). ISEAS -Yusof Ishak Institute.

Yamada, G., & Palma, S. (2018, March 28). Is China's Belt and Road working? A progress report from eight countries. *Nikkei Asia*. https://asia.nikkei.com/Features/Cover-story/Is-China-s-Belt-and-Road-working-A-progress-report-from-eight-countries.

Yuen, F. K. (2019). Power as prestige in world politics. *International Affairs, 95*(1), 119–142.

Zakaria, F. (2019). The self-destruction of American power. *Foreign Affairs, 98*(4), 10–16.

CHAPTER 11

The Legacy of Colonialism: Malaysia's Foreign Policy Under Tunku Abdul Rahman

Rahul Mishra and Peter Brian M. Wang

Introduction

Consistency is one of the defining features of the foreign policy of a stable and confident nation. Malaysian foreign policy, at least in the recent past, is no exception to that. Malaysia's foreign policy has remained relatively consistent and coherent over the years, at least in rhetorical terms. Malaysia's current foreign policy is described as "***independent, principled and pragmatic*** [...] ***founded on the values of peace, humanity, justice, and equality***" (Ministry of Foreign Affairs, 2019). Malaysia's foreign policy objective remains to "***safeguard Malaysia's sovereignty and national interests***" while contributing "***towards a just and equitable community of***

R. Mishra (✉)
Asia-Europe Institute & Centre for ASEAN Regionalism (CARUM), University of Malaya, Kuala Lumpur, Malaysia
e-mail: rahul.seas@gmail.com

P. B. M. Wang
National Institute of Public Administration (INTAN) & Asia-Europe Institute, University of Malaya, Kuala Lumpur, Malaysia

R. Rasiah et al. (eds.), *Contesting Malaysia's Integration into the World Economy*, https://doi.org/10.1007/978-981-16-0650-2_11

nations" with multilateralism, regionalism, the United Nations, the Association of South East Asian Nations (ASEAN), and deepening economic integration functioning as important vehicles to effect this. Since independence, Malaysia's foreign policy has evolved to effectively and peacefully deal with internal and external challenges, yet it retains many aspects and principles from its formative years.

Thus, both continuity and change define the contours of the Malaysian foreign policy. However, some scholars have termed Malaysian foreign policy as paradoxical, especially today in the context of its relations with both China and the US. Malaysia's relations with China and the US, particularly in the defence and security domain, have been a matter of academic and policy debates. Scholars have highlighted how Malaysia has moved to expand its long-standing military partnership with the US, it has also developed and slowly institutionalised Malaysia-China defence cooperation despite its growing anxiety about Beijing's more assertive maritime actions, especially since 2013 (Kuik, 2016: 157).

These paradoxes are also apparent when we discuss Malaysia's foreign policy in relation to its colonial past. The impact of colonialism on this part of the world, as elsewhere, has been significant. As Acharya and Buzan (2019: 19) write:

> *Through the process of colonialization, […] the Europeans tried, and up to a point succeeded in, remaking the world in their own political and economic image, though far less so culturally.*

Its impact can be seen when we compare between Shaharil Talib's description of the precolonial world of Southeast Asia (Talib, 1997) against the reality that faced the Southeast Asian nations at the time of their independence. A region whose people have once upon a time shared similar cultural beliefs and rituals, customs, language and political structures (the mandala system)—and still do—was by the end of the Second World War a conglomeration of states that were governed under different political structures and ideologies, with some in direct opposition to each other.

However, in the literature on Malaysia's foreign policy which includes analyses that view it from multiple angles (i.e. from an overall developmental perspective; or with focus on specific periods or leadership; or those that focus on its relationship with regional or multilateral organisations), colonisation is listed as one of the many factors; the other important factors being geopolitics, domestic politics, leadership and pragmatism, etc.

Malaysia's foreign policy shifts from 1957 to 2008 are succinctly captured by Saravanamuttu in his two seminal works The *Dilemma of Independence: Two Decades of Malaysia's Foreign Policy 1957–1977* (Saravanamuttu, 1983) and *Malaysia's Foreign Policy: The First Fifty Years: Alignment, Neutralism, Islamism* (Saravanamuttu, 2010). Saravanamuttu's historical analysis is complemented with Alles' (2014) use of first-hand accounts in analysing the Malaysian foreign policy. Both arrive at similar conclusions; that (like any other modern nation state) Malaysia's foreign policy is shaped by both endogenous (i.e. domestic politics and debates on economic interests and concerns) and exogenous factors (i.e. relations with neighbours and systemic factors such as the Cold War which transformed into the unipolar liberal international order with the collapse of the Union of Soviet Socialist Republics (USSR), and is again turning into a multipolar world or a "Multiplex World" as Acharya has termed it (Acharya, 2014). Both mention Malaysia's colonial past, but none attribute it more significance than other influencing factors.

Saravanamuttu, for instance, while discussing Malaysia's foreign policy under Tunku Abdul Rahman, identifies his anti-communist position, leaning towards the Western bloc and strong commitment to international and regional cooperation as major reasons for his foreign policy position (Saravanamuttu, 1983). The most Saravanamuttu attributes to colonialism is to Malaysia's posture, specifically with regard to its position on Algeria, West Irian and South Africa, which he describes as "*forthrightly Third-World oriented*" (Saravanamuttu, 1983: 44). Alles' (2014) brief treatment of this same period shares Saravanamuttu's views on the role of the Tunku's anti-communist and pro-Western position and like Saravanamuttu pays scant attention to colonialism.

Strangely, the Tunku himself while highlighting anti-colonialism as one of Malaysia's foreign policy motivations, does seem to confine it to justifying support for his own stronger views on the struggle against communism (Rahman, 1965: 660):

> *The people of Malaya, I said, wanted independence for their own country; if this could be achieved, they would be responsible for the fight against Communism, and they would win. Any delay in achieving independence could only benefit the Communists, as Communism thrived and flourished on colonialism.*

Or as part of efforts to identify with other Third-World countries (Rahman, 1965: 665):

> *We are very conscious of brotherhood with the Afro-Asian nations. We feel at one with them in campaigning against colonialism, apartheid, disease, hunger and human misery.*

Going against the grain, instead of merely being one of many, the objective of this chapter is to show how indelibly linked Malaysia's colonial experience is with Malaysia's foreign policy during this period. We will delve into some of the major foreign policy issues faced by Malaysia during this period and provide arguments to show that even within these issues, the legacy of colonialism must be accorded due recognition. Among the issues this chapter touches on are Malaysia's positions in relation to the United Nations, regionalism, communism and the Non-Aligned Movement (NAM). Any discussion of Malaysia's foreign policy during this period cannot escape discussing the Tunku himself. Despite concerns of scholars like Saravanamuttu on overstating the role of the "*small stable elite comprising four or five men*" (Ott, 1972: 225) his own body of work belies this, having himself written an insightful piece on the role of Tun Dr. Ismail Abdul Rahman in the formulation of Malaysia's foreign policy during the period in question. In order to establish that in addition to the exogenous and the endogenous factors, the Tunku's personality and background also contributed in shaping Malaysian foreign policy, this chapter will also explore the role of the Tunku by analysing him in his own words, contained in the literature mentioned above, his articles published in *The Star* and in an article he contributed to the *Foreign Affairs* magazine in 1965.

Impact of Colonialism

Shaharil Talib, in his paper titled, "The Asiatic Archipelago: History Beyond Boundaries", describes the Asiatic archipelago as a single entity that existed and functioned "*beyond boundaries*". Quoting Raffles, he argues (Talib, 1997: 125–126):

> *I cannot but consider the Malayu nation, as one people, speaking one language, though spread over so wide a space, and preserving their character and customs, in all maritime states lying between the Sulu seas, and*

the southern ocean, and bounded longitudinally by Sumatra and the western side of Papua or New Guinea.

Talib argued that Raffles, based on his extensive research on the archipelago's maritime tradition and institutions, found similarities which were best encapsulated in the Maritime Code of Malacca. This is important as it reveals that within the myriad system of kingdoms that characterised the archipelago, there existed an overarching framework of law(s) that governed the actions of man both on land and on sea. For both these laws, the authority of the "Raja" (King) over the land, and that of the "*Nakhodah*" (Captain) was not to be questioned (Talib, 1997: 125–126),

> *If these laws are attended to, no one can question the authority of the Nakhodah, for as the Raja is on shore, so is the Nakhodah at sea. This authority has been conferred by the Sultans of the land, upon all Nakhodahs, in order that they may administer the laws on-board their respective vessels. Whoever does not admit this authority offends against the law.*

According to Talib, the source of state power and wealth was derived from its control over resources, manpower, shipping, routes, trade, commodities and markets but each cluster of kingdoms operated multilaterally. He writes (Talib, 1997: 127):

> *The history beyond boundaries of the Asiatic Archipelago is the interplay between markets and resources extracted by manpower at the production end and between the commodity trade carried by sea through trade routes. This is the unchanging theme of the material conditions of the archipelagic history. The rise and fall of kingdoms are the control or loss of control over markets, manpower, resources, commodity trade and shipping routes.*

This, however, changed during the period of colonialism, which transformed the region forever. The region was carved up by first the Anglo-Dutch Treaty of 1824, and again by the Anglo-Siamese Treaty of 1909. The consequences, as Talib writes, were far-reaching. It created boundaries where none existed before and severed social and political ties among ruling families. It transformed trade patterns from what was once "*an intra-Asian multilateral trade emporium*" to "*a bilateral Asian-European trade pattern*" (Talib, 1997: 132). More importantly, as a result of colonialism the region lost some of its initiatives in world affairs.

Instead it became a subject to the external forces, some of which developed in regions on the other side of the world. In the specific case of Malaysia, the impact of the treaties mentioned above had the effect of creating the future state of Malaysia and, as we will see in the following sections, colouring Malaysia's relations with its neighbours.

Malaysia's Foreign Policy (1957–1970)

In analysing and assessing the first phase of post-independence Malaysian foreign policy between 1957 and 1970, Malaysian foreign policy experts including Saravanamuttu and Alles have generally focused on four major themes, namely: Malaysia's position at the United Nations; approach towards emerging patterns of regionalism; responses to communism, and; responding to the emergence of the Non-Aligned Movement as the third front beyond the Western and the Soviet blocs. Scholars like Jeshurun, although approaching the study of Malaysia's foreign policy from very different angles, tend to also focus on the same areas to an extent. This chapter delves into these issues, highlighting the commonly accepted opinions/views held by scholars and then review these in relation to colonialism.

Malaysia's Position at the United Nations

Malaysia became a member of the United Nations (UN) in 1957, and swiftly established its image of a strong advocate for a stronger UN. The active role that Malaysia (then the Federation of Malaya) played in strongly backing the then UN Secretary-General, Dan Hammerskjold, who was under attack by the USSR, is very thoroughly documented and analysed (Saravanamuttu, 1983). Malaysia's contribution of troops to the UN peacekeeping mission in Congo was also impressive considering that Malaysia itself was at the time facing a communist insurgency at home (Jeshurun, 2007). According to Saravanamuttu, Malaysia's strong support for the UN was driven by the belief that the UN "*embodied the aspirations of the small, developing states*" (Saravanamuttu, 1983: 44) while its contribution towards the Congo peacekeeping mission was for the purpose of "*establishing the new state's status in the world community*" (Saravanamuttu, 1983: 58). Although colonialism is not highlighted overtly as a determining factor, a quote contained in the book leaves no doubt that

Malaysia's experience with colonialism was crucial. Malaya's UN delegate had stated that (Saravanamuttu, 1983: 40):

> *As a nation which has just attained its independence from colonial rule,* [...] *the Federation of Malaya has dedicated and continues to dedicate itself to the just cause of peoples and nations everywhere for the right to self-determination and freedom* [...] *the cause of freedom has become one of the cardinal principles that form the cornerstone of* (my) *government's foreign policy.*

Malaysia's Approach Towards Emerging Patterns of Regionalism

Ever since its independence, Malaysia has been a strong advocate for regionalism in Southeast Asia, first pushing for the establishment of the Southeast Asia Friendship and Economic Treaty (SAEFET), and later with the Association of Southeast Asian States (ASA), both of which did not gain the traction that the Tunku may have hoped for. This inability to gain traction was clearly due to the failure in obtaining Indonesian support for both the initiatives. It is clear from the literature that Indonesia or more accurately, Sukarno viewed the Philippine and Thailand's membership in the South East Asia Treaty Organisation (SEATO) and Malaysia's defence arrangements with Britain (i.e. Anglo-Malayan Defence Agreement—AMDA) as major stumbling blocks; this despite efforts undertaken to temper the Tunku's original intention, which according to Saravanamuttu, was aimed at building a broad "*grouping of non-communist (if not, anti-communist) states*" (Saravanamuttu, 1983: 42).

Here again we witness the role played by colonialisation in determining Malaysia's foreign policy success or failures. At one end of the spectrum, Malaysia's adherence to maintain relations with its former colonial rulers, and at the other, Indonesia's desire to break free from its past, both inevitably brought about this failure to take off. This was the case until 1967 when the ASEAN was formed; a feat only possible due to a change in government in Indonesia, and with it the replacement of the pro-eastern bloc and anti-colonial Sukarno.

For the Tunku, the dispute with the Philippines over Sabah was a major stumbling block in ensuring regional peace and cooperation. Highlighting its significance, he writes (Rahman, 1978b: 220):

> *This (The Philippine claim over Sabah) had soured relationships between two countries of one racial origin, and to no useful purpose. The governments of these countries have changed so much since the Sultanate of Sulu, and it is difficult to entertain a claim based on pure history without logical support. Were such a claim possible, others would start making similar claims. So it was a matter of great happiness to all people in Malaysia to hear coming from the mouth of President Marcos himself "that action is being taken to renounce the claim on Sabah.*

The Tunku's perceptions of the Philippines turned more positive after Ferdinand Marcos, the then President of the Philippines, offered to relinquish his country's claims on Sabah as part of efforts to remove obstacles towards greater ASEAN unity but one that he never followed through. In some of his writings, the Tunku also mentioned the role of race and religion in shaping the decision as to who should take control of Sabah. He stated (Rahman, 1978a: 136):

> *The Philippines's claim to Sabah was first brought up during the time of President Macapagal in the early 1960s, and it was done on behalf of the heirs of the Sultan of Sulu. I turned it down on the grounds that I could not answer for the people of Sabah, and for the same reason the Philippines President could not claim the state for somebody who did not enjoy the power or the sovereign status of a sultan any more…the transfer of Sabah could not give the heirs the sovereign rights over the State to enjoy and to rule in the name of the Philippines government when it can no longer claim it for himself.*

Since this chapter does not focus on domestic and ethno-religious politics, this issue will not be explored further.

Malaysia and Communism

Communism and communist insurgency at home were undoubtedly the major determining factors behind independent Malaysia's foreign policy in its first decade. During the early part of the Tunku's tenure as the Prime Minister, Malaysia's foreign policy position on communism even extended to providing active support to states in conflict with communist states such as the People's Republic of China (PRC), i.e. South Vietnam, India, Tibet and to some extent Taiwan, and going as far as not recognising the PRC and questioning its membership in the UN (Saravanamuttu, 1983).

This even extended to domestic measures, including prohibiting the Bank of China from operating in the country (Jeshurun, 2007).

It is difficult to see how Malaysia's experience with colonialisation would have contributed towards its opposition, towards communism and the PRC, except when viewed in the context of Malaysia's own struggle in dealing with the Communist insurgency ("the Emergency") at home that lasted from 1948 to 1960. This had a huge impact not only in pushing Malaysia closer to the Western bloc but also significantly affecting its relations with communist states such as the PRC, and to some extent coloured its relations with Sukarno's Indonesia which was an active member of the NAM and had good ties with several communist countries. The Tunku may have seen that as a part of a larger international Communist conspiracy. He writes (Rahman, 1965: 666),

> *The Communists consider us an obstacle to be reckoned with in their grand design to subject all Asia to their influence. Obviously Malaysia from their point of view has to be "crushed." The Communists were quick to seize the opportunity to implement this "crushing" vicariously through Indonesia* [...] *We cannot ignore the fact that the Indonesian Communist Party is the third largest in the world and closely collaborates with Peking.*

We must bear in mind that the struggle against communism went beyond ideology for it also potentially posed a threat to what Saravanamuttu identifies as Malaysia's "*major foreign policy objectives [which] were the protection of its political sovereignty and its territorial boundaries against outside interference and aggression*" (Saravanamuttu, 1983: 28). For a country that had just been freed from the clutches of colonialism, these would have seemed legitimate concerns. In Tunku's own words (Rahman, 1965: 666),

> *We in Malaysia have been made well aware by actual aggression, infiltration, subversion and sabotage of the Communist determination to bring about the extinction of our country.*

Clearly, the challenge of communism and communist insurgency at the domestic front substantively influenced Tunku's foreign policy priorities. One may argue that if such a situation had not arisen in Malaysia, his response would have been softer—at least towards some countries of the communist and the NAM bloc. However, as argued in the foregoing paragraphs, even the absence of a communist threat at the domestic front would not have brought the Tunku closer to the USSR and the Eastern bloc. His dislike for the communist countries was manifested even in the way he treated the member countries of the Non-Aligned Movement. His dislike for communism was one of the reasons why Malaysia did not participate in the NAM meetings. The Tunku himself alluded to that on several occasions. Having said that, his relations with leaders such as Jawaharlal Nehru of India were cordial because of the personal rapport (both of them were educated in Britain and were from elite background) and Commonwealth linkages.

Malaysia and the Non-Aligned Movement

With regard to Malaysia's relationship with the Non-Aligned Movement, it is necessary for us to split Tunku Abdul Rahman's tenure into two periods, namely, the period from independence to just before the establishment of Malaysia (1957–1962) and the period from the establishment of Malaysia to his easing from office (1963–1970). Despite the Tunku's promise to United Malays National Organisation (UMNO) that Malaysia would pursue a foreign policy that was free from external influence and which would be "*guided by the spirit of Bandung and Geneva*" (Jeshurun, 2007: 23), the points raised above reveal that Malaysia which was dependent on its former colonial master for its defence and security needs and based on its position vis-à-vis the PRC, one that was influenced by a strong anti-communist policy. The strength of the Tunku's Western orientation should not be underestimated. According to Liow, one of the reasons why Indonesia disliked Tunku's foreign policy was what it perceived as a "*benevolence to the west*", further exacerbated by Tunku giving more emphasis to the SEAFET than Bandung (Liow, 2005: 101).

In this respect, Tunku's absence from the Bandung Conference which he attributed to Malaya not yet being an independent nation (Rahman, 1965), perhaps needs to be re-examined. With the formation of Malaysia in 1963 and the resulting response from the Philippines and Indonesia, Malaysia had to pursue a less selective foreign policy that involved among others reaching out to African, Asian and even some Eastern European countries, as it sought support around the world for its cause. "Konfrontasi" also prompted a slow shift towards the PRC whose existence Malaysia no longer called into question on the condition it did not interfere in the domestic affairs of the region (Saravanamuttu, 1983). This eventually culminated with the establishment of diplomatic ties with China in 1974 during the tenure of Tunku's successor, Tun Abdul Razak.

This new spirit of neutralism was reflected in other aspects of Malaysia's foreign policy, including its position in relation to regionalism, notably the efforts surrounding the creation of a Zone of Peace, Freedom and Neutrality (ZOPFAN) which came after, and which remains outside the ambit of this paper. This shift in policy is often cited as proof of Malaysia's pragmatic approach but when you consider that what really drove it was "*Konfrontasi*", which as explained earlier was a response, at least in the case of Indonesia, to what it saw as neocolonialism, then the legacy of colonialism should not be discounted.

The Tunku's dislike of the Non-Aligned Movement had several motivations. Two reasons figure prominently in that list. First that several countries of the bloc had a socialist leaning, and; second, that Sukarno, with whom the Tunku experienced difficulties in terms of developing a working relationship, was a key figure in the NAM. Difficult relations with Sukarno and challenges posed by communists within the country—were two aspects that greatly shaped his attitude towards the NAM—although initially he was open to the idea of NAM. The Tunku himself had stated once that when NAM started as the Bandung conference in 1955, it was a small but a successful group as (Rahman, 1978b: 147),

> *....it gave a definite shot in the arm to those countries, which were then working for independence, such as ourselves, or fighting for independence, like Algeria, as the Bandung Declaration demanded freedom for all race.*

It is a well-known fact that the Tunku held strong negative views against the communists and considered them his (and Malaysia's) enemies. Such sentiments were echoed in his remarks after the August 1976 NAM conference held in Colombo, which was attended by the then Prime Minister, Hussein Onn and Tengku Rithauddeen—the then foreign minister of Malaysia. The Tunku said that the "Afro-Asian group made no secret of their partiality towards the communist camp". Criticising the NAM's stand on the Malaysian proposal on making the Southeast Asian region a zone of peace, freedom and neutrality, he stated (Rahman, 1978b: 146):

> *Malaysia's case for a neutrality zone in Southeast Asia had the backing of the ASEAN countries and most other democratic nations. This objective had been repeatedly stated and declared over the past few years, at least since Tun Razak became Prime Minister in 1970. One would think that the so-called Non-Aligned Nations would have welcomed the proposal. Being small and weak themselves, only through neutrality can they maintain their freedom. As a matter of fact, their attitude was rather to be expected because this Afro-Asian body, which goes under the guise of being non-aligned, is in fact a communist satellite organisation.*

Terming the NAM a "communist satellite organisation" is a little too much. Apparently, John Foster Dulles was the only other prominent leader whose terming of the NAM as an "immoral" bloc got popular media attention. Nevertheless, this clearly tells us how much the Tunku abhorred the communists. He even (successfully) convinced the leaders of India, Pakistan and Ghana, who were attending the Commonwealth conference with him in London, to not attend the 1964 NAM conference. His dislike for Sukarno is not a secret either. He believed that Sukarno was not only against the idea of the formation of Malaysia but was also maligning Malaysia's image, which wasn't completely false. His views about Sukarno largely (and unfortunately) shaped his ideas about the NAM as a multination platform. He believed that once Sukarno's "Crush Malaysia" policy failed and he failed to harm Malaysia, he then "hit upon the idea of calling another (NAM) conference in 1964" (Rahman, 1978b: 148). He further stated that Sukarno's sole objective was to "enlist the support of other countries for his rabid ideas against 'neo – colonialism', quoting Malaysia as an example" (Rahman, 1978b: 148).

It is important to clarify here that multilateral organisations do not revolve around the whims and fancies of middle and small powers. Sukarno's Indonesia, which was unable to exercise its hegemony even within the Southeast Asian region, was in no way on the list of top thought leaders of the NAM. The three key leaders of the NAM during Sukarno's time were Jawaharlal Nehru (India), Gamal Abdel Nasser (Egypt) and Josip Broz Tito (Yugoslavia) who shaped the vision and direction of the NAM (New York Times, 1956). Sukarno may have played a role in trying to influence the leaders in convening another conference but was certainly not the representative face of the NAM. Moreover, since early 1961, particularly during the India–China War of 1962 and later during the Konfrontasi—when India supported Malaysia, Sukarno turned against India but could not gain much support of the NAM members. For the Tunku though, Konfrontasi was a major event, which by no means could have been overlooked. However, the fact that it overshadowed the Tunku's perceptions of the third force in the bipolar Cold War system is rather intriguing. These perceptions also brought him closer to the Western countries particularly the United Kingdom and its two former colonies—Australia and New Zealand. In his essay titled "No way for the Reds", he writes (Rahman, 1978b: 133–134).

> *In 1963 Malaysia was formed. Thereupon Sukarno started trouble...The extent to which we went in trying to appease the "devil" had no limits. He was intent on achieving what he wanted to do - that is "Crush Malaysia". But with the united efforts of our people and with support from our Commonwealth friends, Britain, Australia and New Zealand, we managed to prevent Soekarno from carrying out any large-scale operations against us.*

Indeed, Malaysia's Commonwealth friends, particularly Britain, Australia and New Zealand supported Malaysia in dealing with Indonesia. First the bilateral defence agreement (Anglo-Malaya Defence Agreement) with Britain, and later the Five Power Defence Arrangement (FPDA) played a great role in Malaysia's military-strategic preparedness and security. From the above, it is clear that even though FPDA was signed in 1971 and Malaysia was not a signatory to the SEATO, it was very much a security partner of Australia and New Zealand.

Malaysia and the West

From the foregoing sections it is clear that the Malaysian foreign policy under Tunku Abdul Rahman reflected a very strong pro-Western leaning which was very distinctively different from the foreign policies of some of the other Southeast Asian states, particularly Indonesia. Sidel (Sidel, 2012), who examined the varying trajectories of nationalism as it developed within Southeast Asia,[1] attributed this to how each chose to negotiate their international relations, specifically in relation to their

[1] Sidel categorised Burma's, Cambodia's and Indonesia's attempts as struggle to achieve economic autonomy and political neutrality, Malaysia's, Singapore's, the Philippines' and Thailand's as neocolonial, while Vietnam, Laos and Cambodia as anti-imperialist and socialist.

"*(re)integration into the world capitalist economy and the Cold War geopolitical order*" (Sidel, 2012: 143). What is noteworthy is the idea that different negotiating approaches did emerge and this to some extent had influenced not only the form of nationalism that emerged but also the relationship between these states and the West, including their former colonial rulers. Saravanamuttu highlights two aspects where Malaysia's relationship with (or more accurately its dependency on) the West is very clearly present. Firstly, in the area of defence and security through the AMDA and secondly, in the area of development and trade, where the West remained an important market for Malaya's exports (particularly tin and rubber), and source of imports as well as a source for development funds (Saravanamuttu, 1983).

The above supports our contention that Malaysia's foreign policy was constrained by conditions that were a direct consequence of colonialism. This dependency on the West, particularly in the area of defence and security, was further enhanced after the formation of Malaysia as troops from Britain, Australia and New Zealand were required to deal with the *Konfrontasi*.

Although Malaysia formally became an independent country on 31 August 1957, unlike several other former British colonies, its security was still tied to the UK. For all practical purposes, the UK was still a security provider to Malaysia on which the policymakers relied upon from 1957 until the late 1960s. The security of Malaysia was managed through the Anglo-Malaya Defence Agreement. According to Wariya (1989):

> *...The obligation to defend the two most important core values that a nation like Malaya would like to preserve, that is, national independence and territorial integrity, was the task of London. This availability of external security assistance to Malaya was subsequently extended to cover Malaysia as of 16 September 1963.*

With regard to a more independent security policy formulation, it is clear that the British withdrawal from the Suez marks a clear beginning of a new phase. Wariya argues (Wariya, 1989):

> *It was agreed that should Malaya come under attack from any foreign power, as had happened during the "Confrontation" with the Indonesians following the formation of Malaysia in the 1960s, the British would help to counter external aggression. It can be argued that the leadership in Malaysia only*

> *began to undertake the primary responsibility for national security after 1970 when AMDA was terminated as a result of the British withdrawal from East of Suez.*

Clearly, this had a strong impact on Malaysia's foreign policy orientations. The Malaysian foreign policy approach was closely knit with the British outlook on the regional security and the international order—an aspect clearly manifested in Tunku Abdul Rahman's foreign policy.

Even within the ASEAN mechanism, the Tunku seemed to have more confidence in the Western powers and their allies than the rest including the member countries of ASEAN. Expressing his enthusiasm, the Tunku notes (Rahman, 1978b: 220–221):

> *It is heartening that Australia, New Zealand and Japan, are taking interest in this Southeast Asia grouping for the economic and political well-being of the region. These countries can do so much for ASEAN. They are much more advanced politically, economically and in all other aspects of importance in the world today...furthermore, a cursory examination or even a detailed investigation would reveal that ASEAN has come together for economic, political and cultural ties. The member states are not well-armed and prepared to make war on countries, nor are they carrying on any armed struggle against any country. Their time is occupied in trying to keep their own homes free from communist subversive activities.*

The Tunku's approach towards the West was not that of all-out support. Just like his relations with the NAM countries, he attempted to customise his preferences even within the Western bloc. This pattern is seen so strongly in his policies that at times it seems contradictory. For instance, while the Tunku was alright with seeking military support of the British through the AMDA (Anglo-Malayan Defence Agreement), which was signed in 1957 (and later superseded by the 1971 Five Power Defence Partnership Agreement involving Britain, Australia, New Zealand, Singapore), his government did not support the SEATO (South East Asia Treaty Organisation) which had all these countries as members. His acknowledgment and appreciation of the contributions made by the Australian and New Zealand governments, as mentioned earlier, do not get well with the refusal to sign the SEATO pact. As Malaysia was dependent on key Western members of the SEATO for its security, the refusal to sign SEATO would not have led to any substantial change on the ground.

Even with regard to the AMDA, while the Tunku was keen to secure the British (and its allies') support, others in his cabinet were not open to such an idea. For instance, young nationalist leaders such as Aziz Ishak were critical of the continued British presence on the Malaysian soil. However, the Tunku carried on with the plan though not without concerns and criticisms emanating every now and then (Storey Ian, 2011). The contradiction between seeking AMDA on the one hand and opposing SEATO on the other stands unresolved. The Tunku was honest in not denying his government's indirect links with the SEATO. In a statement in the parliament, he said (Legislative Council Debates, 1958),

> *...all I can say is that we are not in SEATO. In this respect, if SEATO countries are involved in any war, we are not committed to the war, but on the other hand, if Britain entered the war and one of the countries which we are committed to defend, like Singapore, a British territory, or Borneo, is attacked, then we are treaty bound to fight. Perhaps you may say that we are indirectly connected with SEATO, but I can say quite openly here and assure the House that we are not in SEATO.*

Technically, it was not possible for Malaysia to steer clear of the SEATO arrangements. However, despite knowing that it would not be possible to do such a thing, he chose the middle path and did not formally join the SEATO even though Malaysia was a part of the security mechanism for all practical purposes.

Tunku Abdul Rahman, Sukarno and the Young Turks: The Personality Factor

The Tunku's personality, his family and educational background massively influenced his outlook on foreign policy as on other matters. The Tunku was born into royalty (i.e. he was the seventh son of Sultan Abdul Hamid Halim Shah, the twenty-fifth ruler of the Kedah Sultanate) and according to Sheppard (2007) enjoyed a privileged life. Moving to England at the young age of 17, it is no wonder that England should have made a deep impression on him and his outlook. Certainly, it influenced the way he carried himself, at least from in the eyes of his contemporaries. Liow writes, "*He has commonly been described as a 'relaxed, aristocratic Anglophile who, as Sir Henry Gurney once suggested, carried the imprimatur of English politicians'*" (Liow, 2005: 89). For sure, these factors play a huge role in shaping the decision-making abilities of leaders. The Tunku was no exception to that. Jeshurun (2007: Xi) opines, "the personalities of the leaders of our nations have invariably shaped and directed the path of Malaysian foreign policy since 1957".

Despite concerns of scholars like Saravanamuttu on overstating the role of the "*small stable elite comprising four or five men*" (Ott, 1972: 225), a proper assessment of Malaysia's foreign policy cannot avoid considering the role of the movers and shakers of the Malaysian foreign policy scene. Both Saravanamuttu and Jeshurun highlight, for instance, the role played by men like Tun Dr. Ismail and Ghazali Shafie in the formulation of Malaysia's foreign policy in the early post-Independence phase. Nevertheless, both Liow and Ahmad (1985) share the view that it was the Tunku who played the more pivotal role. Liow writes (Liow, 2005: 90),

> *To be sure, the policy formulation process did include several other key members of the political elite, namely, Deputy Prime Minister and Minister of Defence Tun Abdul Razak and Home Minister Tun Dr Ismail. [...] Be that as it may, while it was possible that 'the importance of idiosyncratic variables vary from issue-area to issue-area' in Malaya, in general it was the Tunku who dominated the entire process.*

Highlighted this aspect in 1985, Ahmad writes (Ahmad, 1985: 2),

All major decisions had always been taken by the Tengku himself and he rarely discussed them with the Cabinet. [...] Ott, without citing sources, said the Tengku sometimes consulted Cabinet but, then, only to obtain consensus and to legitimise his decisions.

Ahmad (Ahmad, 1985: 20) further states, "Endorsement from his Cabinet colleagues was automatic because of their common Western orientation".

Much has already been said of the Tunku's pro-Western and anti-communist stance. These leanings had an impact on Malaysia's early relations with the PRC as well as other communist states. It should be noted too that this was also a factor in Malaysia's poor relations with Indonesia, even before "*Konfrontasi*". Jeshurun notes (Jeshurun, 2007: 43):

> *While one should not make too much of the degree to which personality clashes might severely affect the bilateral relationship between Indonesia and Malaya,*

it was an open secret that the Tunku and Sukarno could not get along, either personally, socially or as national leaders.

This is hardly surprising since the two men were definitely not cut from the same cloth. While the Tunku was part of the aristocracy and received British education (he studied law at Cambridge University) which led him to have a far more favourable view and (some might say friendlier) relationship with the West, Sukarno was a son of a teacher, received his education mostly in Indonesia and generally had a more negative view of Western imperialism. This can be viewed as a legacy of colonialism, or more precisely how the experience of colonialism might differ from country to country, class to class and individual to individual. In addition to the Tunku, the role of Tun Dr. Ismail who shared the Tunku's anti-communist and pro-Western stances is also well documented (Saravanamuttu, 2007: 10). These men—the Tunku himself and Tun Dr. Ismail[2]—all shared certain similarities. They were all Western-educated, pragmatic and conservative and represented Malaysia's elites (Saravanamuttu, 1983). While differences did emerge, most notably in relation to China,[3] these men still shared the view on the importance of maintaining ties with the West.

Eventually, the real challenge came not from his peers but from much younger members of UMNO ("Young Turks"), men like Dr. Mahathir Mohamad and Musa Hitam who did not belong to the aristocracy, were not Western-educated, were anti-colonial and who criticised the Tunku's foreign policy for being too tied to Britain's. Likewise, the Tunku felt "*He* [Mahathir] *was a "nobody. His father was a subordinate officer in Kedah. I did not mix with his father. We had a club in Kedah, a special club for civil servants, for royalty and so on. They had a subordinate club*" (Wain, 2009: 3).

[2] Ott (1972) include Tun Abdul Razak, Tun Tan Siew Sin and Khir Johari while Jeshurun (2007) includes also Ghazali Shafie.

[3] It was Tun Dr. Ismail who proposed for the shift towards non-alignment and neutralisation of Southeast Asia from its previous hardline position on China, a proposal that received full support from Tun Razak but not from Tunku (Saravanamuttu, 1983). By 1971, these differences ceased to be an issue. With Tun Razak at the helm, Malaysia began to fully pursue a policy of non-alignment and efforts to improve ties with the PRC eventually culminating with the establishment of diplomatic relations and the historic visit of Tun Razak to the PRC in 1974.

Clearly, the elite perceptions heavily influenced foreign policymaking during the early years of Malaysian foreign policy formulation. Wariya (1989) notes:

> *Reviewing the statements made by those concerned regarding threats to national security since independence, it can be concluded that the perception of the ruling elites of what they considered as threats to the vital interests of the state can be viewed from a number of perspectives. The definition of threat is seen not only from the military dimension but also that of economics, politics and social norms. In fact, anything that is seen by the ruling class as endangering the fundamental values of the state can be regarded as threats to national security.*

Beyond the realm of Western influence, the Tunku seems to have developed a stereotype that Westerners are better than Asians. His views on Malays confirm the same. The Tunku writes (Rahman, 1978: 224),

> *Whatever we may think of ourselves, however good we think we are, I may be excused for saying that the European are still far ahead of us in methods and systems and organisational ability. For this reason I say there is nothing to be ashamed of, if we learn these things from them.*

However, the Tunku must be given credit for leading the initiative of according Bahasa Melayu as much importance as English as the official language of the newly independent Malaysia.

The descriptions and views presented above seem to confirm the suspicions held by the Tunku's contemporaries that he was an anglophile, favoured by the West (Liow, 2005). Ahmad (1985) in his book titled, "*Tengku Abdul Rahman and Malaysia's foreign policy, 1963-1970*" describes some of the far more disparaging opinions held by others, which saw Tunku as a product of a pampered aristocratic upbringing who was thrust into a leadership role by accident but was considered the ideal choice by both the British administration and pro-colonial Malay leaders who were eager to see Malaya's struggle for independence come to naught. This portrait, however, may not be totally fair nor offer us an accurate picture.

In a paper by Ho (2014) which explored Tunku's use of symbolism as a means of communication, the author offers a different portrait. The paper which focuses on two speeches, i.e. a speech to UMNO delegates on 5 April 1953, and another speech delivered on the interracial harmony event on 16 February 1957 (few months before Independence), looked into Tunku's use of three words/phrases "*ribut taufan*" (storm), "*kota*" (fort) and "*racun*" (poison). In relation to the first ("*ribut taufan*"), the author concludes that it references the challenges awaiting the party (UMNO) as it pushed forward with its plans to achieve independence. This opposition would come from a diverse group made up of the British, the Malay administration (i.e. the Sultans and several Chief Ministers) and those within his own party that supported its former leader Dato' Onn Jaafar. In relation to "*kota*" (fort), this was referring to the British use of "divide and rule" to keep the races in Malaya divided, a problem that Tunku suggested could only be overcome through education. Lastly, "*racun*" (poison) was a reference to what Tunku considered the main challenge in achieving independence, namely, "*takut, bimbang dan tak percaya*" (fear, worry and distrust), specifically between the Chinese and the Malays.

What this paper does is highlight three key challenges facing the Tunku at the time leading towards independence, namely: Opposition from the elites (British and Malay elites) and lack of unity among the main races (Chinese and Malays) driven by the fear and distrust they held for each other. The former challenges the view that the Tunku's efforts were part of this larger neocolonialist endeavour to retain British influence within the region. The actions by the British in freeing radical Malay leaders from prison in 1955 which may have fuelled opposition Malay parties (all of which is mentioned in Ho's paper) seem to challenge this idea as well. The latter highlights the domestic challenges faced by the Tunku in uniting the major races, separated by their differences which extended beyond culture and religion to include economic disparities, the last being a by-product of the colonial administration of Malaya.

Conclusion

Malaysia's foreign policy in the early post-independence period can be described as a paradox. Unlike other countries, which took steps to break free from their former colonial rulers and pursue an independent foreign policy, Malaysia instead maintained a pro-Western foreign policy and retained positive relations with Britain to the extent that it relied on Britain for its national security and defence. It even pursued an anti-communist agenda, which saw relations with the PRC and to some extent Indonesia, suffer for it. Scholars have offered a range of explanations, most notably the influence of geopolitics, domestic politics, leadership and pragmatism while giving scant attention on colonialism. This chapter has attempted to establish that colonialism has had a far deeper and meaningful impact on Malaysia's foreign policy than we may wish to give it credit for. It also contributed to the shaping of the foreign policy outlook of the movers and shakers (i.e. Malaysia's elite) responsible for Malaysia's foreign policy; in this case—Malaysia's first Prime Minister, Tunku Abdul Rahman. The Tunku's proclivity towards the West is unquestionable, and can be truly appreciated when compared to his contemporaries and those that came after. While his pro-Western leanings can be explained as resulting from the ongoing communist insurgency, the reality was that the options available to Malaysia were limited by the dependent relationship that existed between Malaysia and its former colonial master, brought about as a direct consequence of colonialism. This pro-Western policy has unsurprisingly encouraged some to view the Tunku as being a British tool to maintain their influence in the region. Nevertheless, as arguments made in this chapter have revealed, this reasoning is not well supported when one considers the challenges faced by the Tunku not only among the British administration, but also among certain sections of the Malay elites, to his efforts to achieve independence and subsequently lead it towards greater peace and stability despite lack of resources at disposal. Added to that was the poor relations between races which was a direct by-product of colonialism. This colonial legacy can also be seen today, as Malaysia's current foreign policy retains many of the principles and values that shaped Malaysia's foreign policy as it emerged from the yoke of colonialism.

References

Achraya, A. (2014). *The end of American world order*. Cambridge: Polity Press.

Acharya, A., & Buzan, B. (2019). *The making of global international relations*. Cambridge: Cambridge University Press.

Ahmad, A. (1985). *Tengku Abdul Rahman and Malaysia's foreign policy, 1963–1970*. Kuala Lumpur: Berita Publishing.

Alles, D. (2014). The construction of Malaysia's foreign policy since 1957. In S. Lemiere (Ed.), *Misplaced democracy* (pp. 27–50). Petaling Jaya: Strategic Information and Research Development Centre.

Ho, W. S. (2014). Penggunaan simbol dalam teks ucapan Tunku Abdul Rahman: analisis teori relevans. *Jurnal Bahasa, 14*(1), 60–92.

Jeshurun, C. (2007). *Malaysia: Fifty years of diplomacy 1957–2007*. Singapore: Talisman Publishing Pte. Ltd.

Kuik, C. C. (2016). Malaysia between the United States and China: What do weaker states hedge against? *Asian Politics & Policy, 8*(1), 155–177.

Legislative Council debates 1958, 4. S. (n.d.).

Liow, J. C. (2005). Tunku Abdul Rahman and Malaya's relations with Indonesia, 1957–1960. *Journal of Southeast Asian Studies, 36*(1), 87–109.

Ministry of Foreign Affairs, Malaysia. (2019). Malaysia's foreign policy. *Ministry of Foreign Affairs Malaysia*. https://www.kln.gov.my/web/guest/foreign-policy. Accessed 10 Oct 2019.

New York Times. (1956, July 19). https://www.nytimes.com/1956/07/19/archives/nehru–tito-nasser-limits-conference-hopes-nehru-opens-talk.html. Accessed 23 Sept 2020.

Ott, M. C. (1972). Foreign policy formulation in Malaysia. *Asian Survey, 12*, 225–241.

Rahman, T. A. (1965). Malaysia: Key area in Southeast Asia. *Foreign Affairs, 43*(4), 659–670.

Rahman, T. A. (1978a). Fate of the fellow Muslims. *The Star*, p. 5.

Rahman, T. A. (1978b). *Viewpoints*. Kuala Lumpur: Heinemann Educational Books (Asia) Ltd.

Saravanamuttu, J. (1983). *The dilemma of independence: Two decades of Malaysia's foreign policy, 1957–1977*. Kuala Lumpur: Penerbit Universiti Sains Malaysia.

Saravanamuttu, J. (2007). Tun Ismail: Early Architect of Malaysian foreign policy. *The Journal of Diplomacy and Foreign Relations, 9*(1), 7–16.

Sheppard, M. (2007). *Tunku: His life and times: The authorized biography of Tunku Abdul Rahman Putra al-Haj*. Petaling Jaya: Pelanduk Publications.

Sidel, J. T. (2012). The fate of nationalism in the new states: Southeast Asia in comparative historical perspective. *Comparative Studies in Society and History, 54*(1), 114–144.

Storey Ian, E. R. (2011). *Five power defence arrangements at forty*. Singapore: ISEAS.

Talib, S. (1997). The Asiatic archipelago: History beyond boundaries. *Jati-Journal of Southeast Asian Studies, 3*, 123–137.

Wain, B. (2009). *Malaysian maverick: Mahathir Mohamad in turbulent times*. Singapore: Springer.

Wariya, C. (1989). Leadership change and security in Malaysia: From the days of the Tunku to Dr Mahathir Mohamad. *Contemporary Southeast Asia, 11*(2), 160–185.

Index

R. Rasiah et al. (eds.), *Contesting Malaysia's Integration into the World Economy*, https://doi.org/10.1007/978-981-16-0650-2

The manufacturer's authorised representative in the EU is Springer Nature Customer Service Centre GmbH, Europaplatz 3, 69115 Heidelberg, Germany. If you have any concerns regarding our products, please contact ProductSafety@springernature.com

Printed and bound by CPI Group (UK) Ltd, Croydon, CR0 4YY
30/09/2026
02225326-0008